My Dear President

My Dear President

LETTERS BETWEEN PRESIDENTS AND THEIR WIVES

Gerard W. Gawalt

**BLACK DOG
& LEVENTHAL
PUBLISHERS**
NEW YORK

IN ASSOCIATION WITH THE LIBRARY OF CONGRESS

To the first ladies of the Gawalt/Cavanaugh family

MARIE REGINA CHALOUX GAWALT
AND ARLITA GERALDINE DODGE CAVANAUGH;
MY WIFE, JANE FRANCES CAVANAUGH GAWALT;
MY DAUGHTERS, SUSAN, ANN, AND ELLEN;
AND MY GRANDDAUGHTERS, CAITLIN, SARAH,
EMMA, MARY ELIZABETH, AND ABIGAIL.

Copyright © 2005 Library of Congress, Washington D.C.

All photos courtesy of the Library of Congress

ISBN-13: 978-1-57912-552-3
ISBN-10: 1-57912-552-2

Library of Congress Cataloging-in-Publication Data
My dear President: letters between presidents and their wives / [compiled by] Gerard W. Gawalt;
in association with the Library of Congress.
   p. cm
  Includes bibliographical references and index.
  ISBN 1-57912-552-2 (alk. paper)
 1. Presidents--United States--Correspondence. 2. Presidents' spouses--United States--
Correspondence. 3. Married people--United States--Correspondence. 4. Presidents-- United
States--Family relationships. I. Gawalt, Gerard W. II Library of Congress

  E176.1.M98 2006
  973.09'9--dc22

                               2005057223

Cover and interior design: Liz Driesbach

Manufactured in the U.S.A.

Published by
Black Dog & Leventhal Publishers, Inc.
151 West 19th Street
New York, New York 10011

Distributed by
Workman Publishing Company
708 Broadway
New York, New York 10003

g f e d c

CONTENTS

The Letters

FOREWORD

"Every thing around and within reminds me that you are absent," wrote a forlorn James Madison to his wife, Dolley Payne Madison, early in his presidency. Politics and the process of "hello and good-bye" were two constants in the lives of our fourth president and first lady, as they have been for first couples from George and Martha Washington to George and Laura Bush.

The letter from which this quote is extracted is part of the Library of Congress's collection of the personal papers of twenty-three U.S. presidents. *My Dear President* draws upon the library's magnificent and unparalleled holdings of manuscripts, books, microforms, prints, and photographs—as well as those of other presidential, university, and private libraries—to open a unique window into the special familial relationships of our first families.

This book is the latest in a long list of Library of Congress publications drawing upon the personal papers of America's presidents, the most recent of which are a companion to this work, *First Daughters: Letters Between U.S. Presidents and Their Daughters*, and an illustrated biography, *Thomas Jefferson: Genius of Liberty*. Each of these books includes numerous illustrations from the library's unique collection of American prints and photographs. If this and other books whet your appetite for the library's historic material, be aware that the library's digital initiative is now making available free of charge to persons of all ages and nations the papers of five presidents—George Washington, Thomas

Jefferson, James Madison, Andrew Jackson, and Abraham Lincoln—through its Web site at http://www.loc.gov.

Forty-two of our presidents have been married, and the couples' letters and other written and recorded communications reveal the depth and intensity of their relationships. More often than not, presidential marriages developed into political as well as personal partnerships.

The more than two hundred documents and illustrations gathered here exhibit a wide range of sentiments, ideas, and plans, both momentous and mundane. Sometimes intense, sometimes distant, sometimes deeply personal, sometimes coolly professional, the letters and their accompanying images offer unique insight into the nation's first families. Brought together for the first time in a single volume that spans the nation's 230-year history, these documents, many published here for the first time, may surprise, entertain, enlighten, and perhaps sadden you—but they will never disappoint as, time and again, the presidential couples rise to the singular challenges of their personal and public lives.

The book's thematic groupings organize the experiences of the spouses into such such broad categories as marriage, education, family, sorrow, and travel; and showcase the struggles the families faced to maintain equilibrium in their lives while climbing and remaining atop the political mountain. While very few of these men initially set out to become president, none was able to resist the pull of the nation's highest office.

My Dear President, like its companion book, *First Daughters*, includes only a small number of the thousands of letters exchanged by presidents and their wives, which is why the library's digital archive is such a valuable resource. As time marches on, it is my hope that more and more institutions that have preserved historic papers will follow our lead and make them available through the Internet.

From the invention of the telegraph to today's complex communications systems, private messages are increasingly expressed through ephemeral electronic transmissions, presenting unprecedented challenges to recorders of our national history and heritage.

Indeed, the transition from written letters transported by human hands to verbal or written messages transported by electronic means is made clear in the course of this book. This anthology documents the innermost thoughts, plans, and experiences of the nation's most public figures, continuing the Library of Congress's tradition of providing ever increasing access to the richness and humanity of our cultural heritage.

James H. Billington,
Librarian of Congress

INTRODUCTION

Forty-three men have become president of the United States, and forty-two of them were married. Invariably, these partnerships were instrumental in their rise to prominence. The letters and other known communications of these presidential couples help us understand their personal and political lives—their successes and failures, triumphs and losses, joys and sorrows, everyday and exotic experiences. These communications provide a window through which to study, understand, and simply enjoy the lives of these privileged individuals without the distorting prisms of intermediary observers. While perusing these documents, we can focus on the private thoughts, as opposed to the public words and actions, of the letterwriters.

Americans often wonder what impact a first lady has on a president. It might reassure us to feel that our president has a trustworthy partner, or frighten us to think that he might be dependent on his spouse. (Many of us look forward to the day when we will have to substitute the word "spouse" for "first lady.") This book draws upon thousands of personal letters, memoranda, telegrams, cables, cards, reported conversations, and telephone and teletype messages in the collections of the Library of Congress, other public institutions throughout the country, private family collections, and published works, to allow readers to share in these special relationships and better understand the nature of the presidency. Often, these means of communication have been the primary substitute for presence and the primary avenue for expressing the authors' innermost thoughts and concerns—after all, the life of the president is filled with obligations that carry him far from home. For this reason, these missives have become invaluable as a source for readers of all kinds, from serious historical researchers to the merely curious.

Handwritten letters constituted the primary means of communication for most of our nation's history. Indeed, for many people, including Mary Lincoln, letter writing was considered an art, and much care was devoted to the task. If one of our early presidents sent out a letter that had been written by a secretary—even if dictated by the president himself—an apology was required. At the end of the nineteenth century, the cable, telephone, and telegraph began to replace letters. Presidents McKinley and Theodore Roosevelt were the first to show a preference for the telegram and telephone, and, over the next century, electronic communication increasingly dominated. While Mamie Eisenhower would still complain when her husband sent her a message via cable or teletype, subsequent presidential couples seldom communicated by letter.

The dramatic rise in the use of electronic communication has made it necessary to expand the definition of "letters" for the purposes of this volume. Reported or reconstructed telecommunications and conversations have been included on a limited basis for the sake of completeness, from the overseas cables and teletype messages of Dwight D. Eisenhower to the personal conversations and telephone calls of the Nixons, Fords, and Clintons. We have, of necessity, relied on the accuracy of the conversations as reported in personal memoirs, when no other extant copy was available for verification.

The search for letters and written messages proved challenging. Presidential families are always concerned with their privacy, never more so than when it comes to the first lady. Jackie Kennedy Onassis requested in her will that her letters to her husband not be published, a request honored in this book. Often a surviving spouse—Martha Washington, for one—destroyed the couple's personal correspondence. Likewise, Thomas Jefferson removed virtually all written traces of his wife, Martha, keeping only a few lines that they had written together when she was on her deathbed. (Her household account book was salvaged, however, and was later used by Jefferson to make legal notes and by his granddaughters to keep kitchen accounts at Monticello.) Often, family members held on to the cherished correspondence of their mothers when they sold or donated their fathers' papers to collections or public institutions—and some of these were subsequently misplaced or locked away from the public. Dolley Madison's son, John Payne Todd, tried to sell her correspondence but her nieces, acting, they said, under their Aunt Dolley's specific orders, destroyed most of it. Sadly, very few letters written by Dolley Madison, Mary Lincoln, Julia Grant, and Eleanor Roosevelt are available to us. No letters of Elizabeth Monroe, Eliza Johnson, Florence Harding, Grace Coolidge, Bess Truman, or Barbara Bush are available.

On the other hand, some presidential couples retained their letters by the hundreds, including John and Abigail Adams, John Quincy and Louisa Catherine Adams, James and Lucretia Garfield, Rutherford and Lucy Hayes, and William and Helen Taft. Most presidential couples were more selective, retaining many of their communications but discarding just as many, failing to grasp the importance that these documents might have to future generations.

My Dear President, like its companion volume, *First Daughters*, gathers a wide range of messages (chiefly letters) expressing a variety of sentiments, ideas, hopes, plans, and simple daily events from these American icons. The letters included here, from thirty-six presidential couples, were selected from thousands. Whenever possible, the entire text of a letter has been retained, but when necessary, excerpts of written or recorded communications—and even reported conversations or telephone messages—have been included to provide readers with the best examples of these familial exchanges. It would have been a shame to omit the conversations and telephone messages of Hillary and William Clinton and Gerald and Betty Ford; or the cable and teletype messages of the Grants, the Roosevelts, and the Eisenhowers.

Because this book is not a "scholarly edition" of letters, no attempt at completeness was contemplated, but a special effort was made to represent as many presidential couples as possible. And we have certainly made every effort to retain the accuracy and completeness of each letter. Special care was taken to select letters or messages that form an exchange, and all available correspondence was thoroughly combed in order to find the most interesting and informative for the scholar as well as the general public.

All of the letters and other messages are reproduced here with a minimum of editorial intrusion. Neither spelling nor grammar has been modernized or corrected whenever the original document was available. We've added a brief introduction to each entry, in order to set the context and help explain the complex relationships out of which they sprang.

The letters have been grouped thematically, allowing readers to observe the sometimes static, sometimes evolving conventions of private and public life. Letters and messages expressing fondness and love highlight all courtships and marriages, and many of these are included here. Some are merely flirtatious, others more explicit; some are more formal, others off-the-cuff; some are inspiring, others downright silly; some are elated, others evoke sadness. From the flirtations of John and Abigail Adams—both masters of the double entendre—to the gushing devotion of the Wilsons and Reagans, the evolving nature of courtship and the constancy of love and marriage are on display. Times have changed since the day when John Tyler hesitated to write to his future wife, Letitia, without her permission; the Wilsons, Tafts, Johnsons, and Reagans of the twentieth century couldn't seem to write often enough!

Not all presidential marriages were without their rough spots: James and Lucretia Garfield seemed to spend more time making up than making love. When Abigail Adams flirtatiously wrote, "If you want more balm, I can supply you," the desire simply rises from the words. Readers cannot escape the intensity of Lyndon Johnson's declaration to Bird Taylor, "I am very madly in love with you."

War played a major role in the lives of many presidential couples, from George Washington proudly marching off to Boston; James Madison fleeing a burning Washington, D.C.; Ulysses S. Grant, Rutherford Hayes, Chester Arthur, Benjamin Harrison, and James Garfield leading the Union to victory; to the ultimate Rough

Rider, Theodore Roosevelt; Harry Truman's service in World War I; and Dwight Eisenhower, John Kennedy, Lyndon Johnson, Gerald Ford, Richard Nixon, Ronald Reagan, and George H. W. Bush leading America to victory in World War II. The wives of these brave men had to endure their husbands' departures into battle. John Tyler, the only U.S. president to serve in a rebellious government, wrote, "These are dark Times Dearest." Abraham Lincoln led the Union to victory only to be chided by his wife, Mary, [to] "put a fighting General in." Lincoln, of course, ventured to the front lines, and reported, "the battle now rages furiously." For their part, the wives did battle on the home front, providing support and advice to their husbands and the nation, awaiting that day when they could, as Rutherford Hayes put it, "all be together again for good!"

Even without war, presidents have tended to be away frequently. These ambitious men, often married to ambitious women, traveled far and wide and left their spouses to run the family business, whether that was a plantation, a professional firm, a radio station, or simply the family investments. These letters show the strains of separation and the joys of reunion as the men, bolstered by their wives and families, sought greater recognition and higher offices. But there was longing for their spouses and a hope for a quick return. As James Madison wrote to Dolley, "Every thing around and within reminds me that you are absent." Or as Ronald Reagan wrote plaintively to his wife, Nancy, "As it is I'm sitting here on the 6th floor beside a phony fireplace looking out at a grey wet sky and listening to a radio play music not intended for one person alone."

And then there was politics! Always politics! Politics inevitably became the focal point of the lives and letters of these couples. A few presidents, including Ulysses S. Grant and Dwight Eisenhower, were propelled by military triumphs to the highest office in the nation. But most of them, even George Washington, worked their way up step by step, with their wives pushing and pulling them over the steepest and rockiest ground. Letters show the couples in the midst of toil, trouble, and triumph. Even in victory, these men were sometimes chided by their wives: Abigail Adams wrote to John in the midst of debate over the Declaration of Independence, "I can not say that I think you very generous to the Ladies." More frequently, the couples worked hard in tandem: Eleanor Roosevelt wrote to Franklin, "My feeling is that we have to get going and quickly." Often the wives displayed as much, if not more, political courage than their husbands. As Bird Johnson wrote to Lyndon on the eve of the Democratic Party Convention in 1964, "To step out now would be wrong for your country. I am not afraid of Time or lies or losing money or defeat." But their political experience is perhaps best summarized by the blunt-speaking Harry S. Truman, "Ain't that sompin."

All presidents must deal with the threat and fear of assassination—and a number of our leaders have actually faced such an attack. John Tyler reported that President Jackson, when approached by a would-be assassin, "immediately raised his cane and put at him," while Theodore Roosevelt, after being shot in the chest, brushed off his wound, finished his one-hour speech, and telegraphed his wife from the hospital emergency room to report that his injury "isn't a particle more serious than one of the injuries any of the boys used continually to be having." But always the threat hovered in the background.

Preservation of a president's papers has always presented its own particular challenge. Even before there were presidential libraries (some call them presidential pyramids), presidential papers were considered vital to our national government. George Washington's papers were sought out more to check the veracity of the claims of hopeful Revolutionary War pensioners than for their intrinsic value in understanding the founding of our nation. But, for two centuries, Congress has affirmed the importance of the papers and has acted to safeguard them.

Presidential papers were first acquired by Congress in 1834, when it purchased Washington's public papers for $25,000. Subsequently, and before the days of the presidential libraries, Congress and its library acquired the major collections of personal papers of twenty-three presidents, from Washington to Calvin Coolidge, along with smaller collections of the ephemera of the others. The library has also published many books about the presidents and made their papers available in books, on microfilm, and now via the Internet.

These publications tend to focus on one president or presidential couple, but this book, like *First Daughters*, instead presents a range of material that spans our nation's history, from the election of the first president in the eighteenth century through the end of the twentieth.

Over the course of more than two hundred years, many outward aspects of our nation have changed. We have grown from a small insignificant republic limited to the eastern third of North America into a large and powerful democracy stretching across the continent. But we are still led by a duly elected president, who, more often than not, is ably assisted by a wife. This book attempts to further our understanding of the familial culture that enabled these couples to reach the pinnacle of national politics and power. There was a time when it was easy to think of first ladies as mere appendages of their presidential husbands, but that is virtually impossible today. These letters stand as a concrete testament to their complex roles and numerous contributions.

THE CORRESPONDENTS

GEORGE WASHINGTON (1732–99) was born in Westmoreland County, Virginia, the son of Augustine Washington and Mary Ball. After a distinguished career as a commander of Virginia troops during the French and Indian War, Washington settled down as a planter and politician at Mount Vernon Plantation in Fairfax County, Virginia, and married Martha Dandridge Custis, a wealthy widow with two children. A leader of the revolutionary movement

MARTHA WASHINGTON STANDS ON A PLATFORM TO GREET
GUESTS AT ONE OF THE RECEPTIONS THAT HELPED SET THE FORMAL
SOCIAL TONE FOR THE NEW FEDERAL CAPITAL.

against Great Britain in Virginia, he was appointed commander in chief of the American revolutionary forces in 1775. After leading the revolutionaries to victory, he was the unanimous choice in 1789 to serve as president of the United States under the newly adopted federal constitution. Following two terms as the nation's first president, he retired to his home, Mount Vernon. President Washington served from 1798–99 as head of the federal army raised to fight a feared French invasion.

MARTHA DANDRIDGE CUSTIS WASHINGTON (1731–1802) was born in New Kent County, Virginia, the daughter of John Dandridge, a planter, and Frances Jones. In 1750, Martha married Daniel Parke Custis, a wealthy planter, with whom she had four children, two of which, John Parke and Martha, survived. When her husband, Daniel, died in 1757, Martha became one of the wealthiest people in Virginia. After a brief courtship, she married George on January 6, 1759, at her plantation, presciently named White House. Martha helped her husband run a very successful plantation with more than three hundred slaves. George and Martha never had children of their own but reared her two children by her first husband, and four grandchildren. Martha accompanied her husband to every winter quarter during the American Revolution and set the style for many first ladies to come. Her wish "to grow old in solitude and tranquility together" was never granted. After George's death, she carried out his wish to free all of his slaves, but never freed the dozens of slaves she personally owned.

JOHN ADAMS (1735–1826), born in Braintree, Massachusetts, the son of John Adams and Susanna Boylston, graduated from Harvard College and practiced law before becoming immersed in revolutionary politics. He married Abigail Smith, who became his confidante, political advisor, and business manager. Adams was a member of the Continental Congress, where he helped write the Declaration of Independence, before becoming American minister in Paris, Holland, and London. After eight years as President Washington's vice president, Adams was elected to the presidency in 1796. An undeclared war with France and numerous political battles marked his presidency. John and Abigail were the first presidential couple to occupy the President's House, now the White House, in Washington, D.C.

ABIGAIL SMITH ADAMS (1744–1818), born in Weymouth, Massachusetts, to the Rev. William Smith and Elizabeth Quincy, became a leading advocate of women's political, educational, and marital rights. Educated at home by her father and mother, Abigail was recognized in her own time as a person with unusual intellectual and literary talents. Married to John Adams on October 25, 1764, she became the mother of six children and the first woman to be both the wife of a president and the mother of one; but she is best known as her husband's chief supporter and advisor during his years of political and diplomatic service. She was deeply involved in virtually all of his political and governmental decisions, even leaking favorable stories to the press. Of all the expert advice she offered her husband, she is best known for urging him to "Remember the Ladies" in writing a new Code of Laws. Abigail corresponded widely with noted men and women of the day, including Benjamin Rush and Thomas Jefferson. Like the wives of many successful men, Abigail also managed the family farm, real estate concerns, and other business ventures.

THOMAS JEFFERSON (1743–1826), son of Peter Jefferson and Jane Randolph, was born in Albemarle County, Virginia, and educated in private schools and at the College of William and Mary before studying law with George Wythe. He practiced law as well as ran a very large plantation operation with the help of numerous slaves and overseers. Jefferson married Martha Wayles Skelton, and the couple had six children. A political leader in revolutionary Virginia, Jefferson drafted the Declaration of Independence while a member of the Continental Congress and served as a wartime governor of Virginia and American minister to France. Upon his return to the United States in 1789, he became Secretary of State, then vice president in 1797, before being elected president in 1800. Jefferson's two presidential terms were highlighted by the acquisition of the Louisiana Territory, the Lewis and Clark Expedition, an undeclared war against the Barbary

Pirates, and deteriorating relations with Great Britain and France over boundaries and maritime rights.

MARTHA WAYLES SKELTON JEFFERSON (1748–82) was born in Charles City County, Virginia, to John Wayles and Martha Eppes. Her first husband, Bathurst Skelton, died in 1768, and on January 1, 1772, she married Thomas Jefferson. The couple had six children, but only two of them, daughters Martha and Maria, lived to maturity. No portrait of Martha, nor any of her letters, survives—only the literary excerpt printed in this book and her household accounts and recipe book give a hint as to the talents and qualities she used in helping to run Monticello and support her husband's political endeavors. She died from complications of childbirth and puerperal fever before American independence was achieved.

JAMES MADISON, JR. (1751–1836), was born at Port Conway, Virginia, to James Madison and Eleanor Rose Conway, reared as the son of a prosperous planter, and educated in private schools and the College of New Jersey (now Princeton University). Madison returned to his family plantation, Montpelier, sporadically studied law, and became one of the most influential revolutionaries. Popularly known as the "Father of the United States Constitution," Madison was instrumental in the establishment of the federal government in 1787–89. In 1794, he married Dolley Payne Todd. A leader in the U.S. Congress, where he engineered the adoption of the Bill of Rights, and Secretary of State under Thomas Jefferson, Madison was elected president in 1808. His two terms were marked by the War of 1812, often called the Second War of American Independence. During his retirement he continued to offer political advice but ignored pleas to set an example for the nation by freeing his slaves, despite being a leader of the American Colonization Society.

DOROTHEA (DOLLEY) PAYNE TODD MADISON (1768–1849), was born at New Garden, North Carolina, to Quaker parents John Payne and Mary Coles, and raised in Goochland County, Virginia, and Philadelphia. Married in 1790 to John Todd, she had two sons, but only John Payne lived to maturity.

After her husband's death from yellow fever in 1793, she met and married Congressman James Madison, Jr., then a well-established political leader. Dolley Madison helped serve as hostess during Jefferson's administration and then blossomed as the first lady for eight years, turning the President's House into the social center of the capital. During the British attack on Washington, D.C., she bravely stayed behind to help rescue the furnishings in the President's House. Dolley provided her husband with traditional support and in later years served as his private secretary. After his death, she arranged for the publication of his papers and returned to Washington, where she supported herself by selling her husband's papers to the federal government, and selling off slaves and land at Montpelier.

JAMES MONROE (1758–1831), the eldest son of Spence Monroe and Elizabeth Jones, graduated from the College of William and Mary (1776). After serving in the American Revolutionary army, where he was wounded in the Battle of Trenton, New Jersey, Monroe practiced law in Virginia, where he became a protégé of Thomas Jefferson and rival of James Madison. Monroe married Elizabeth Kortright. He served in the Continental Congress; in the U.S. Senate; as American minister to France, Spain, and England; and as Secretary of State in the administration of James Madison. Elected to the presidency in 1816, Monroe served two terms, marked by peace at home and abroad and known as the Era of Good Feeling. President and Mrs. Monroe are credited with the restoration of the President's House after it was burned during the War of 1812.

ELIZABETH KORTRIGHT MONROE (1768–1830), the daughter of Laurence Kortright, a once wealthy West India merchant, and Elizabeth Aspinwall, married James Monroe in 1786, when he was a member of the Continental Congress. Elizabeth and James had three children but only two daughters lived to maturity. Accustomed to an elegant, urban lifestyle, Elizabeth Monroe sought to enhance her surroundings, whether in Paris, Washington, or Fluvanna County, Virginia. President and Mrs. Monroe refurnished the President's House with French furniture, fixtures, and china after it had been restored from British destruction, established a kind of formality in the president's social events, and introduced French style to Washington society.

JOHN QUINCY ADAMS (1767–1848) was the son of John Adams, the second president of the United States, and Abigail Smith. While accompanying his father on diplomatic missions abroad, John Quincy attended private schools, going on to graduate from Harvard College. With the support of his father, John Quincy served as an American minister to the Netherlands, Prussia, and Russia, and as chief negotiator of the Treaty of Ghent, ending the War of 1812. While teaching at Harvard, Adams served as a U.S. senator (1803–8) and then as President Monroe's Secretary of State when he helped formulate the Monroe Doctrine. Elected to the presidency by a controversial vote of the U.S. House of Representatives in 1825, Adams endorsed public works projects and a very high tariff. Defeated for a second term by Andrew Jackson, he returned to serve in the U.S. Congress, where he was a leader of the antislavery faction. He suffered a fatal stroke while at his seat in the House chamber.

    LOUISA CATHERINE JOHNSON ADAMS (1775–1852), the only foreign-born first lady, was raised in London and Nantes, France, by her American parents, Joshua Johnson and Catherine Nuth. Louisa met John Quincy while he was on a diplomatic errand in London and quickly captivated the young New Englander. She proved to be a worthy intellectual partner and, like her mother-in-law Abigail Adams, chaffed at the traditional roles allotted to the wife of a successful man. Louisa suffered through many miscarriages and infant deaths, with only three sons reaching maturity. She wrote poetry and prose, and introduced dancing at presidential receptions. Her talent as a writer is evident in her many letters to her husband, family, and friends.

ANDREW JACKSON (1767–1845), son of Andrew Jackson and Elizabeth Hutchinson, was born and raised in the Waxhaw region along the North and South Carolina border. During the Revolutionary War he was wounded and briefly imprisoned by the British army. Schooled at home and by life, he studied law in Salisbury, North Carolina, and was admitted to the Bar in 1787, before heading west to Nashville, Tennessee, where he practiced law, ran a plantation, and served as a U.S. representative and senator. He twice married Rachel Donelson Robards (see below). Jackson came to fame as a frontier duelist and militia general, leading highly successful armies against the Creek, Chickasaw, Choctaw, and Seminole Indians and against the British at New Orleans. Narrowly defeated by John Quincy Adams for the presidency in the House of Representatives in 1825, Jackson railed against that "corrupt bargain" until the 1828 election, when he soundly beat Adams. Jackson's two terms were marked by the destruction of the Bank of the United States, the Black Hawk War, a political battle against Southern nullification of federal law, and the infamous expulsion of the Cherokees from their lands east of the Mississippi River.

RACHEL DONELSON ROBARDS JACKSON (1767–1828) was born in Halifax County, Virginia, the daughter of John Donelson and Rachel Stockley, and raised in Kentucky and Tennessee. After a brief, allegedly abusive marriage to Lewis Robards, she met Andrew Jackson, who "married" her in 1791 while her divorce proceedings were underway. Officially married in 1794, the couple had no children but adopted one of Rachel's nephews. Their union was an object of political attack throughout Jackson's career. Although only informally educated, Rachel ran the family plantation during Jackson's frequent absences. She died shortly after his victorious presidential campaign in 1828.

JOHN TYLER (1790–1862), the son of John Tyler and Mary Armistead, was born at Greenway, the family plantation in Charles River County, into a Virginia family with a long tradition of public service. A graduate of the College of William and Mary, Tyler successively married Letitia Christian and Julia Gardiner, and was the father of fourteen children who lived to maturity—the most of any president. After long service as a U.S. representative and senator, Vice President Tyler became president upon the April 5, 1841, death of President William Henry Harrison. His White House years saw the Webster-Ashburton Treaty settling the northern boundary of the United States, the annexation of Texas in 1845, and the Treaty of Wanghia granting the United States access to trade and the right of extraterritoriality in China. Tyler has the distinction of being the only U.S. president ever to serve in the Confederate government.

LETITIA CHRISTIAN TYLER (1790–1842), born at Cedar Grove in New Kent County, Virginia, to Robert Christian and Mary Brown, married John Tyler on March 29, 1813. Letitia usually remained at home during Tyler's many trips to Richmond and Washington, maintaining the manse and mothering seven children who lived to adulthood. Having suffered a debilitating stroke in 1839, Letitia remained in the family quarters at the White House during her husband's term, except when she attended her daughter Mary's wedding in 1842.

JULIA GARDINER TYLER (1820–89) was the daughter of David Gardiner and Juliana McLachlan of New York. Educated at private schools, Julia appeared as a model in clothing advertisements before she met and married the recently widowed President Tyler in 1843. Tyler's older children had a hard time accepting Julia into the family, but the president and his new first lady had seven children, making Tyler the president with the most offspring. Despite her New York origins, Julia was a staunch advocate of slavery and states' rights. After her husband's death she spent the Civil War years at the family home on Long Island, later successfully reviving the family's landed estate in Virginia.

JAMES KNOX POLK (1795–1849), born in Mecklenburg County, North Carolina, to Samuel Polk and Jane Knox, was educated in Presbyterian private schools and at the University of North Carolina before studying law in Nashville, Tennessee. A lawyer and plantation owner, Polk served in the Tennessee assembly, the U.S. Congress, and as governor of Tennessee, before being elected president in 1844, pledging to annex lands in America's Southwest and Northwest. His notable accomplishments as president included victory in the Mexican War (1846–48), and signing the Oregon Treaty with Great Britain in 1846. His brief retirement ended in death from cholera while on a trip to New Orleans.

SARAH CHILDRESS POLK (1803–91), born near Murfrees-boro, Tennessee, to Joel Childress and Elizabeth Whitsitt, was educated at public schools, by tutors, and at the Moravian Female Academy in North Carolina before marrying James Polk on January 1, 1824. For most of Polk's political service Sarah was by his side, encouraging him to victory and consoling him in defeat. Her letters reflect her key role as a keen political observer, secretary, and aide, as well as her role in running the family properties. Although she banned cards, dancing, and liquor from the White House, she entertained regularly and enthusiastically.

FRANKLIN PIERCE (1804–69), born in Hillsborough, New Hampshire, to Benjamin Pierce and Anna Kendrick, was educated at Bowdoin College, read law, and began to practice in Hillsborough. In 1834 he married Jane Means Appleton and embarked on a long political career in the New Hampshire legislature, the U.S. House of Representatives, and the U.S. Senate before his election to the presidency in 1852. After a tenure marked by the inflammatory Kansas-Nebraska Act and the failure of his plan to annex Cuba, Pierce retired to New Hampshire but continued to oppose the use of force to save the Union. He suffered personally from the early death of his three sons, and the mental and physical frailty of his wife.

    JANE MEANS APPLETON PIERCE (1806–63), born in Hampton, New Hampshire, to Rev. Jesse Appleton, the president of Bowdoin College, and Elizabeth Means, was educated at home and with private tutors. After an eight-year courtship, Jane married Franklin Pierce over the objections of her mother and family. Always of delicate health, she nonetheless bore three sons, whose early deaths contributed to her apparent mental fragility and depression. A very religious person, this first lady seldom left the White House except for church, but she did attend many of the formal and informal entertainments at the President's House.

ABRAHAM LINCOLN (1809–65), born in Hardin County, Kentucky, to Thomas Lincoln and Nancy Hanks, attended frontier public schools while working on his father's and neighboring farms, worked in a general store, and then read law. He began his practice in Springfield, Illinois. In 1842 he married Mary Todd. After serving in the Illinois legislature and the U.S. Congress, Lincoln ran for the Senate in 1858 but was defeated by William Douglas. Elected to the presidency in 1860, Lincoln faced Southern rebellion and secession. President Lincoln led the Union forces to victory against the Confederacy, abolished slavery in the Confederacy with the Emancipation Proclamation, and was assassinated by John Wilkes Booth on the eve of the absolute surrender of all Southern forces.

MARY ANN TODD LINCOLN (1818–82), born in Lexington, Kentucky, to Robert Smith Todd and Eliza Parker, was educated at Shelby Female Academy and Charlotte Mentelle's finishing school for young women before moving to Springfield, Illinois, in 1839. Three years later, she married Abraham Lincoln, and the couple had three children, but only their son Robert lived to adulthood. During the course of their marriage, she became mentally fragile and paranoid. Nevertheless, Mary's surviving letters indicate a willingness to offer her husband advice, even on the removal of generals and the care of refugee former slaves. Following the president's assassination, she struggled psychologically and financially, until 1870 when she was finally granted a federal pension. After her son Robert had her declared "insane" by an all-male jury, Mary enlisted the help of Myra Blackwell, the first woman lawyer admitted to practice before the Supreme Court, who wrested control of her life back from her son. Thereafter, she lived a peripatetic life in Europe and America.

ANDREW JOHNSON (1808–75), born in Raleigh, North Carolina, to Jacob Johnson and Mary McDonough, was trained as a tailor and self-educated with the help of his wife, Eliza McCardle. When he was fifteen, Johnson ran away from his apprenticeship as a tailor and traveled to South Carolina, Alabama, and Tennessee, finally settling in Greenville, where he operated a tailor shop, prospered, and invested in real estate. Johnson entered politics in Greenville, serving as alderman, U.S. representative, Tennessee governor, and U.S. senator. His valiant efforts to keep

Tennessee in the Union brought him an appointment as military governor of Tennessee and, in 1864, the nomination for vice president on the ticket with Abraham Lincoln.

Like Harry S. Truman nearly a hundred years later, Johnson became president near the end of a major war and after barely one month in office. Johnson's term in office was marked by the end of the Civil War and his own tumultuous relations with Congress, ending with his impeachment and the failure by one vote to convict him and remove him from office. At the end of his presidency, in 1869, Johnson ran unsuccessfully for the U.S. Senate, but then in 1875 became the first former president elected to the Senate, serving for only five months alongside twelve senators who had voted "guilty" in his impeachment trial.

ELIZA McCARDLE JOHNSON (1810–76) was born in Leesburg, Tennessee, the only child of John McCardle and Sarah Phillips, and was educated at Rhea Academy in Warrensburg. When she was sixteen she married Andrew Johnson, whom she taught to read and write. Her family gave her full credit for Andrew's success, and the couple had five children. Afflicted with tuberculosis, Eliza remained at home during most of her husband's career, minding the family and business affairs. Often caught between warring armies during the Civil War, she nevertheless succeeded in preserving her home and family. As first lady, Eliza remained in the background, letting her daughter Martha preside over most of the public functions at the White House.

HIRAM ULYSSES S. GRANT (1822–85), the son of a prosperous tanner and store owner, Jesse Grant, and Hannah Simpson, graduated from West Point in 1843. After serving in the army until 1854, including service in the Mexican War, he operated a farm in Missouri and then went to work for his father in Galena, Illinois. In 1848, Grant married Julia Boggs Dent. Grant's commanding service in the Civil War led to the defeat of the Confederacy and his subsequent election as president of the United States in 1868. Grant was the last president to have owned a slave, whom he freed in 1859. After two terms in the White House notable for the "reconstruction" of the former Confederacy and for corruption within the government, he went on an extended global tour. Grant was nearly nominated for president again at the 1880 Republican Convention in Chicago, but James Garfield beat him out on the thirty-sixth ballot. In 1884, facing a bleak financial future after the failure of his son's brokerage firm and a bleaker medical future (he had been diagnosed with throat cancer), Grant wrote his memoirs at the urging of Mark Twain, and they proved to be highly successful and profitable.

JULIA BOGGS DENT GRANT (1826–1902), was born near St. Louis, Missouri, to Frederick Dent, a prosperous plantation owner and merchant, and Ellen Wrenshall. Educated at the private school of Phillip Mauro in St. Louis, she married Hiram Ulysses Grant after a four-year engagement, during which they met only once and despite the opposition of both sets of parents. Unable to accompany her husband to his West Coast military assignments and unhappy with the military life style, she urged him to resign and become a planter in Missouri. The couple had four children who led prosperous and productive lives. When the Civil War erupted, she once more suffered through long periods of separation, but often visited General Grant at headquarters. While first lady, Julia entertained lavishly, proudly stood by her husband, and thoroughly enjoyed her role as a social leader. At the end of Grant's presidency, Julia and Ulysses traveled widely and lived luxuriously. After his death, Julia continued her peregrinations on behalf of veterans, and wrote her memoirs.

RUTHERFORD BIRCHARD HAYES (1822–93), the son of Rutherford Hayes and Sophia Birchard, was born and raised in Delaware, Ohio, by his mother and uncle, Sardis Birchard. Educated at Kenyon College and Harvard Law School, Hayes practiced law in Cincinnati, Ohio, where he married Lucy Ware Webb. After serving as a Union major general in the Civil War and enjoying a long political career in Ohio, Hayes became president in 1877, after one of the nation's most disputed elections. (It ultimately had to be settled by a special electoral commission.) Despite Hayes's positive attempts at government reform, his reputation was permanently sullied by this dubious election, which apparently brought him the White House in dubious exchange for ending the federal military occupation of the Southern States and the protection of Freedmen. Hayes enjoyed a short but happy retirement at Spiegel Grove in Fremont, Ohio.

LUCY WEBB HAYES (1831–89), born in Chillicothe, Ohio, to James Webb, a physician, and Maria Cook, graduated from Cincinnati Wesleyan Women's College. The first First Lady to graduate from college, she worked with the poor before her 1852 marriage to Rutherford B. Hayes. The couple had five children who lived to maturity. A vigorous opponent of slavery, she convinced her husband to join the Republican Party and spent the Civil War at home, maintaining the family and manse, and hoping for the safe return of her husband. She was instrumental in his successful political career and entertained without alcohol at the White House. Lucy Hayes began holding the annual Easter Egg Roll at the White House; it had hitherto been held at the capitol grounds. A believer in women's higher education and women's suffrage, she nevertheless refused to support them publicly in deference to her husband's political career.

JAMES ABRAM GARFIELD (1831–81) was born on an Ohio farm, the son of Abram Garfield and Eliza Ballou. Educated at local schools and Williams College, he taught at the Eclectic Academy in Hiram, Ohio, and studied law before the Civil War propelled him to the rank of major general and a future political career in the U.S. House of Representatives (1863–80). Securing the 1880 Republican presidential nomination over Hiram Ulysses S. Grant in 1880, Garfield had just begun his first year in office when he was shot at the Baltimore and Potomac Railroad Station in Washington, D.C.; he died two months later. In 1858, he married Lucretia Rudolph, and the couple had five children who lived to maturity. Garfield's courtship and marriage were rocky, but James and "Crete" were a formidable intellectual duo, as their letters testify.

LUCRETIA RUDOLPH GARFIELD (1832–1918), born in Garrettsville, Ohio, the daughter of Zebulon Rudolph, the founder of the Eclectic Academy in Hiram, Ohio, and Arabella Mason, was a classmate of James Garfield at the Geauga Seminary at Chester, Ohio, and the Eclectic Academy. Lucretia Rudolph taught school in Hiram and Cleveland before her marriage to James Garfield. Despite Garfield's infidelities, Lucretia supported her husband's political ambitions and managed households in Washington and Ohio and raised five children. After Garfield's assassination, Lucretia divided her time between Ohio and California, lecturing on literature and working for the Red Cross.

CHESTER ALAN ARTHUR (1829–86), born in North Fairfield, Vermont, the son of William Arthur and Malvina Stone, was educated at the Lyceum in Schenectady, New York, and Union College before studying law in New York City. Arthur practiced law in New York City and married Ellen Lewis Herndon in 1859. He was active in Republican Party politics and served in the Civil War, before being appointed Collector of the Port of New York in 1871. In 1880, he was elected vice president on the ticket with James Garfield and, when Garfield was assassinated in 1881, became president. Arthur is best known for his support of the creation of the modern civil service in the Pendleton Act of 1883. After leaving the presidency, he resumed the practice of law in New York City.

ELLEN LEWIS HERNDON ARTHUR (1837–80), was born in Culpepper Court House, Virginia, the daughter of William L. Herndon and Frances Hansbrough. Privately educated, Ellen was a talented soprano, singing with the Mendelssohn Glee Club in New York City. While her husband served in the Union Army, Ellen sympathized with the Southern Rebellion. Chester and Ellen Arthur had two children who lived to maturity. Ellen died of pneumonia on January 10, 1880, while Arthur was away on a business/political trip.

STEPHEN GROVER CLEVELAND (1837–1908), born in New Jersey to Richard Cleveland, a Presbyterian minister, and Ann Neal, was the only president to be elected to nonconsecutive terms of office (1885–89, and 1893–97). He attended private schools in Fayetteville, New York, before becoming a lawyer in Buffalo. Despite having purchased a substitute soldier for service in the Civil War (then a legal practice), Cleveland was elected governor of New York in 1883 and president in 1885. Cleveland was the first president to be wed in the White House, where he married his "niece" and ward, Frances Folsom. His administrations were highlighted by regulation of commerce, higher education, and labor, and the financial panic of 1893.

FRANCES FOLSOM CLEVELAND (1864–1947), born in Buffalo, New York, the daughter of Oscar Folsom, a close friend of Grover Cleveland, and Emma Harmon, was educated at public and private schools before graduating from Wells College. On June 2, 1886, she married her "Uncle Cleve" (who had served as a financial advisor to her mother) in the first White House wedding of a president. The couple had five children who lived to maturity. The Clevelands mainly lived in their own Washington house during his first presidential term. Frances served on the board of Wells College for fifty years and helped found the University Women's Club. Frances Cleveland financially supported the Women's Christian Temperance Union, a strong advocate of woman suffrage. In 1913, she married Thomas Preston, Jr., a college professor, gave public speeches supporting World War I, and supported Alfred E. Smith for president.

BENJAMIN HARRISON (1833–1901), the son of John Scott Harrison and Elizabeth Irwin, was born in North Bend, Ohio, the home of his grandfather, former president William Henry Harrison. Educated at Miami University in Ohio, Harrison became a lawyer in Indianapolis, Indiana. In 1853, he married Caroline Lavinia Scott, and following her death, married his first wife's niece, Mary Scott Lord Dimmick in 1896. After military service in the Civil War, he became a U.S. senator before winning the Republican nomination for the presidency and defeating Stephen Grover Cleveland in 1888. His presidency is known for the first billion-dollar federal budget, the Sherman Anti-Trust Act, and the admission of the most (six) states to the federal union during a single presidential term.

CAROLINE LAVINIA SCOTT HARRISON (1832–92), the daughter of the Rev. John W. Scott and Mary Neal, was educated at Oxford Female Institute, a school founded by her father.

She married Benjamin Harrison, a former student of her father's at Farmers' College. They were the parents of a son and a daughter. The couple were the first to erect a Christmas tree at the White House, and electricity was installed at the White House during a renovation overseen by them. Plagued by ill health, she died just two weeks before the end of her husband's unsuccessful reelection campaign.

MARY SCOTT LORD DIMMICK HARRISON (1858–1948), born in Honesdale, Pennsylvania, the daughter of Farnham Lord and Elizabeth Scott, was a niece of Caroline Harrison, and served as her aide during the presidential term of Benjamin Harrison, whom she married to the great consternation of Benjamin and Caroline's children. Mary and Benjamin were the parents of a daughter, Elizabeth, who became a lawyer and founder of an investment newsletter for women.

WILLIAM McKINLEY, JR. (1843–1901), born in Niles, Ohio, the son of William McKinley, an iron manufacturer, and Nancy Allison. He was educated at public schools, Poland Seminary, and Allegheny College before studying law and practicing in Canton, Ohio. He married Ida Saxton. McKinley was the last Civil War veteran elected to the presidency and served in the U.S. House of Representatives and as governor of Ohio before winning the presidential election of 1896. Reelected in 1900, with the Spanish-American War hero Theodore Roosevelt as his running mate, McKinley was assassinated in 1901 in Buffalo, New York. His first administration is best known for the Spanish-American War, the annexation of Hawaii, the acquisition of the Philippines, and the Boxer Rebellion in China.

IDA SAXTON McKINLEY (1847–1907), the daughter of James Saxton, a Canton banker, and Catherine DeWalt, was educated at Brooke Hall Seminary in Medina, Pennsylvania. She married William McKinley before a thousand guests in 1871, and the couple had two daughters who died in infancy. A semi-invalid after the death of her second child, Ida McKinley nonetheless led White House entertainments and frequently accompanied her husband on his political travels, including his ill-fated trip to

Buffalo in 1901. She feared for her husband—a fear that was realized when he was shot and killed in Buffalo, New York, by a self-avowed anarchist.

THEODORE ROOSEVELT (1858–1919), the son of Theodore Roosevelt and Martha Bulloch, was born in New York City, graduated from Harvard College, and in 1882 embarked on a long career of public service. He first married Alice Hathaway Lee, then Edith Kermit Carow. First a New York State assemblyman, Roosevelt held various state offices, rising to governor in 1898, and led a regiment of "Rough Riders" to victory in the Spanish-American War. After serving only six months as William McKinley's vice president, he became the youngest president of the United States when McKinley was assassinated in 1901, and served until 1909. Roosevelt is best known for negotiating an end to the Russo-Japanese War, sending the American naval fleet around the world, the building of the Panama Canal, and for his motto, "Speak softly and carry a big stick." He tried for reelection in 1912 on a third-party ticket, but was defeated. In retirement, he traveled the world in search of adventure.

ALICE LEE ROOSEVELT (1861–84), born in Chestnut Hill, Massachusetts, the daughter of George Cabot Lee, a banker, and Caroline Haskell, was privately educated and raised within Boston Brahmin society. Against her parents' wishes, she married Theodore Roosevelt on October 27, 1880. After a short but intense marriage, to judge from the surviving documentation, Alice died from childbirth complications and Bright's disease on February 14, 1884, after delivering a daughter, Alice.

EDITH KERMIT CAROW ROOSEVELT (1861–1948), born in Norwich, Connecticut, to Charles Carow, a wealthy businessman, and Gertrude Elizabeth Tyler, was educated at the Comstock School. After a long friendship, Edith and Theodore Roosevelt were married on December 2, 1886, in London. The couple had four children who lived to maturity. Edith worked hard to further Theodore's career while maintaining home and family. Edith entertained untiringly and oversaw a complex renovation of the White House, while traveling extensively with her husband. After Theodore's death, she continued to travel and entertain, as well as campaigning for Republicans and donating money to charities and the arts.

WILLIAM HOWARD TAFT (1857–1930), born in Cincinnati, Ohio, the son of Alphonso Taft, President Grant's U.S. Attorney General and Secretary of War, and his second wife, Louisa Maria Torrey, was educated at Yale University and the University of Cincinnati Law School. Long service as a federal judge, U.S. solicitor general, and commissioner general of the Philippines brought him an appointment as Theodore Roosevelt's Secretary of War, and he was Roosevelt's choice to succeed him in 1909. After one term as president, he was defeated by Woodrow Wilson when Taft's own mentor, Theodore Roosevelt, ran as a third-party candidate. Taft later served as Chief Justice of the U.S. Supreme Court, 1921–30, the only former president to hold that position.

HELEN HERRON TAFT (1861–1943), born in Cincinnati, Ohio, the daughter of John Williamson Herron, a lawyer and partner of Rutherford B. Hayes, and Harriet Collins, was educated at Miss Nourse's School, Miami University in Ohio, and the Cincinnati College of Music. After teaching school in Walnut Hills, Ohio, she married William Howard Taft on June 19, 1886. While mothering three children and running the family household, she shepherded Taft to the White House, where she entertained extensively. Helen traveled widely with her husband and often went abroad with her children while her husband traveled elsewhere on official business.

THOMAS WOODROW WILSON (1856–1924), born in Staunton, Virginia, to the Rev. Joseph R. Wilson, a Presbyterian minister, and Jessie Janet Woodrow, was educated at Davidson College, Princeton University, University of Virginia Law School and Johns Hopkins University (PhD 1886). He married Ellen Louise Axson and then Edith Bolling Galt. Wilson taught at Bryn Mawr College and Princeton before becoming president of Princeton and then governor of New Jersey in 1911. In 1912, he was the first (and only) person with a doctorate to be elected president. Wilson's two terms in office were marked by victory in World War I and his failure to secure U.S. ratification of the Versailles Treaty and entrance into the League of Nations. His presidency saw the passage of three Constitutional Amendments, including the seventeenth for the direct election of senators and the nineteenth, which provided for women's right to vote.

ELLEN LOUISE AXSON WILSON (1860–1914), the daughter of the Rev. Samuel Axson and Margaret Janet Hoyt, was educated at local schools and studied art in New York. Before her marriage, she taught school and drew crayon portraits to support herself. Ellen married Woodrow on June 24, 1885, and dedicated herself to "a service of love." The couple had three daughters, and Ellen home-schooled them, while supporting Wilson's academic and political careers. As the first lady, she worked to improve conditions for government employees and for the enforcement of child labor and school attendance laws. She died of Bright's disease and tuberculosis of the kidneys.

EDITH BOLLING GALT WILSON (1872–1961), the daughter of William Bolling, a lawyer, and Sallie White, was educated by tutors and at Martha Washington College in Abingdon, Virginia, and Powell Girls School in Richmond, Virginia. Before she married Woodrow Wilson, she was widowed by Norman Galt, a wealthy Washington, D.C., jewelry store owner. Edith married Wilson on December 18, 1915, with the full emotional support of the groom's daughters. During World War I, she volunteered with the Red Cross, even selling wool from the sheep that grazed on the White House lawn for the organization's benefit. When Wilson suffered a series of severe strokes in the last years of his presidency, the first lady virtually ran the country in her husband's name while he was bedridden and semicomatose, even helping to force the resignation of Secretary of State Robert Lansing for calling Cabinet meetings and questioning the president's ability to govern.

WARREN GAMALIEL HARDING (1865–1923), was born in Corsica (Blooming Grove), Ohio, to George Tyron Harding and Phoebe Elizabeth Dickerson, both of whom were physicians. Harding was educated in public school and at Ohio Central College, and was a sports (primarily golf) and card fanatic. In 1891, he married Florence Mabel Kling DeWolfe, a divorced woman. He was a co-owner and publisher of the *Marion Star*. Active in Republican politics, he served as a state senator, Ohio lieutenant governor, and U.S. senator before his election to the presidency in 1920. His administration was marked by the diminution of the League of Nations and the Teapot Dome Scandal, among other scandals. President Harding died while on a cross-country "Voyage of Understanding" to meet the American people.

FLORENCE (DUTCHESS) MABEL KLING DEWOLFE HARDING (1860–1924), was born in Marion, Ohio, the daughter of Amos Kling, a wealthy banker, and Louisa Bouton, and was educated at public schools and the Cincinnati Conservatory of Music. When she was nineteen she married Henry DeWolfe and divorced him six years later, supporting herself by giving piano lessons. She then married Warren G. Harding and, though the couple had no children of their own, they helped raise Florence's son, Marshall. Despite her husband's numerous affairs, Florence supported Harding's political career, accompanying him to the Republican Convention in Chicago and campaigning with him. Mrs. Harding was a strong advocate of women's rights and supported organizations protecting animals. She was also instrumental in reopening the White House to tourists, and she entertained extravagantly.

JOHN CALVIN COOLIDGE (1872–1933), born in Plymouth, Vermont, the son of John Calvin Coolidge, farmer/storekeeper, and Victoria Moor, was educated at pubic schools and St. Johnsbury Academy before graduating from Amherst College. Coolidge studied law in Northampton and practiced there. In 1905, he married Grace Goodhue. Coolidge served in the Massachusetts legislature and as governor of Massachusetts before his election as vice president in 1921. When Warren Harding died in office, Coolidge was sworn in as president by his father, a local justice of the peace. In 1924, Coolidge won election to the presidency, and is known for having set limits on immigration, instituted tax cuts, and signed the Kellogg-Briand Pact of 1928, renouncing war. His reputation for frugality with both money and words can be seen in the letters to his wife, Grace.

GRACE ANNA GOODHUE COOLIDGE (1879–1957), was born in Burlington, Vermont, the only child of Andrew Goodhue, an engineer, and Lemira Barrett. She attended public schools and graduated from the University of Vermont, and was working as a teacher of the deaf at the Clark School in Northampton, Massachusetts, when she met Calvin Coolidge, whom she married in 1905. The couple had two sons, one of whom, Calvin, died while his father was seeking reelection in 1924. As first lady, Mrs. Coolidge entertained extensively and maintained a menagerie of animals. After the sudden death of her husband in 1933, Grace lived comfortably on their savings and continued her lifelong work on behalf of the deaf, particularly at Clark School. She supported Republican candidates and served as a volunteer for Waves in training at Smith College.

HERBERT CLARK HOOVER (1874–1964) was born in West Branch, Iowa, the son of Jesse Clark Hoover, a salesman, and Huldah Minthorn, and was reared by his uncle, Dr. John Minthorn in Newberg, Oregon. Educated at public schools, Friends Pacific Academy, and Stanford University, Hoover traveled the world and became wealthy as a mining engineer and geologist. He led relief efforts for displaced persons during World War I and served as Secretary of Commerce for President Warren Harding, before his election as president in 1928. The stock market crash, the Veterans Bonus March on Washington, and the Great Depression marked his administration. During his long retirement in California and New York, Hoover chaired a major relief effort for displaced persons during World War II and two major post–World War II commissions to streamline the federal government.

LOU HENRY HOOVER (1874–1944), was born in Waterloo, Iowa, and raised in California, the daughter of Charles Delano Henry, a banker, and Florence Weed, and was educated in public schools, at a California teacher's college before becoming the only female geology student at Stanford University. It was there that she met Herbert Hoover, whom she married in 1899. The couple had two sons. Lou Hoover shared her husband's work as a mining engineer, traveling the world as both his wife and business

PRESIDENT AND MRS. HERBERT HOOVER POSE DURING HAPPIER TIMES
IN 1929, BEFORE THE STOCK MARKET CRASH LATE IN THE YEAR.

associate, living chiefly in China and London. During World War
I, they returned to the United States and Lou became a champi-
on of the Girl Scout movement, serving at one point as president
of the National Girl Scout Council. It can be argued that she was
the most cosmopolitan first lady, but she was shocked by the
nation's blaming her husband for the Great Depression.

FRANKLIN DELANO ROOSEVELT (1882–1945) was born
at Hyde Park, New York, the second child and only son of James
Roosevelt, lawyer and financier, and Sara Delano. After graduating from the Groton School and Harvard College, Roosevelt attended
Columbia Law School and practiced in New York City before enter-
ing the political fray as a Democrat. (His cousin, former president
Theodore Roosevelt, was a Republican.) Franklin married his distant cousin, Anna Eleanor Roosevelt, in 1905. After serving in the
New York Senate (1911–13), as assistant Secretary of the Navy
(1913–20), and, despite his having contracted crippling polio in
1921, he served as governor of New York (1929–32) and became
president in 1932, in the midst of the Great Depression. He won

reelection three more times. (Amendment XXII, which limits presidents to two elected terms in office, would not be added to the Constitution until 1951.) His New Deal, including the Social Security Act, and the successful campaigns of World War II highlighted his presidency, the longest in American history.

ANNA ELEANOR ROOSEVELT ROOSEVELT (1884–1962), born in New York City, the daughter of Elliott Roosevelt, the younger brother of Theodore Roosevelt, and Anna Hall, was educated at Allenwood School in London. Before her marriage to distant cousin Franklin D. Roosevelt, she volunteered for the Consumers' League and local settlement houses. Eleanor and Franklin were the parents of five very successful children. During World War I she worked daily for the Red Cross. In addition to her roles as a mother and as the wife of an ambitious politician, she spent most of her life working for rights that would benefit women, the working people, the poor, and victims of discrimination. While first lady, Eleanor initiated the practice of holding press conferences with women reporters, and maintained a career as a lecturer and radio personality. Eleanor was the longest-serving first lady, and after her husband's death President Harry Truman appointed her the nation's first delegate to the nascent United Nations organization.

HARRY S. TRUMAN (1884–1972) was born in Lamar, Missouri, the son of John A. Truman, a farmer, and Martha Ellen Young. Raised in Independence, Missouri, where he attended public schools, he held a number of clerical jobs before returning to the family farm. He served in the U.S. Artillery in France during World War I and attended Kansas City Law School. Married in 1919 to Elizabeth Virginia Wallace, Truman pursued a political career beginning as a judge in Jackson County in 1922. In 1935, he was elected to the U.S. Senate, where he served until he became vice president of the United States in 1945. President Roosevelt's death, just one month after Truman took office, propelled him into the presidency on April 12, 1945. Although actually elected president only once, in 1948, Truman, like Theodore Roosevelt, served nearly two full terms before declining to run for reelection in 1952. The end of World War II, the dropping of the atomic bomb, the reconstruction of

Europe, and the onset of the Cold War were highlights of his presidency. As president, Truman strongly supported Constitutional Amendment XXII that limited a president to two full terms in office.

ELIZABETH VIRGINIA WALLACE TRUMAN (1885–1982) was born in Independence, Missouri, the daughter of David W. Wallace and Margaret Gates. She attended public schools and Barstow School in Kansas City. After a very long engagement, she married Harry Truman, and the couple had one daughter. Bess, as the first lady was known, shied away from the public role of politician's wife, but when her husband became a U.S. senator, she helped to run his office and manage his staff. As first lady, she helped to draft his speeches, campaigned for his reelection, and oversaw the reconstruction of the White House (1949–52).

DAVID DWIGHT EISENHOWER (1890–1969), born in Denison, Texas, the son of David Eisenhower and Ida E. Stover, was educated at public schools in Abilene, Kansas, and at West Point Military Academy. Making a career of the U.S. Army, Dwight Eisenhower (by then he had reversed his first and second names) rose to become supreme Allied commander of Allied Military Forces (non-Russian) in Europe during World War II. Without any political experience, he was elected president in 1952 and served two terms, during which he oversaw an end to the Korean War, the continuing cold war, American involvement in Vietnam, the construction of the interstate highway system, and continued postwar prosperity. He retired to his farm in Gettysburg, Pennsylvania.

MARIE (MAMIE) DOUD EISENHOWER (1896–1979), born in Boone, Iowa (the last First Lady born in the nineteenth century), to John Doud, a meat packer, and Elivera Carlson, was raised in Denver, Colorado, and San Antonio, Texas. She attended public schools and Miss Wolcott's School for "ladies of refinement." Married in 1916 to Dwight Eisenhower, she raised one son to maturity while traveling to military posts around the world. Mamie thrived in the White House, entertaining extensively but eschewing public political speeches. She renovated the family quarters—the perfect officer's wife. After the presidency, the Eisenhowers fulfilled a lifelong dream by retiring to a farm in Gettysburg, Pennsylvania.

JOHN FITZGERALD KENNEDY (1917–63), born in Brookline, Massachusetts, the son of Joseph P. Kennedy and Rose Fitzgerald, was educated at private schools, Choate, Princeton University, and Harvard University. After service in the navy during World War II, he was elected to the U.S. Congress in 1947. After serving in the House and the U.S. Senate, he was elected president in 1960, and assassinated in 1963. His administration was marked by the failed Bay of Pigs invasion of Cuba, deeper military involvement in southeast Asia, the Cuban missile crisis of 1962, the civil rights movement, and the Berlin crisis.

JACQUELINE LEE BOUVIER KENNEDY (1929–94), born in Southampton, New York, to John Bouvier and Janet Lee, was educated at private schools, Miss Porter's School, Vassar College, and George Washington University. Before her marriage to John F. Kennedy on September 12, 1953, Jackie worked as a newspaper photographer. Two of the couple's children reached maturity.

PRESIDENT JOHN F. KENNEDY AND FIRST LADY JACQUELINE GREET A CROWD OUTSIDE THE NATIONAL THEATRE IN WASHINGTON, D.C., ON SEPTEMBER 25, 1962.

Jackie campaigned in person and in the media during her husband's presidential bid. As first lady, she was known for her youth, elegance, style, and overseas travel. She was particularly interested in supporting the arts, historical restoration, and furthering women's rights. In 1968, she married Aristotle Onassis.

LYNDON BAINES JOHNSON (1908–73), the son of Sam E. Johnson, Jr., and Rebecca Baines, was educated at public schools in Johnson City, Texas, and Southwest Texas State College. After a brief teaching career, he went to Washington as a congressional aide. Johnson became a U.S. representative in 1937, serving until his switch to the U.S. Senate in 1948. After becoming Majority Leader of the Senate, he was elected vice president in 1960. When President John F. Kennedy was assassinated on November 22, 1963, Johnson became president and was reelected in 1964. The passage of a strong Civil Rights Act and the escalation of the war in Vietnam marked his presidency.

CLAUDIA ALTA (LADY BIRD) TAYLOR JOHNSON (1912–) was born in Karnack, Texas, the daughter of Thomas Jefferson Taylor, a prosperous storekeeper, and Minnie Lee Patillo. After her mother's death when she was five, she was raised by a doting father and other relatives and attended public school, St. Mary's Episcopal School for Girls, and the University of Texas. She married Lyndon Johnson in 1934, raised two daughters, and supported her husband's political career. In 1943, Lady Bird used part of her inheritance to buy a radio station in Austin, which she personally supervised and developed into a prosperous communications empire of radio and television stations. She continued her role as political partner and promoted a national beautification and conservation campaign, which she continued to spearhead after President Johnson left office. In 1982, she retired from public life and as chairman of the LBJ Holding Company.

RICHARD MILHOUS NIXON (1913–94) was born in Yorba Linda, California, the son of Frank A. Nixon and Hannah Milhous. After graduating from Whittier College in 1934, Nixon received his law degree from Duke University Law School in 1937.

In 1940, he married Thelma "Pat" C. Ryan and served from 1942 to 1946 in the U.S. Navy. He began his long political career in 1946 by winning a seat in the U.S. Congress, where he served as a representative and senator until 1953. Elected vice president as Dwight D. Eisenhower's running mate in 1952, he was narrowly defeated by John F. Kennedy in his 1960 presidential bid. Staging a remarkable political comeback, Nixon was elected president in 1968, only to narrowly avoid impeachment in 1974 before his resignation on August 9, 1974, in the culmination of the Watergate scandals. He was later pardoned by President Gerald R. Ford and in his retirement wrote and traveled extensively, once again reviving his career and reputation. During his presidency, he ended the war in Vietnam, reopened diplomatic relations with the People's Republic of China, and became enmeshed in political crimes and scandal.

THELMA (PATRICIA) CATHERINE RYAN NIXON (1912–1993) was born in Ely, Nevada, the daughter of William Ryan, miner/farmer, and Kate H. Bender, and raised in Artesia, California. Pat Ryan was educated at public schools, Fullerton Junior College, and the University of Southern California. She worked for two years as a stenographer and X-ray technician in New York City. After graduating from the University of Southern California, she taught in Whittier High School. In 1940, she married Richard M. Nixon and the couple raised two daughters. During World War II, she followed her husband from base to base, worked as a price analyst for OPA, and after the war she supported his political career. From his first campaign for Congress in 1946, "Pat" Nixon was part staff, part political wife. Although she did not like the public scrutiny that political candidates and their families were subjected to, she actively supported Nixon's candidacies. After his forced resignation, the first lady settled into private life in San Clemente, California.

GERALD RUDOLF FORD, JR. (1913–), was born Leslie Lynch King, Jr., the son of Leslie Lynch King and Dorothy A. Gardner. He became Gerald R. Ford after his mother divorced King and married Gerald Rudolf Ford, who adopted her young son and changed his name. Ford graduated from the University of Michigan, coached football at Yale University, and graduated from Yale Law School in 1941. After navy service in World War II, he practiced law in Grand Rapids, Michigan. He was elected to the U.S. Congress in 1948 and that same year married Elizabeth "Betty" Bloomer Warren. The couple had four children. Ford was congressman until 1973, when be became vice president of the United States, replacing Spiro Agnew, who had stepped down in the face of corruption charges. When President Nixon was forced to resign on August 9, 1974, Ford was sworn into office. He and his appointed vice president, Nelson Rockefeller, were thus the first presidential team to serve without a national election. The restoration of national confidence, the pardoning of former president Nixon, the American evacuation of South Vietnam, and the celebration of the Bicentennial of American Independence marked Ford's term in office.

ELIZABETH ANN (BETTY) BLOOMER WARREN FORD (1918–) was born in Chicago, Illinois, the daughter of William S. Bloomer and Hortense Neahr. A professional model and dancer, she was educated at Bennington College School of Dance and in Martha Graham's New York School. In 1942, she married William C. Warren, whom she divorced in 1947. During her engagement to Gerald R. Ford, she helped in his first congressional campaign. They were married on October 15, 1948, and spent their honeymoon on the campaign trail. A dedicated campaigner, she supported her husband's rise to the presidency, meanwhile becoming an outspoken supporter of women's rights, including abortion and the Equal Rights Amendment, and was a prominent advocate of breast cancer awareness and research. She also became a public voice for fighting women's drug and alcohol addiction.

JAMES EARL CARTER, JR. (1924–), was born in Plains, Georgia, the son of James Earl Carter and Lillian Gordy and educated in the Plains public schools and at the U.S. Naval Academy. After service in the navy, Carter returned to run the family peanut warehouse business in Plains. He married Eleanor Rosalynn Carter in 1946. Carter served in the Georgia State Senate and as governor of Georgia (1971–75) before his election to the presidency in 1976. His administration was marked by the nuclear crisis at Three-Mile Island, the Iranian Hostage Crisis, the Panama Canal Treaty of 1977, and the 1978 Camp David Accords between Egypt and Israel. Since his defeat by Ronald Reagan in 1980, Carter has become an advocate for peace, a supporter of Habitat for Humanity, and an environmental advocate, as well as an accomplished author.

ELEANOR ROSALYNN CARTER (1927–) was born in Plains, Georgia, the daughter of Frances Allethea Murray and William E. Smith, and was educated at the Plains public schools and Georgia Southwestern College. She married James Carter, and the couple had four children. Rosalynn considered herself a "political partner" to her husband and helped him reach the presidency in 1976. She has been a longtime advocate in the fight against mental illness. Since leaving the White House, Rosalynn has written several books, including her autobiography, *First Lady from Plains.*

RONALD WILSON REAGAN (1911–2004) was born in Tampico, Illinois, the son of John E. Reagan and Nelle Wilson. After spending an active youth in Dixon, Illinois, he graduated from Eureka College, then embarked on a successful career as a film actor. He married Jane Wyman in 1940 and Nancy Davis in 1952. Reagan served as a Republican governor of California from 1967 to 1975, before his election to the first of two presidential terms in 1980. Reagan survived an assassination attempt in 1981, and his administration was notable for the release of the Iranian hostages, the Iran-Contra scandal, the Grenada invasion, tax reform, and an arms race that bankrupted the Soviet Union, leading to its collapse and an end to the cold war.

ANNE FRANCIS (NANCY) ROBBINS DAVIS REAGAN (1921–) was born in New York City, the daughter of Kenneth Robbins, a car salesman, and Edith Luckett, an actress, and was adopted by her stepfather, Dr. Loyal Davis. She attended Chicago Girls' Latin School and graduated from Smith College. Before marrying Ronald Reagan, she was a successful stage and screen actress. The couple raised two children to maturity, and helped to raise Ronald Reagan's two children from his first marriage to Jane Wyman. "Nancy" Reagan supported her husband's acting career and his political rise to the presidency. During his presidency, the first lady played an active but behind-the-scenes role in his administration, influencing the selection of officials and the adoption of public policies.

GEORGE HERBERT WALKER BUSH (1924–), born at the family home in Milton, Massachusetts, the son of Prescott S. Bush and Dorothy Walker, graduated from Yale University after overseas service in the U.S. Navy during World War II. He was the founder and CEO of an oil exploration and drilling company before his 1966 election to the U.S. House of Representatives. After serving as U.S. ambassador to the United Nations, chairman of the Republican National Committee, chief U.S. liaison in China, and director of the CIA, he was elected vice president in 1980, serving two terms with President Reagan. Bush was elected president in 1988. His term in office saw the breakup of the Soviet Union and America's victory over Iraq in the First Gulf War. Following his non-reelection in 1992, he has written and traveled extensively and supported his son, George W. Bush in his victorious campaigns for the presidency in 2000 and 2004.

BARBARA PIERCE BUSH (1925–) was born in New York City, the daughter of Marvin Pierce, an engineer, and Pauline Robinson. She was educated at Rye Country Day School and Ashley Hall in South Carolina, before attending Smith College. In 1945, she married George H. W. Bush and the couple had five children. Barbara supported her husband as a businessman and in all his political activities, traveling widely and acting as a trusted personal adviser. After her husband's defeat in 1992, the first lady gracefully retired to Houston, Texas, and Kennebunkport, Maine, and continued her charitable work and service for nonprofit organizations.

WILLIAM JEFFERSON CLINTON (1946–), born in Hope, Arkansas, the son of William Jefferson Blythe and Virginia Cassidy, was educated at public schools, Georgetown University, Oxford University, and Yale University School of Law. Clinton practiced law and served as attorney general and governor of Arkansas before his election to the presidency in 1992. His presidency will be remembered for his plans for national reform of health care, a foreign policy of "nation building," the restoration of a federal budget surplus, and his victory in an impeachment trial in the U.S. Senate. In retirement, he has written his memoirs and spoken and traveled widely.

HILLARY RODHAM CLINTON (1947–), born in Chicago, Illinois, the daughter of Hugh Rodham and Dorothy Howell, was educated at public schools, Wellesley College, and Yale University Law School. While teaching law at the University of Arkansas Law School and practicing law, she was instrumental in running William Clinton's campaigns for public office. In 1975, she married him and the couple had one child, Chelsea. While Clinton served as attorney general and governor of Arkansas, Hillary continued to practice law in Little Rock at the Rose Law Firm and became a national advocate for children. She was a chief adviser to her husband during his presidential campaigns and his two terms as president, chairing his commission on health care reform. She embarked on her own career as an author in 1996 with *It Takes a Village.* Hillary Clinton became the only first lady elected to the U.S. Senate, when she won election in New York during the final year of her husband's presidency.

HAPPINESS RADIATES FROM GEORGE AND
BARBARA BUSH AS THEY WALK FROM THE CHURCH
IN RYE, NEW YORK, AFTER THEIR WEDDING
ON JANUARY 6, 1945.

CHAPTER 1

LOVE AND MARRIAGE

~♪

"To be an unloved wife, O Heavens."
—Lucretia Rudolph to James Garfield,
September 1, 1857

"My purest queen, no man was worthy of your love."
—Theodore Roosevelt to Alice Lee,
October 17, 1880

*"What I would not give this
morning for just one clasp of your hand."*
—Woodrow Wilson to Edith Galt,
May 6, 1915

*"Will you love me when
I'm shriveled and ridiculous looking?"*
—Pat Nixon to Richard Nixon,
June 1944

FROM the suggestive to the overstated, the expressions of love, fondness, and mutual attraction fill thousands of pages exchanged during the courtship and marriage of presidential couples. Viewed collectively, they form a tapestry of love and affection between two centuries of America's men and women, from eager youth to solid maturity. Celebrity and success seem almost irrelevant as one reads these highly personal messages.

*A*bigail Smith, who married John Adams on October 25, 1764, wrote this flirtatious letter to John while he was away in Boston undergoing inoculation for smallpox.

Weymouth, 16 April, 1764.

My Friend,

I think I write to you every day. Shall not I make my letters very cheap? Don't you light your pipe with them? I care not If you do. 'Tis a pleasure to me to write. Yet I wonder I write to you with so little restraint, for as a critic I fear you more than any other person on earth, and 'tis the only character in which I ever did or ever will fear you. What say you? Do you approve of that speech? Don't you think me a courageous being? Courage is a laudable, a glorious virtue in your sex, why not in mine? For my part, I think you ought to applaud me for mine. Exit Rattle

Solus your Diana

And now pray tell me, how you do? Do you feel any venom working in your veins? Did you ever before experience such a feeling? (This letter will be made up with questions, I fancy, not set in order before you, neither.) How do you employ yourself? Do you go abroad yet? Is it not cruel to bestow those favors upon others, which I should rejoice to receive, yet must be deprived of?

I have lately been thinking whether my mamma—when I write again I will tell you something. Did not you receive a letter to-day by Hanes?

This is a right girl's letter, but I will turn to the other side and be sober, if I can.

But what is bred in the bone will never be out of the flesh, (as Lord m. would have said.)

As I have a good opportunity to send some milk, I have not waited for your <u>orders</u>, lest, if I should miss this, I should not catch such another. If you want more balm, I can supply you.

Adieu; evermore remember me with the tenderest affection, which is also borne unto you by your A. Smith

JOHN QUINCY ADAMS
TO
LOUISA CATHERINE JOHNSON

*J*ohn Quincy Adams, American minister to the Netherlands in 1797, and Louisa Catherine Johnson exchanged these "love letters" just months before they were married in London. Louisa, who had been born in London, became the only foreign-born first lady.

The Hague 19 May 1797.

Since my last Letter, I have received none from you my amiable friend; nor have I any thing new to tell you at this time to repeat the assurances of my affection, and my hopes that you are well, and to observe the rule of suffering no week to pass without writing something are the principal objects for which I now write.

I proposed in my last Letter to your father what appears to me the only expedient that may enable us to meet in Europe. I place but little dependence upon it and calculate upon finding a further trial of Patience and Resignation imposed upon us.

I have been expecting in consequence of what you wrote me to see Mr. Hall here, and therefore not answered his last Letter. I still postpone the answer under the same expectation.

My brother will soon be upon his return from Paris, after which I shall set seriously about my departure. I shall be here however time enough to receive the answer to my last Letter. You have often heard, I suppose of Dutch Fairs we have had one here the last Ten days; it is a time of great amusement and festivity and accordingly as you judge, well agrees with me. It is however now at length come to a close.

Farewell, my kind friend, remember me affectionately to all the family, and believe me ever your's. A.

London May 26th 1797

Your letter of the 12th is arrived, and I flatter myself that our difficulties are ended.

Why my beloved friend did you tell me to choose, what I have always declared requires no amount of hesitation to determine, no my Adams, I have long ardently wished you might be enabled to return, and I have repeatedly assured you, that no personal inconvenience, would prevent my accompanying you, if possible—need I then say more to convince you, that your return would make me happy, and that I anticipate it with the utmost pleasure. I only fear my friend, that you will find <u>me</u> a troublesome companion.

In regard to your temper &c. I can only say that the more I know you, the more I admire, esteem, and love you, and the greater is my inclination, to do every thing in my power to promote your happiness, and welfare.

Mama, and my sister, desire their love, and say they hope to see you shortly–for myself, my best friend, I would say a great deal if I knew how to express it, but it is impossible, and I must simply stile myself yours unalterably, Louisa C. Johnson

*J*ohn Tyler, son of a wealthy, distinguished Virginia family and a member of the Virginia Assembly, broke one of the major courting conventions of the day when, without permission, he wrote this charming, almost desperate letter of love to Letitia Christian, whom he would marry just three months later.

Richmond Dec. 5. 1812

Although I could not entirely obtain your permission to write to you, yet I am well aware that you will not be displeas'd at my exercising a privilege so valuable to one standing in the relation that I do to you. To think of you and to write to you are the only sources from whence I can derive any real satisfaction during my residence in this place. The prerogative of thinking of those we love, and from whom we are seperated, seems to be guaranteed to us by nature, as we cannot be deprived of it, either by the bustle and confusion of a town or the important duties which attach to our existence.

Believe me, my L-, that this observation has been completely verified by me since I last saw you, for altho' defen'd with noise, and attention to the duties of my station yet you...the subject of my serious meditations and the object of my fervent prayers to heaven. From the first moment of my acquaintance with you I felt the influence of genuine affection; but now, when I reflect upon the sacrafice which you make to virtue and to feeling, by conferring your hand on one who has nothing to boast of, but an honest and upright soul, and an heart of purest love, I feel gratitude superadded to affection for you. Indeed, I do esteem myself most rich in possessing you. The mean and sordid wretch who yeilds the unspeakable bliss of possessing her whom he ardently loves may boast of his ill-acquired wealth and display his treasure in all the pride of ostentation to the world. But who shall administer to him in the hour of affliction? Whose seraph smile shall chase away the fiends which torment him? The partner of his bosom he neither esteems or regards—and he knows not the balm which tender affection can bestow. Nature will still be true to herself, and as your favorite Thompson expresses it "Nought but love can answer love, or render bliss secure."

You express'd some degree of astonishment my L-, at an observation which I once made to you "that I would not have been willingly wealthy at the time that I address'd you." Suffer me to repeat it. If I had been so, the idea of your being actuated by prudential considerations in not rejecting me would have eternally tortured me. But I exposed to you frankly and unblushingly my situation in life, my hopes and fears, my prospects and dependencies, and you nobly disregarded them. To insure you happiness is now my only object—and whether I float or sink in the stream of fortune, you may be assur'd of this, that I shall never cease to love you. Forgive me for these remarks, which I have been irresistibly led to make.

Col. Christian will deliver you this, together with the two first volumes of the forest of Montablano. I would not trouble him with the last two volumes because I was fearful of incommoding him and because I shall be at your father's on Wednesday evening, if the business of the Legislature be not very important. You will feel much sympathy for the unfortunate Angelina and admiration for the character of good Father patrick. Fedr...inexplicable until you read the ...

Suffer me to assure you of my constant esteem and affection, and believe me to be Yrs. Most affectionately, John Tyler

*U*lysses S. Grant and Julia Dent were in the midst of a four-year engagement when Ulysses wrote this charming, long letter. Neither set of parents approved of the marriage, but the couple finally went ahead with their nuptials on August 22, 1848.

[Fall, 1845]

My Dear Julia

There is one subject that is ever upermost with me and I have alluded to it several times before but I could not resist this fine opportunity, when I know you will get my letter, to mention it again. I take an extra sheet for it not that I have said so much on the first but: I cant tell why.

I was so much in hopes that I would have a letter from you that I could scarsely bear to leave the office without one, I wanted to write such a long one to you and wanted it to be an answer; but I know very well My Dear Julia that letters are a long time travelling as far as we are separated, and then too ladies think themselvs punctual if they answer a letter in a month after it is received. This is no reproach upon you Julia for I have had two—and beautiful ones too—since the 4th has been in Texas; but you will write oftener even than this in the future wont you. You often heard me say how delighted I always am to get a letter and now that you are so far away I believe I feel still more anxiety about hearing from you. It is not true that absence and distance conquer love.

The subject spoken of as being ever upermost, is my love for <u>my Dear Julia</u> and the consequence (matrimony) of a love so pure. It is now about a year and half Julia since I first confessed my love for you, and since that time we have been engaged, and yet but little has been said as to when we should be united. We have always lived in hopes that your Pa would remove the only obstacle in our way and I took his answer to me as almost a complete removal.

He told me that before giving a positive answer he would have to speak to you. I thought that he would decide as you wished, and I thought I well knew how that was. I cant believe yet my <u>Dear Dear Julia</u> but that he will give his consent. I would do anything to gain his permission to our engagement but if he should still refuse: have you ever decided how we then should or ought to act? I shall always recollect Miss C.O.F's views upon this subject; it was you told me them, and I perfectly agree with her. I think we should try to gain the consent of all interested parties as long as there was hopes but only allow the best of reasons to change our intention. Do you think with me on this subject? The Army seems to be the only objection and really I think there can be no happyer place to live. As I told you in my last letter I am at this time thinking strongly of resigning but I do not think I will ever be half so well contented out of the Army as in it.

I shall not believe my Dear Julia that the difficulties alluded to above will ever be met with. I will continue to think that when my Regiment is permanant at some post where the officers have their families that you will consent to go there too, and there will be no serious objections made. We have loved each other now so long and without any abatement, so far as I am able to answer, that it seems to me they (I mean your Father & Mother) must agree that even admiting that we might possibly be unhappy after marriage we would be still more so were they to break off the engagement, I say we because I measure your love by my own Julia. It may be vanity but I do not think so.

It is now 8 o'clock A.M. and I have to march on Guard this morning so that I can have but a few minuets more to write.

I have been reading the Wandering Jew but I have only got 15 Numbers of it. If you have the numbers after fifteen will you send them to me. I have no way of geting them except by writing to my friends to send them and what one more properly than Julia?

Give my love to Ellen. Ask her how Mr. Some one in the country is coming on. Write soon and very often and I will do the same—Adieu.

Your most affectionate Ulysses

CHESTER A. ARTHUR
TO
ELLEN LEWIS HERNDON

*C*hester Arthur was in St. Joseph, Missouri, on a political fact-finding mission for the Republican Party, when he wrote his only surviving letter to his fiancée, Ellen, then living on East 23rd Street in New York City.

St. Joseph, Mo. Sunday. Aug. 30. 1857.
My dearest Nell.
We are at St. Joseph again, in our way down the river. We left Omaha early on Friday morning and arrived here today about noon.

It is a great waste of time to travel on the river. It is so low that the boat can make but slow progress, but even then it is much preferable to staging in this new country. We shall leave here for Leavenworth about eighty miles below, as soon as a boat arrives.

PRESIDENT CHESTER ARTHUR LEADS A PARTY ACROSS THE
NEWLY COMPLETED BROOKLYN BRIDGE IN 1883.

ELLEN LEWIS HERNDON ARTHUR DIED OF PNEUMONIA
AT AGE FORTY-TWO IN 1880, JUST MONTHS BEFORE
HER HUSBAND WAS NOMINATED AS THE VICE-PRESIDENTIAL
RUNNING MATE OF JAMES GARFIELD.

I am desirous to learn as much as I can about the affairs and condition of Kansas and we shall probably be at Leavenworth, Lawrence & Lecompton several days.

I did not receive any letter from you Nell, up to the time I left Omaha. I ought not to have written to you to direct a letter to me there, but when I wrote from Milwaukee I expected to stay at Omaha much longer than we did. We were there not quite a week. We took the first boat that came after we were already to go, for we might have been obliged to wait many days for another.

It was hard to go away knowing that in a day or two more, the long-wished for letter would come. It is a great trial to be so long without a word to tell me that my darling, dearer to me than all the world beside is safe and well.

I hope you get my letters regularly and that you have lost none of them. I think if you send a letter to me at St. Louis immediately on your receiving this, I shall get it before I leave there on my way home. I trust you are well, darling, though at times I feel anxious & fearful for you.

This is your birth-day—my own precious darling—my own Nell. The remembrance came with my first awaking in the early morning—as the thought of you always does and as I kissed your dear image, darling, my heart was full to overflowing with love and prayer for you! And when I looked out, and saw it was a glad, bright morning and everything looked fresh & beautiful, I thought it a happy omen! How full of joy & happiness the world seemed to me, for I felt that you are <u>my own Nell</u>—that <u>you love me!</u> I said "I am content." I was happy and thanked God that he had so blessed me!

The day has fulfilled its morning promise, it has been most bright and beautiful even to the last rays of its gorgeous sunset, still lingering on the sky.

Who is there, dear, darling, Nell, who can, today, so anxiously & lovingly wish you all earthly happiness—richer blessings with each returning year & God's blessing and protecting care, here & hereafter—as your own loving Chester—May these blessings all be yours and, oh, if any part of that earthly happiness be in my keeping, my darling, my precious one, it is a precious, sacred trust dearer than life itself!

I have never been with you on your birth-day—two years ago, I can not realize it now,—neither of us had heard the others name. A year ago, I was away from you, though my heart was with you <u>then</u>, and now I am a long, long way from you. Yet <u>nearer</u> than ever before, darling! I would that the next may find me <u>with you</u>, that I may tell you all I would wish, all that my heart is now too full for me to write—My heart is full indeed for my thoughts have been of you all the day.

I sat down to write two hours ago, but I could not.

The sun went down & I sat in the coming on of the still, soft Sabbath evening dreaming of the soft, moonlight nights of June, a year ago in our old place in the window-seat—of the happy, happy days at Saratoga—the golden fleeting hours at Lake George and all the precious days I have been with you, since, a year ago today, I wrote you wishes for your happiness.

It has been a happy year to me. The happiest of my life, It has given me the priceless blessing of your love, and it has been a happy year to you, dearest love, for I believe you when you tell me that it is happiness to you, to know that I love you, fondly, truly, devotedly, always—that you are my own darling Nell!

I know you are thinking of me now. I feel the pulses of your love answering to mine. If I were with you now, you would go & sing for me: "Robin Adair"—then you would come & sit by me—you would put your arms around my neck and press your soft sweet lips over my eyes—I can feel them now.

Yes darling, my heart is indeed full to night, full of love for you, of happiness and gratitude for your love. Swelling with all these recollections & with the thought, that with God's blessing, I shall soon hold you to my heart again! The hours grow longer every day.

Good night. May God bless & keep you always my darling. Your own Chester

---

LUCRETIA RUDOLPH
TO
JAMES GARFIELD

---

*L*ucretia Rudolph and James Garfield were in the midst of a long engagement, punctuated by Garfield's dalliances with other women, when his young fiancée wrote this sad letter confronting his breach of their engagement.

Cleveland, September 1, 1857

My dear James:

Yes, <u>mine</u> forever, though a destiny cruel and relentless separate us as far as the east is from the west. Whatever our earthy relations may be, we are one and belong to each other, and in view of this truth I no longer fear to reveal to you every thought. I know that my motives will be understood however freely I may speak. The fear which has so long sealed my lips that James might construe any expression of my real thoughts and feelings into a design on my part to gain my own selfish ends no longer haunts me. I believe that you trust me now, and I know that in my own heart has been awakened that confidence which brought such sweet peace to my spirit two years ago. James, do you know that it was the withdrawal of that confidence in me which pressed home to this grieving heart the keenest dagger! How many many times I felt that if you would only love me just enough to come and tell me all, I could endure to know the worst; but to see you shrink away from me as though you could not endure my presence, and hide from me the truth, was almost more than I could bear. May Heaven spare me from ever living again such hours of bitter anguish. Pardon me for alluding to them. It is the last time. They have told upon my heart the lesson I trust they were sent to teach. Their mission has been fulfilled; let them pass unnoticed longer. I would much rather rest with you beside Erie's moonlit waters and feel my heart throbbing against your own, while I talk to you tonight. But I will not wait until it may be so blessed before saying some things so long unsaid.

James, the bright ideal of life and love which are here held up before us was indeed very beautiful; but was it the true one? Can the human heart hear the tests to which it may be submitted by it? I had hoped it might. Indeed, I had almost, yes, entirely trusted that a love as pure and deep as I believe ours to have been could never never meet with anything that could possibly turn it from its course or prove ever the slightest interruption. I was telling Mother this and remarked that it might be an error. Her reply was if there was no danger of any such thing happening if two loving hearts could find only in each other all that would satisfy, there would have been no necessity for the marriage vow.

May be it is so. If there could be no temptation, no danger of turning to another, why register in Heaven the vow of constancy? I blame you for nothing, for whatever you may have done I believe your heart's faithfulness; and allowed the generous and gushing affection of your warm impulsive nature to go out in all its fullness towards another than the one to whom you had pledged your all. All innocently as this was done, I can not blame you, and could the effect which all the past of our intimacy might have over you be blotted out, I would say to you this hour, go and marry Rebecca; and hereafter trust not your heart so far. Rebecca is a good and noble girl, in many aspects far my superior but she loves you no better than Crete. If, however, you love her better, if she can satisfy the wants of your nature better, and more than all, if you can with her become a good and noble man in spite of all the Past, Crete can give you up. And pronounce upon your Love a sister's blessing. You told me that judgment prompted you to another course, that to feel yourself an honourable, generous man you must take me alone to your heart. Let feeling dictate whatever it might. I have thought I could never allow that, that I could never be your wife unless every feeling of your heart seconded the decisions of reason. Perhaps I asked too much, but, James, to be an unloved wife, O Heavens, I could not endure it. I am not exacting. It would excite no spirit of jealousy in my heart to know that my husband admired and even loved a thousand others, and know that they possessed traits superior to mine, but I do feel it to be my right to claim this sole assurance, that I am his choice; and that however much he may find to be more admired in others he will not turn away from me to them, but rather seek to correct my faults, and make me like them. I want to find in my husband that strength of love, which can steel itself against every attraction that might come between us, which will hold me nearest his heart in spite of every impulse which an ardent nature might feel. Now, James, I freely pardon any error your ignorance of the human heart may have led you to commit, but I do hope whatever course you may take, that hereafter you will be more guarded for your own happiness if nothing more. It pains me to see you so miserable as you are at times, and sometimes I feel that I could dare almost anything, even for the hope of making you happy again. But could I—could I become your wife and see that best hope fail! Oh no, no, no. If it would not fail, may God help me to know it. Then I will make the trial. James, write to me very soon. Keep nothing back that is in your heart.

A word about our schedule then I will close. I am very pleasantly situated with over 90 little fellows in charge. The school will be divided in a few days when I shall have a fine time. I am not going to fail. You needn't have a fear of it. I had no intention of it when I was talking so. And you do you grow discouraged and disheartened at the prospect before You? I do not wonder that you feel like letting the trustees choose to go to destruction before the eclectic if they will. But Jams don't do so. Let your "power" be felt, and you will be appreciated some time, and reap the reward of your labors. Don't <u>work</u> too hard. Take care of your health. If for no other purpose, at least for the good you may do. I do not think I shall attend the Bedford meeting. You can tell Charles where I am so he can find me. Shall I expect you two weeks from next Saturday? Direct to care of Harlon Wright.

Yours most lovingly, Crete

JULIA   GRANT

TO

ULYSSES   S.   GRANT

---

*I*n the only surviving letter to her husband, Julia Grant writes a loving anniversary note and he responds in kind.

[May 22 1875]

Dear Ulys

How many years ago to day is that we were engaged?
Just such a day as this too was it not?

Julia

Thirty-one years ago. I was so frightened however that I do not remember whither it was warm or snowing. Ulys.

THEODORE ROOSEVELT
TO
ALICE LEE

*J*ust five days before their marriage, Theodore Roosevelt wrote this frenetic letter to his nineteen-year-old fiancée.

October 17, 1880. Oyster Bay

My Dearest Love,

You are too good to write me so often, when you have so much to do; I hope you are not all tired out with the work. But at any rate you will have two weeks complete rest at Oyster Bay, and then

ALICE HATHAWAY LEE BECAME THE FIRST WIFE OF
THEODORE ROOSEVELT ON OCTOBER 29, 1880, AT THE UNITARIAN
CHURCH IN BROOKLINE, MASSACHUSETTS. SHE DIED FROM CHILDBIRTH
COMPLICATIONS ON FEBRUARY 14, 1884, THE FOURTH
ANNIVERSARY OF THEIR ENGAGEMENT.

you shall do just as you please in everything. Oh, my darling, I do so hope and pray I can make you happy. I shall try very hard to be as unselfish and sunny tempered as you are, and I shall save you from every care I can. My own true love, you have made my happiness almost too great; and I feel I can do so little for you in return. I worship you so that it seems almost desecration to touch you; and yet when I am with you I can hardly let you a moment out of my arms. My purest queen, no man was worthy of your love; but I shall try very hard to deserve it, at least in part. Goodbye, my own heart's darling. Your Loving Thee

---

WILLIAM   HOWARD   TAFT
TO
HELEN   HERRON

William Taft and Helen Herron dated each other for more than five years before their engagement in June 1885 and marriage on June 19, 1886, exchanging hundreds of letters. The following focus on their engagement and future wedding trip.

[July 1, 1885]

My darling Nellie,

I have walked the streets this morning with the hope of seeing you and with little other excuse. I received a letter this morning in which I hope you will be interested and to part of which you are entitled. I am only a postman. I hope, Nellie dear, that you will derive as much pleasure from reading it as I do. Mother is justly incensed at me for showing you her first letter as you were. It showed about as delicate an appreciation of your feelings and hers as a brute of a man is likely to have. If you have forgiven me for it, I can rely upon forgiveness from Mother. I think Mothers sometimes welcome sins in their sons, because it is such a pleasure to them to forgive. I was confident that Mother would say nothing of what I told but you see that I was mistaken. When you come to consider their isolated positions and the circumstances, perhaps it was too much to expect of her. I hope that you will not feel very badly over it. They will not be at home until October and can not let it leak before that time even if they would. I have a letter from Horace this morning in which he still advises against the Fabian policy, insisting that it was a policy to be pursued by only a weak army and one frequently defeated. I hope to be able some day to assure him that in one respect at least I resemble Scipio more than Fabius Maximus. I am very glad that this letter has come before you leave. It is as I knew it would be. You will be welcomed lovingly into the family and their love and respect for you will grow as they know you better. I believe that yours will for them. The fact is you maybe compelled to piece out the feelings of the member who has pushed you to that fatal step, with the virtues of some others of the family. Rufus has been in to say that he expected to call tonight. I told him that you had spoken of a driving party, giving him the notices but that I was not certain that it would be carried out. He said he would not call under those circumstances. I did not understand from you definitely whether you expected us tonight to supper or not. It is to know this that I write. Indeed it was the only reason for the note. I find that I caught a little cold last night. If so, I am afraid that you did too. If we could have reversed our hours of rising this morning it would have been better for your health and my business reputation. Maria understood, I suppose, that our horse was lame and could come but slowly. Let me hear from you please, by telephone or note what your plan is for tonight. Till then. Your loving Will

Washington, March 5th. 1886

My dear Will,

I was very much surprised to have your letter arrive as usual this afternoon, although I had changed my place of residence, I had left my address at the hotel with directions to forward letters, but thought that I would probably be without one for a day or two. I have been worried, my dear but the letter I wrote the day before yesterday was some what abrupt. My opinion is the same, still but I might have given it more in detail, and with more deference for your opinion and feelings. For after all I want to do what you consider best. I think I don't blame myself with the flekleness usually ascribed to women, for my desire to build was founded on two mistakes. I over estimate the expense of furnishing, but I hardly think do. Then as to the trip this summer. If we decide to Shorten our stay, and that you must not hesitate to do, my dear Will, if it seems best. You are only too good to take me at all. I think it would be better to go only to England and give up Paris. The time is altogether too short, it seems to me, and Allie thinks so too, to do so much in. We should simply have to tear from place to place to do all on that place in two weeks. And we are going for rest, you know, and must take our time. I care more about the travelling than I do the house—for it will be a very long time probably, before we can go any where again. Yesterday I tried on my wedding dress and veil and all, and looked, as I supposed I would Like a fright—but of course you won't think so, so it doesn't make any difference. I don't know that—that is true though now I think of it for love doesn't blind you to defects of that kind I believe. Forgive my teasing.

The rest of the morning I wandered along 6th Avenue looking at the shops, which, are very fascinating. Allie & I went out again in the afternoon and bought me an etching—a wedding present from Uncle Nathan. I don't know whether you will like it or not. It is Called, "The picture of an Oak," by Forel, and is a magnificent oak tree with a cow lying under it. I inclose a picture of it which I cut from the catalogue. There was the loveliest head of Psyche which I wanted awfully but I hadn't ten dollars to divest. Rufus sent Elsie a Carafe as a wedding present. I don't see how he had the face to sit up there and tell Annie that lie about proposing to Edith, putting himself in such a magnanimous light. I am more disgusted with him that ever, but that does not prevent my being very sorry that he lost that money. It was pretty hard times— I am very glad your widow got her divorce. Allie and I piloted ourselves across the ferry and accomplished the journey here in safety after a tearful parting with the Aunts, and I came to Mrs. Feudenbergs. By the way I must tell you the cheekiest thing. You know Jennie wanted to give us a sideboard, so I got the address of a number of old curiosity shops and told Aunts M & P what I wanted to look for. We went off all over and I asked for sideboards and talked it over with them, and all. Two were much preferable to the others. When Allie arrived what was my surprise to hear Aunt Mary tell Allie she wanted to give her a sideboard and to go and look at the nearest one. Eva might look at the others, as she Allie had not time and select the one she liked the best. Did you ever hear anything so cool after I had gotten the addresses, taken them there and all? It was too much and I told Allie I thought it was very cheeky. I don't think she was very pleased, as she was crazy for the piece.

I have taken a long enough time for you, now is goodnight. I am sorry you object to the end of my letters. I will endeavor to change it. Helen

*W*oodrow Wilson, a graduate student at Johns Hopkins University, wrote this longing letter to Ellen Louise Axson, a budding artist, when they had been engaged only a few
days and Woodrow had just written Ellen's father seeking his permission for the match.

Baltimore, Md. Sept. 21st 1883

My darling,

I was about to date my letter the 20th, but it is after midnight
and I must of course be strictly accurate. A quarter past twelve
is not the best time for beginning a letter, but you shall have that
time, since I've had none other to give you. I am not at present
my own master, for I am a guest in a friend's house. An old (though
young) college friend has taken me in keeping since my arrival
and insisted upon my staying at his house until I can find a boarding place to my taste; and I am, therefore, likely to spend some
days as I have spent to-day. The whole of this morning was consumed in looking up all sorts of houses in all sorts of localities
where I had learned that board and lodging were to be had if
sought by single gentlemen; and dinner was scarcely over in time
to admit of its digestion before it was high season to dress for
the evening. For this evening Miss Woods had company here to
a late tea and I must needs be dragged into making myself agreeable to young ladies and polite young gentlemen who were utter
strangers to me. I did my duty nobly (myself being the judge)
but it consumed a tediously long time in the doing, it seems to
me. I was all the time longing to write my letter to you; but I
believe I <u>did</u> succeed in contributing to the pleasure of some of
the party, because I am just now, I must inform you, in splendid
spirits and anything seems easy to do! It must be that, if you are
feeling light-hearted and happy—for we were both in the mountains. Is it so with you too?

ELLEN AXSON WILSON, WHO STUDIED AT THE ART STUDENTS LEAGUE IN NEW YORK AND TAUGHT ART, DREW THIS SKETCH OF WOODROW WILSON BEFORE THEIR MARRIAGE IN 1885.

I shall have nothing to do at the University until next Wednesday (for, as you remember, I told you, instructions are not resumed until a week after the opening of the University), so that I can make haste slowly in settling in quarters. In the meantime I am unreasonably chaffing at being kept here where there is no work a-doing when I would give all the world to be with you. And the way I am being carried captive to kindness the while! Tomorrow afternoon I am to be carried out into the country to play lawn tennis with the young ladies who were here to-night, after which I know not what things lie in store for me.

I wrote to your father yesterday, my darling; and I believe I never did harder work. I wanted to say what I had to say as earnestly, simply, and respectfully as possible, and I succeeded only in being unusually awkward and stiff. But I trust he read the letter indulgently, making due allowances for the circumstances under which it was written and the peculiar difficulties of the subject.

I have heard nothing from you yet. There has scarcely been time for a letter to reach me since you got to Rome; but it has occurred to me that possibly you may have been hesitating to write before I had given you some particular address in the city. I shall, however, be sure to get anything that may come to the general post office until I have a street and number. I am very hungry for a line of love from you. I don't believe I can ever make you know how passionately I love you, my own darling; for no expression of word or deed can convey half of the fulness of my love for you. Good-night. I'll go to bed and dream of the kisses I cannot give you.

Yours with all my full heart, Woodrow

G R O V E R   C L E V E L A N D
T O
F R A N C E S   F O L S O M   C L E V E L A N D

---

*G*rover Cleveland was awaiting his second inauguration when he wrote this dreamy letter to his wife.

12 West Fifty-First Street Jan 2. 1893

Darling

I received the enclosed to day and hope you will dispose of it. You perhaps know that I do not dance very well.

Fairchild dined with me to night. He came some time before dinner and stayed a good while after but I enjoyed his visit very much and walked down with him as far as 30th Street. This is the first time I have been out of the house in two days except to step into the Commanders last evening.

I have tried to work to day but succeeded very indifferently as I have had a good many calls.

I feel Kind of worthless to-night and since it is past twelve think I will go to bed. I've taken to a great habit of dreaming late-ly and most every night I dream of you.

I love you dearly and want to see you very much. Kiss our Dar-ling Child for me and give my love to your mother.

Yours fondly Grover Cleveland

FRANCES FOLSOM CLEVELAND WAS A STRONG ADVOCATE
OF WOMEN'S EDUCATION, SERVING ON THE WELLS COLLEGE BOARD
FOR MORE THAN FIFTY YEARS.

FRANCES FOLSOM CLEVELAND
TO
GROVER CLEVELAND

*T*he only extant letter from Frances (Frank) Cleveland to her husband, is this brief note written at Christmas 1894.

Christmas 1894

A <u>Surprise</u> for My Dearest—from Frank.

WOODROW WILSON
TO
EDITH BOLLING GALT

*J*ust days after fifty-eight-year-old President Woodrow Wilson's proposal to Edith Galt, a widow of forty-three, the couple exchanged these two excited letters and dozens of others before their December 18, 1915, wedding. (This, in spite of the fact that they saw each other daily.)

6 May '15

Oh, dear kindred spirit, my sweet incomparable friend, what would I not give this morning for just one clasp of your hand, just one little greeting exchanged face to face, one word with the sound of your voice in it! But I have slept a little now and can speak more clearly than I did last night, when my need, my fathomless need, was crying out in me. I was thinking of myself then, now I think of you (and, ah, how sweet it is to think of you!) That note you wrote me yesterday before the dawn ("before the dawn"!)

Lies before me my little charter of liberty! And I realize that I have not answered it—except in my heart. I can hardly see to write for the tears as I lift my eyes from it, the tears of joy and sweet yearning. <u>Yes</u>, my dear loving friend, "we <u>will</u> help and hearten each other." My heart sends you back your words—oh, with what gladness and pride. "I pledge you all that is best in me—to help, to sustain, to comfort." "Into the space that separates us I send my spirit to seek yours. Make it a welcome guest!" How welcome a guest your spirit is, my dear. I hope God will give me the grace to show you—without selfishness of any sort. And how proud I am to be its host—and its haven of welcome—how proud and happy! For there never was a more beautiful spirit, a spirit more altogether lovely. I will be its knight,—serve it, not myself, and feel myself grow a better, purer man in the service!

> "I claimed and claim thee; ready now to pay
> The perfect love and leaves no self to slay!"

Yesterday, in my deep need and longing, I let myself think of my own life and the work I need the full, unbounded equipment to do that I can have only when my heart is satisfied; but now what I hope is my real and finer self is awake in response to your sweet pledge. It goes out to meet you, with outstretched hands. <u>I love you</u>, not myself. I shall live to help <u>you</u>— "to help, to sustain, to comfort," to gladden, not to burden or distress,—to help you, if I can, to realize the lovely things that are in you and you have not seen yourself. It grieves me that you should ever have been unhappy, that clouds should ever have shadowed you who are by nature and every sweet gift so radiant and full of the perfect light that shines in the heart of a completely gifted woman. If I can never have the privilege of shielding you from all the world, I can at least shield you from anything that is selfish in me and let no shadow darken your thoughts that may gather in my sky. It will be my study and my joy to make you <u>glad</u> that you met me. My love shall never stand in your way. You have had too little joy in your life; I shall try to add to its stock, not take away from it! The wonderful woman I recognized and loved, and sought selfishly to claim,

I shall seek to enrich, not impoverish. Nothing that she demands of me, though it were utter sacrifice, will seem hard to give if she desires or needs it or will be made happier by it. I would rather see light—the light of joy and complete happiness—in those eyes than have anything I can think of for myself.

I seem to have been put into the world to serve, not to take, and serve I will to the utmost, and demand nothing in return. It is a man may show himself worthy, perhaps, to call himself Your devoted friend Woodrow Wilson

"Being thy slave, what should I do but tend
Upon the hours and times of your desire?
Nor services to do, till you require.
Nor dare I chide the world without end hour
Whilst I, my sovereign, watch the clock for you,
Nor think the bitterness of absence sour
When you have bid your servant once adieu;
Nor dare I question with my jealous thought
Where you may be, or your affairs suppose,
But, like a sad slave. Stay and think of nought
Save, where you are how happy you make those!
So true a fool is love, that in your Will,
Though you do any thing, he thinks no ill."

EDITH GALT

TO

WOODROW WILSON

May 6th, 1915

I have just read and read again your triumphant note of the early morning—so full of tenderness, of yearning, of the "hunger and thirst of the heart"—and yet vibrant with <u>strength</u> and the blessed surety that you have <u>found yourself</u>!

A YOUNG EDITH BOLLING SITS ON HER FRONT PORCH
IN VIRGINIA IN 1887, NEARLY THREE DECADES BEFORE MEETING
AND MARRYING PRESIDENT WOODROW WILSON.

This is what makes me so proud of you, and so sure that all's right with the world! You could not be yourself and not feel as you do today. It is so worthy of you to forget your own hurt in helping me, and my heart is singing with the wonder of your revelation of yourself.

Forgive a pencil I am in my car waiting for Mother so ink is impossible.

On my heart rests a golden rose, and in my heart is a treasure of pure gold. May I never tarnish this pure trust, but guard it with my life, and leave the rest to God. E. B. G.

FRANKLIN D. ROOSEVELT

TO

ELEANOR ROOSEVELT

---

*P*resident Roosevelt wrote this note to his wife, excusing himself for not finding a present for their twenty-eighth wedding anniversary.

The White House, Mar 17, 1933

Dearest Babs:

After a fruitless week of thinking and lying awake to find whether you need or want undies, dresses, hats, shoes, sheets, towels, rouge, soup plates, candy, flowers, lamps, laxation pills, whisky, beer, etchings or caviar.

I GIVE IT UP !

And yet I know you lack some necessity of life—so go to it with my love and many happy returns of the day! F. D. R.

This couple had known each other for exactly one month when Lady Bird wrote this flirtatious letter to her future husband.

Friday, Oct. 5 [1934]

Dearest!

No letter today! I am <u>so</u> disappointed. I wonder why you didn't write? Are you too busy—or have you perhaps already left for Texas—or why? I had no idea how peculiarly <u>empty</u> a day would be without a letter from you. If you miss a letter from me as much as I do yours—I'll make sure you get one every day!

When I think that I said I wouldn't write every day I am quite amused. I meant it most certainly. I'd never written to anyone <u>every</u> day and I thought it <u>most</u> absurd! And now I find myself looking forward to the time of day when I write you. Its the nicest time of day except around eleven o'clock when I go down after the mail—yours usually comes on that train.

Today I took Isabel and Nig and Panky and Willy Floyd to the Fair. They were as tickled over it as I'd be over seeing Broadway! While they were there I went to see Somerset Maugham's "Of Human Bondage." It was skillfully played but quite harrowing. Dear, when it comes and you've time I want you to see "The World Moves On." I remember you don't like shows but I'm sure you'll like this one. The love-making is in the most flawless good taste I've ever seen on the screen. It made me feel very set-up about the human race to watch them.

The books came today and I am delighted! I shall begin one tonight. They are library books, aren't they? Is the limit two weeks? I shall hurry! And thanks, dear.

But, Lyndon, the clippings didn't come. Perhaps they will be waiting for me tomoro when I go down. I shall look forward to it.

I've been reading "Early Autumn" and am enthralled. If we were together, I'd read it to you.

There's nothing I like better than being comfortable in a nice cozy place and reading something amusing or well-written or interesting to someone I like. All good things are better shared, aren't they?

My Bachelor of Journalism degree came the other day and I've lost it! Fancy that! I am sorry because I like President Benedict's signature, bless his heart, and it (the diploma) was a dear sort of souvenir from the Grandest Place on Earth. Anyway, I know what they look like!

My dear, do you know what today it? Its our anniversary! One month ago today we met—

LYNDON B. JOHNSON
TO
LADY BIRD TAYLOR

---

*L*yndon was in the first throes of love when he wrote this passionate letter to his future wife, whom he had met just weeks before.

House of Representatives Washington
Tuesday noon
[October 24, 1934]

My dear Bird;

This morning I'm ambitious, proud, energetic and very madly in love with you. I want to see people—want to walk thro-the throngs—want to do things with a drive. If I had a box I would almost make a speech this minute. Plans, ideas, hopes—I'm bubbling over with them. For fear you might think me too conceited I'll stop there but there is so much more guiding my pen this morning than when I wrote you of my worry about this time last week. You are apparently always so free from concern that when

I feel as I do this morning I think how cruel it was to even let you know how despondent I felt last week.

This morning I've written letters so freely. Just finished one to Alice Wyatt. She will probably think I've reverted to the eighteen year old stage but I could feel no restraint. Dictated all of my mail in a jiffy, had coffee with Joe Railey's secretary, and before lunch I've finished my day at the office. A letter from you on the afternoon mail will make this day such a perfect one.

The postman brought me several interesting, stimulating letters from friends in Texas. I wish you were here to sit on the arm of my chair and read them over my shoulder. People are so good to me. Even one of my best Washington friends, realizing how much I appreciate letters, chose to chide me with an early special before I had my breakfast at the hotel. For almost a week I was busy-busy-working and worrying and the letter says "What I need badly now and then is a special person, a loyal friend to whom I'm particularly attached, to talk to. But when I need him he's sure to be off with bankers, lawyers, and the big men of the nation generally who are laying out a future for him. (Went driving with Mr. Dick's banker friends Saturday.) So that's how the week-end goes when I'm in need of solace. If I go astray, I'll tell you what he will be like. He'll be about fifty, somewhat mellowed in his point of view toward the triumphs of this life, he'll be rather quiet, and he'll actually be interested in what I'm doing." After the work is all done today we will meet and have a highball and most probably talk about you and her author—(and he isn't fifty). Then Ben Crider, a boy who helped me in school, writes at length. He has very pleasant work with the Fed. Land Bank and tells me more about his marriage, his work, my family and my friends. Just recently he has been transferred to the hill country from So. Texas. You may remember meeting him when you came to Corpus.

But darling with all the nice things coming at once—I haven't had a letter from you since Saturday—it was written Thursday. Not fussing just checking up on Uncle Sams efficient postal service.

When you write again tell me about Austin and your schooldays there.

Tell me about what you did—when you studied and what you had for entertainment—and just how much a "young man" in law school can have. Tell me you love me if you want to and if you don't I'll believe you do anyway and keep on loving you every minute and it may be "completely" suggestions from loved ones not withstanding.

Here is a big hug-kiss and the everlasting love of Lyndon Baines

---

D W I G H T D . E I S E N H O W E R
T O
M A M I E E I S E N H O W E R

*W*hen General Dwight Eisenhower sent these reassuringly intimate letters to his wife amidst public stories that he had a very close personal relationship with an aide from Ireland, Kay Somersby.

June 25, 1943

My darling:

Soon have to go off on a trip of a week or more and now I'm try-ing to write to you every day, so you'll have letters dropping in occasionally, even if there is a hiatus in my writing.

It seems strange, at times, that a man's longing to see his home and loved ones should seem to build up rather than diminish with the passage of time. I suppose, when a new assignment comes along, the excitement of getting things organized and started keeps the mind off of other things. But as day follows day and routines are established the consciousness of things missed continues to grow until a real case of homesickness results. It comes also, I think, from continued intensive application to difficult problems; to the never ending process of working and working to get a little nearer to the final goal. In any event I certainly miss you these days. How I'd like to drop in on you for a visit—even if it could be only for a few days. But as I look over my future schedule of personal activity—I see no chance at all. But you can never tell—maybe something will happen. The unexpected nearly always occurs in war.

Everett has just left my office after a big business talk. He looks fine, I think, and we had a couple minutes chat about you & Kate. I don't think he is as homesick as I am—but he'd had two trips home (I think) in the past year while I've had none.

Well sweetheart—please take care of yourself. You know I'm delighted your cardiograph record is better than a year ago. I'm glad you had it taken. You are very precious to me!!! I love you, always— Your Lover

FEW LETTERS FROM MAMIE EISENHOWER TO HER HUSBAND ARE AVAILABLE TO THE PUBLIC. THIS BIRTHDAY CARD (THE COVER AND INTERIOR ARE SHOWN HERE), SIGNED BY "YOUR EVER LOVING WIFE MAMIE," REFLECTS THEIR CLOSE PERSONAL RELATIONSHIP.

Algiers June 29, 1943

Darling

Three secretaries are now working on drafts of long telegrams, and this gives me a short breathing space to dash off a note. Jerry Matyks returns home tomorrow and I am especially anxious that he carry a message from me to you.

Day after tomorrow is our wedding anniversary. I've wired to Washington to make sure you have a bunch of roses from me that day. I couldn't very well send "Sheltering Palms" although, here, there is almost every kind of palm. Twenty seven years is a long time on the calendar, but I can remember many details of our wedding day as well as if they had happened this morning. For instance: my difficulty in keeping my white trousers from wrinkling!!

Yesterday I was away all day! It was a busy trip and I was thoroughly tired when I hit the last eve. I was supposed to go out again tomorrow but trip was postponed. Sometimes my journeys are for the day only, sometimes for more than a week. I'll be starting a longer one soon.

Milton sent me a long article, published in the Washington Post, about my job here. It was far more accurate, in describing the character of my work, than are most such stories. The only thing the writer did not seem to know is the extent to which I'm committed to travelling. I truly hope that, before Christmas, there'll be an opportunity for me to come home for a day or so.

Well my love, please be sure I'll be thinking of you on July 1. I love you always—with all my heart. Yours Ike

---

RICHARD NIXON
TO
PAT NIXON

*D*uring World War II, Richard, a naval officer, and Pat were separated for long periods. In 1944, he was stationed in the Pacific Theater. During this time they exchanged these letters of love and longing.

Dearest,

Today was the most wonderful day of all because the picture finally came. It's a swell shot—even though no picture can do justice as well as I tell everyone who sees it. You'll never know how proud I was to show it to all the fellows. Everybody raved—wondered how I happened to rate (I do too.) Jimmy Stewart said you were like a much younger and more beautiful Greer Garson and he's a real judge too. Several asked if you had any sisters! Dearest it's wonderful to see you again and even a picture brings you so very near to me.

PRESIDENT AND MRS. RICHARD NIXON DANCE AT THE JUNE 12, 1971, WHITE HOUSE WEDDING OF THEIR DAUGHTER TRICIA AND EDWARD COX.

PAT NIXON
TO
RICHARD NIXON

[c. June 1944]

Being with you, sweet, is all that matters and the thought of building a life without seems so dull. However, I will have to admit that I am pretty self-reliant and if I didn't love you I would feel very differently. In fact these many months you have been away have been full of interest, and had I not missed you so much and had I been foot loose, could have been extremely happy. So. Sweet, you'll always have to love me lots and never let me change my feelings for you which has been so beautiful all these years. I love the story of Holmes' life and want to buy you the book. I can't resist sending you a page of the condensation—it shows their fun and admiration at past eighty. They had a wonderful life and that is the way I always think of ours. Will you love me when I'm shriveled and ridiculous looking?

HARRY S. TRUMAN
TO
BESS TRUMAN

*I*n 1957, Harry compiled this year-by-year list commemorating his thirty-eighth wedding anniversary with his wife, Bess, who reportedly read this letter daily after the death of her husband until her own death in 1982, as the longest-lived first lady.

Kansas City, Missouri [June 28, 1957]

June 28, 1920 One happy year.
June 28, 1921 Going very well.
June 28, 1922 Broke and in a bad way.
June 28, 1923 Eastern Judge Eating
June 28, 1924 Daughter 4 mo. Old.
June 28, 1925 Out of a job.
June 28, 1926 Still out of a job.
June 28, 1927 Presiding judge—eating again
June 28, 1928 All going well. Piano. Al Smith
June 28, 1929 Panic, in October.
June 28, 1930 Depression still going.
June 28, 1931 Six year old daughter
June 28, 1932 Roads finished
June 28, 1933 Employment Director
June 28, 1934 Buildings finished. Ran for the Senate
June 28, 1935 U.S. Senator, ...
June 28, 1936 Resolutions Philadelphia. Roosevelt reelected.
June 28, 1937 Good time in Washington
June 28, 1938 Very happy time. Margie 14.
June 28, 1939 Named legislation.
June 28, 1940 Senate fight comming
June 28, 1941 Special Senate Committee. Margie wants to sing.
June 28, 1942 Also a happy time
June 28, 1943 Lots of work.
June 28, 1944 Talk of V.P. Bad business
June 28, 1945 V.P. and President. War End
June 28, 1946 Margie graduate & singer. 80th Congress
June 28, 1947 Marshall Plan & Greece & Turkey.
             A grand time 28th Anna.
June 28, 1948 A terrible campaign. Happy day.
June 28, 1949 President again. Another happy day.
June 28, 1950 Korea—a terrible time.
June 28, 1951 Key West—a very happy day.
June 28, 1952 All happy. Finish Jan. 20, 1953
June 28, 1953 Back home. Lots of <u>Roses.</u>

June 28, 1954 A happy 35th
June 28, 1955 All cut up but still happy.
June 28, 1956 A great day—more election
June 28, 1957 Well here we are again as harry Joles would say.
Only 37th to go for the diamond jubilee! H. S. T.

NANCY REAGAN BESTOWED A "PROUD PAPA" AWARD ON HER HUSBAND
AFTER THE 1952 BIRTH OF THEIR DAUGHTER, PATRICIA ANN.

RONALD REAGAN
TO
NANCY REAGAN

*R*onald Reagan wrote this love note to his wife on Valentine's Day in 1960.

Feb. 14–1960

Darling Mommie Poo

Feb. 14 may be the date they observe and call Valentine's day but that is for people of only ordinary luck.

I happen to have a "Valentine Life" which started on March 4 1952 and will continue as long as I have you.

Therefore realizing the importance of this to me, will you be my Valentine from now on and for ever and ever? Ya see my choice is limited, a Valentine Life or no life because I love you very much.
Poppa

RONALD REAGAN
TO
NANCY REAGAN

---

*T*hen California governor Reagan and Nancy exchanged these letters on their fifteenth wedding anniversary.

March 4 1967

My Darling First Lady

I'm looking at you as you lie here beside me on this fifteenth anniversary and wondering why everyone has only just discovered you are the First Lady. You've been the First—in fact the only—to me for fifteen years.

That sounds strange—"fifteen years" it still seems like minutes, they've gone by so swiftly! If I have any regret it is only for the days we've been apart and I've had to awaken without watching you. Someday, you'll have to explain how you can be five years old when you sleep and for fifteen years yet. But then maybe it has something to do with my only being fifteen—because I wasn't living before I began watching you.

Thank you for all my life and living and for happiness as complete as one can have on this earth.

I love you so much and so much more each day. Your husband

My darling husband,

You beat me to it this morning 'cause I was going to write you—
I can never say what I really feel in my heart to you 'cause I get
puddled up—and you always say everything so much better. But
I too can't believe it's fifteen (16!) years. In another way tho' it
seems like forever—I really can't even remember a life before you
now. Everything began with you. My whole life—so you'd better
be careful and take care of yourself because there'd be nothing
and I'd be no one without you.

I love you so much—I never thought I could love you more
than the day we were married but I do—and I'm so proud of
you—every day—I could pop—it just keeps getting bigger and
bigger—those poor other mommies—they don't have a you—
but I do—and I hope you'll always have a me. XXX

*O*nly two days were left in the presidency of Gerald R. Ford when he and his wife
were surprised by their friends with a farewell party in the Grand Hall of the White House.
They had been lured there to pose for a picture with the Marine Band, as reported in
Ford's autobiography:

"[January 18, 1977] Reluctantly, Betty agreed. The South Portico of the White House was dark as our limousine pulled up to
the entrance shortly after ten o'clock that Tuesday night. We took

the family elevator to the first floor. All was quiet; only a few lights were on, but I could see the members of the band waiting for us by the foot of the grand staircase. 'Well, so long as we're here,' I suggested, 'why don't we have a last dance?' She nodded and made a request, 'Thanks for the Memory,' and we began to twirl around the floor.

"Suddenly, from around the hallway on the right, other couples began gliding onto the floor."

GEORGE H. W. BUSH
TO
BARBARA BUSH

$\mathcal{G}$eorge H. W. Bush was a young man of fifty-five when he wrote the first of these two notes to his wife on her birthday; and he was in the first year of postpresidential life when he wrote the second, a forty-ninth anniversary note.

[June 8, 1979]

Happy happy 54th!
love you—I love you very much. Nothing—campaign separations, people, nothing will ever change that.
I can't ever really tell you how much I love you.
Your 55 yr. Old husband. Pop

For: Barbara Pierce   January 6, 1994
From: GHWB

Will you marry me? Oops, I forgot, you did that 49 years ago today! I was very happy on that day in 1945 but I am even happier today. You have given me joy that few men know. You have made our boys into men by bawling them out and then, right away, by loving them. You have helped Doro be the sweetest greatest daughter in the whole wide world. I have climbed perhaps the highest mountain in the world, but even that can not hold a candle to being Barbara's husband. Mum used to tell me: "Now George, don't walk ahead." Little did she know I was only trying to keep up—keep up with Barbara Pierce from Onondaga Street in Rye New York. I love you!

PRESIDENT ABRAHAM LINCOLN AND
HIS WIFE, MARY TODD LINCOLN, GREET GUESTS
DURING THEIR LAST PUBLIC RECEPTION IN THE WHITE
HOUSE ON THE EVENING OF LINCOLN'S SECOND
INAUGURATION, MARCH 4, 1865.

CHAPTER 2

OFF TO WAR

"*It is necessary for me to proceed
immediately to Boston to take upon me the command.*"
—George Washington to Martha Washington,
June 18, 1775

"*These are dark times Dearest.*"
—John Tyler to Julia Tyler,
April 16, 1861

"*The time of our departure draws nearer.*"
—George H. W. Bush to Barbara Pierce,
December 12, 1943

W A R has been a major element of American life for more than
two hundred years. The men who have become president often
proved their leadership capabilities during such times of crisis;
from George Washington to George H. W. Bush, our commanders in chief have often been veterans of active military service.
During wartime, their spouses were often left behind, but some,

like Martha Washington, joined their husbands in military camp. Others, including Julia Grant and Mamie Eisenhower, longed to join their husbands. Still others, including Lucy Hayes, rushed to the army to nurse a wounded spouse. The letters in this chapter reveal the human toll and triumphs of war as having affected both members of a presidential marriage.

GEORGE WASHINGTON
TO
MARTHA WASHINGTON

---

*G*eorge had just been appointed commander in chief of the American Continental Armies when he wrote Martha these two classic letters.

Philadelphia June 18, 1775

My Dearest

I am now set down to write you on a subject which fills me with inexpressible concern—and this concern is greatly aggravated and Increased, when I reflect upon the uneasiness I know it will give you. It has been determined in Congress that the whole Army raised for the defence of the American Cause shall be put under my care, and that it is necessary for me to proceed immediately to Boston to take upon me the command of it. You may believe me my dear Patcy, when I assure you, in the most solemn manner, that, so far from seeking this appointment I have used every endeavour in my power to avoid it, not only from my unwillingness to part with you and the Family, but from a consciousness of its being a trust too great for my Capacity and that I should enjoy more real happiness and felicity in one month with you, at home than I have the most distant prospect of reaping abroad, if my stay were to be Seven times Seven years. But, as it has been a kind of destiny that has thrown me upon this Service, I shall hope that my undertaking of it, is designed to answer some good purpose. You might, and I suppose did perceive, from the Tenor of my letters, that I was apprehensive I could not avoid this appointment, as I did not even pretend to intimate when I should return—that was the case—it was utterly out of my power to refuse this appointment without exposing my Character to such censures as would have reflected dishonour upon myself, and given pain to my friends—this, I am sure could not, and ought not be pleasing to you, & must have lessend me considerably in my own esteem. I shall rely therefore, confidently, on that Providence which has heretofore preservd, & been bountiful to me, not doubting but that I shall return safe to you in the fall. I feel no pain from the Toil, or the danger of the Campaign. My unhappiness will flow, from the uneasiness I know you will feel at being left alone. I beg of you to summon your whole fortitude Resolution, and pass your time as agreeably as possible—nothing will give me so much sincere satisfaction as to hear this, and to hear it from your own pen.

If it should be your desire to remove to Alexandria (as you once mentioned upon an occasion of this sort) I am quite pleased that you should put it into practice, & Lund Washington may be directed, by you, to build a Kitchen and other Houses there proper for your reception. If on the other hand you should rather Incline to spend a good part of your time among your Friends below, I wish you to do so. In short, my earnest & ardent desire is, that you would pursue any Plan that is most likely to produce content, and a tolerable degree of Tranquility as it must add greatly to my uneasy feelings to hear that you are dissatisfied, and complaining at what I really could not avoid.

As Life is always uncertain, and common prudence dictates to every Man the necessity of settling his temporal Concerns whilst it is in his power—and while the Mind is calm and undisturbed, I have, since I came to this place (for I had not time to do it before I left home) got Colo Pendleton to Draft a Will for me by the directions which I gave him which will I now Inclose. The provision made for you, in case of my death will, I hope, be agreeable; I included the money for which I sold my own land (to Doctr Mercer) in the Sum Given you, as also all other Debts. What I owe myself is very trifling—Cary's debt excepted, and that would not have been much if the Bank stock had been applied without such difficulties as he made in the Transference.

I shall add nothing more at present as I have several Letters to write, but to desire you will remember me to Milly & all Friends, and to assure you that I am with the most unfeigned regard,

My dear Patcy Yr Affecte. Go. Washington

P.S. Since writing the above I have received your Letter of the 15th and have got two suits of what I was told was the prettiest Muslin. I wish it may please you—it cost 50/ a suit that is 20/ a yard.

Phila. June 23d. 1775

My dearest,

As I am within a few minutes of leaving this City, I could not think of departing from it without dropping you a line, especially as I do not know whether it may be in my power to write you again till I get to the Camp at Boston. I go fully trusting in that Providence, which has been more bountiful to me than I deserve, & in full confidence of a happy Meeting with you sometime in the Fall. I have no time to add more, as I am surrounded with Company to take leave of me. I retain an unalterable affection for you, which neither time or distance can change. My best love to Jack & Nelly and regard for the rest of the Family concludes me with the utmost truth & sincerity, Yr entire Go. Washington

---

JAMES MADISON
TO
DOLLEY MADISON

---

*P*resident James Madison was still in flight from the British army's devastating attack on the nation's capital, including the sacking and burning of such public buildings as the Capitol and the President's House, when he wrote this letter to his wife.

Brookville Aug. 27. 10OC [1814]

My dearest

Finding that our army had left Montgomery Court House we pushed on to this place, with a view to join it, or proceed to the City as further information might prescribe. I have just recd. a line from Col. Monroe, saying that the Enemy were out of Washington, & on the retreat to their Ships & advising our immediate return to Washington. We shall accordingly set out the Men immediately. You will all of course take the same resolution. I know not where we are in the first instance to hide our heads; but shall look for a place on my arrival. Mr. Rush offers his house in the six buildings, and the offer claims attention. Perhaps I may fall in with Mr. Cutts, and have the aid of his advice. I saw Mr. Bradley at Montgomery Ct. H. who told me that Mrs. Cutts was well. Jamey will give you some particulars wch. I have not time to write.

Truly yours, J. Madison

[P.S.] Given the above it is found necessary to detain Jamey, & sent a Trooper.

A VERY ATTRACTIVE DOLLEY PAYNE TODD
MADISON APPEARS IN THIS ENGRAVING MADE FROM AN EARLY
NINETEENTH-CENTURY PAINTING BY GILBERT STUART.

𝓡achel Jackson was at home when she wrote this letter to her husband, who was leading the American forces against the Creek Indians during the War of 1812.

Hermitage February the 10 1814

My Dearest Life

I received your Letter by Express Never shall I forgit it I have not Slept one night Sinc What a dreadfull scene it was how did I feel I never Can disscribe it I Cryed aloud and praised my god For your safety how Thankfull I was—oh my unfortunate Nephew he is gon how I Deplore his Loss his untimely End—My Dear pray Let me Conjur you by Every Tie of Love of friend ship to Let me see you before you go againe I have borne it untill now it has thrown me Into feavours I am very unwell—my thoughts Is never Diverted from that dreadfull scene oh how dreadfull to me—o the mercy and goodness of Heaven to me you are Spard perils and Daingers so maney troubles—my prayers is unceaseing how Long o Lord will I remain so unhappy no rest no Ease I Cannot sleepe all can come home but you I never wanted to see you so mutch in my life had it not have Been for Stolekel Hayes I should have started oute to Hunts Ville let me know and I will fly on the wings of the pureest affection I must see you pray My Darling never make me so unhappy for aney Country I hope the Campaine will soon End the troops that is now on their way will be sufficient to End the war in the Creek Country you have now don more than aney other man Ever did before you have served your Country Long Enough you have gained maney Laurels you have Ernd them & more gloriously than had your situation have been diferently & instid of your Ennemyes Injuring of you as theay intended it has been an advantage to you— you have been gone a Long time six monthes in all that time what has been your trials daingers and Diffyculties hardeships oh Lorde of heaven how Can I beare it—Colo Hayes waites once more I Commend you to go his providential Eye is on you his parental tender care is gardeing you—my prayers my tears is for your safety Daye and night. farwell my I fell two mutch at this moment our Dear Little Son is well he says maney things to sweet papa which I have not time to mention. The bhest blessings of Heaven await you Crown your wishes—health and happy Dayes untill we meet—Let it not be Long from your Dearest friend and faitfull wife until Death Rachel Jackson

*F*ranklin Pierce, who had enlisted as a private in the volunteers and became a brigadier general in the U.S. Army while leading troops into battle during the Mexican War, wrote this moving letter on the eve of his departure from Boston for Mexico.

Boston Saturday Eveng [December 1846]

My dearest Janie

Your letter came today by express. I cannot trust myself to talk of the departure. My heart is with My own dear wife & boy and will ever be wherever duty may lead my steps. I shall be ready to leave on Monday, but it is quite possible that I may not go to Newport before Tuesday or possibly Wednesday. I have been constantly occupied making arrangements & purchases for myself & Major Sally who has had no opportunity to return from Newport and will sail on Monday. I have seen Robert but have been too much occupied to call on other Friends. I shall write you direct from Newport. Kiss dear Benny give my Kindest regards to Miss Carroll.

And believe me ever with devoted affection yr own Franky

FRANKLIN PIERCE AND HIS WIFE SUFFERED GREATLY OVER
THE EARLY DEATHS OF THEIR SONS, MAKING THEM EMOTIONALLY
FRAGILE DURING THEIR QUEST FOR THE PRESIDENCY.

*I*n this letter to his fiancée, Ulysses S. Grant described the ugly underside of war, and what happens to those who collaborate with the invaders—even if they are victorious.

Tacubaya Mexico June 4th 1848

My Dearest Julia

I wrote you a letter about two weeks ago saying that I should not probably ever write to you again from this part of Mexico. But as there is a Mail going in a few days, and it will probably go faster than the troops will March, I will write to you again and for the last time, from here. Peace is at last Concluded and the most of the troops are on their way to Vera Cruz. On Thursday next the last of the troops in the Valley of Mexico will leave and I think by the 28th or 30th of July I may Count on being in St. Louis. The thought of seeing you so soon is a happy one dearest Julia but I am so impatient that I have the Blues all the time. A great Many of the business people, in fact nearly all of them, want to see us remain in the Country. Already a revolution is looked for as soon as our backs are turned. People who have associated with the Americans are threatened with having their ears & noses cut off as soon as their protectors leave. Gen. Terrace of the Mexican Army lives here in Tacubaya with his family. He has five daughters young ladies who are sociable with officers of the U.S. Army A few weeks ago an Aid-de-Camp of Gen. Velasco threatened to mark their faces as soon as we left. The threat reached the ears of one of the officers who was in the habit of visiting the young ladies and he gave the valient A.D.C. Who was going to make war against innocent females a good thrashing in a Public place, and much to the Amusement of the by standers. Already some barbarities have been Committed such as shaving the heads of females and I believe in one or two Cases they cut their ears off. These are the kind of people that Compose the population of Mexico. Yesterday an officer had his horse Saddle and bridle stolen in broad day light and from the very densest part of the City. Such thefts are common. I most hartily rejoice at the prospect of getting out of Mexico though I prefer the Country and Climate to any I have ever yet seen.

I am going to write you but a short letter dearest Julia because I expect to start at the same time this does. Our March to Vera Cruz I fear will be attended with much fatigue and sickness. Already the rainy Season is beginning to set in and at Vera Cruz there have been several cases of Yellow fever. Every precaution will be taken to keep the troops from getting sick however.

We are all to halt and encamp before we get to the Coast and as fast as transportation is ready the troops will be marched aboard at night and push off immediately.

Give my love to all. Fred is well. Write to me again as soon as you receive this and direct as usual. Whenever a Mail meets us it will be stopped and we will get our letters.

Adieu but for a short time. Ulysses

JOHN TYLER
TO
JULIA TYLER

---

*J*ohn Tyler, the only former president to serve in a rebel government, exchanged these excited letters with his wife as Virginia seceded from the Union and war loomed between the United States and the Southern Confederacy.

Richmond Apl. 16. 1861

Well Dearest, your Letter receivd this morning plac'd me much at ease relative to the dear children. I hope you will still keep an eye upon them and not suffer them to expose themselves to the weather. Our noble boys are of high spirit, and if God spares them I think they will reflect honor on our names. The prospects now are that we shall have war—and a trying one—the battle at Charleston has arous'd the whole North. I fear that division no longer exists in their ranks, and that they will break upon the South with an immense force. Virginia will deserve much credit for boldness if in fact of all this—in debt and without disciplin'd troops, she throws herself into the meleè, taking upon trust the action of the Border Slave States. but events press so rapidly on each others heels that we have, I think, no alternative. Submission or resistance is only left us. My hope is that the border States will follow speedily our lead. If so, all will be safe. The Convention is setting with clos'd doors. Another day may decide our course. To morrow night is fix'd for a great torch light procession and illumination for the battle at Charleston. If to this is added an ordinance of secession there will be an immense outburst I wish the boys could be here. But do not understand me as saying that an ordinance will be pass'd. On the contrary it will be in doubt until the vote. Genl. Scott has resignd. It is as I always thought it would be, He comes to offer his sword to Virginia. I propose to offer suitable resolutions. We learn that the govt. has sent 500 troops to the Navy Yard at Portsmouth.

These are dark times Dearest and I think only of you and our little ones. But I trust in that same Providence that protected our fathers. These rascals who hold power, leave us no alternative. I shall vote secession and prefer to encounter any hazard to degrading Virginia. If the ordinance passes it is to be submitted to the people. Love and kisses to all, Always yr. devoted

J. Tyler

[P.S.] 1/2 after 8 p.m. just adjournd without taking the question.

Sherwood Forest April 27, 1861

Well Dearest the deed is done & the act accomplished by which a New Independence is secured, and Virginia has led the way! to least the Border States. As we ... cannot be present they will soon all drop into the ranks, and fight for that stand they have taken—of a separate & distinct Nation, which the North has driven them to dispute! The South forbore & forbore—forgave & forgave while at last the day of reckoning has come and many there will be at the North that love justice for justices sake who will secretly if they dare not openly encourage & laud the movement which has been only too tardy.

I am glad to see before In your letter the extract of a letter which had been written by Robert. I could see by it that he had thought it proper to break off at once all Southern Correspondence to prove that he was having no hand in the present performances, which is all right while in his adopted State. But have you seen the infamous proposition of Brooks? That steamers shall come up James River to pillage & destroy the places upon it! You may depend upon it the Man has gone stark mad in consequences of the threats of the Mob. In no other way can one account for such infamy. Pray find out whether Miss Randolph that was who married <u>My Mayo</u> is now living in Richmond. Allen has entertained them so much that Brooks must have some particular grudge.

I thought yesterday I gleaned from the papers some peaceful prospects. Letcher's Proclamation to auction seized vessels &c. denoted some change for the better I thought. But I do hope I shall have another letter from you today. That 7th Reg. deserved to be cut to pieces but it seems 'twas not. Since my disappointment is upon her reports the taking of Fort Pickens & the destruction of the 7th New J. Reg. I read the papers much more coolly.

Mr. Gill was about a little while at the Court House yesterday he assist at an Inquest. The body of a man apparently a fisherman came ashore at Mr. Denothat.

I have no letter from Mama. Did you get Julia a cake of soap, box of tooth powder (onis root & prepared chalk) & green veil.

The children are all well. Adieu Dearest, your devoted wife.

JAMES GARFIELD

TO

LUCRETIA GARFIELD

---

*J*ames Garfield commanded the Twentieth Brigade of the Sixth Division in the bloody Battle of Shiloh, in which General Ulysses S. Grant's Union Army turned back an attack by Confederate forces. James wrote this letter to his wife from the battlefield two days after the Confederates withdrew.

Battlefield, 12 miles from Corinth, Miss.
April 9, 1862

My Dear Crete:

I sent a letter to you from Savannah, I just was embarking my Brigade to the battle. We landed from steamers at a place called Pittsburg, nine miles above Savannah, about half past one o'clock. The battle had been raging since early dawn, and the enemy were just begining to fall back slowly. Gen. Woods sent orders for us to proceed to the front with all possible dispatch. I hurried my Brigade on and reached the front before three o'clock. I was there halted to await further orders. For an hour we stood amid the roar of the battle, the shells bursting around us occasionally, and the grape shot falling on all sides of me and my staff. We had ridden forward to watch the indications and await orders, but the tide battle swept over, and as the sun went down our division was ordered to the extreme front where we bivouaced during the worst night of mud and rain I ever saw.

Yesterday morning we pursued the enemy in an armed reconnaissance between three and four miles, where we were attacked by 800 Texan Rangers, and as many more Alabama cavalry. They made a most desperate attack driving back our advance (a Regt. of cavalry and one of infantry) killing 19 and wounding 40 with nearly an equal loss on their Side. They were, however, soon driven back, and their camp destroyed. On the whole this is no doubt the bloodiest battle ever fought on this Continent, in which has been mingled on our side the worst and the best of generalship, the most noble bravery and most contemptible cowardice. Gen. Grant was encamped on the west side of the river with a very large army, and on Sunday morning, very early he seems to have been surprised by an overwhelming force of the enemy who came down with a front line of battle three miles in length and a long column supporting it in the center. Gen. Johnson was in Supreme Command, Beauregard in the Center, Bragg & Hardee on the wings. By some criminal neglect, not yet Explained, their approach was not discovered till fifteen minutes before the attack. Their vast column moved on sweeping Grant's advanced Brigades before it like leaves before a whirlwind. Here and there, some brave officer formed his line and withstood the shock till the long line of dead and wounded was greater than the living. In this way the enemy drove on for four miles, till our force was driven to the steamboat landing, where it must have been annihilated or Captured, but for the two gunboats, which sent shells with terrible effect into the Columns of the enemy and forced him back from the river. This night closed in over a most disastrous day for our arms and our honor. It was the enemy's evident intention to cut off Grant before Gen. Buell should arrive via Nashville and Columbia. In the night, however, our column reached the river and began to cross. Early next morning the battle was resumed, both parties having been strongly reinforced. Inch by inch the enemy were driven back over the ground they had captured, and as night closed in our line of battle, five miles in length, swept the enemy back over a space of six miles. Such a scene as this 30 square miles presents beggars all attempt at description. If I live to meet you again, I will attempt to tell something of its horrors. God has been good to me, and I am yet spared. After returning from our reconnaisance last evening, we slept again on this ground without blankets. It rained heavily for three hours the latter part of the night. Today we are beging. to bury the dead. I presume we shall soon move on Corinth.

My health has never been better, though I am entirely without camp equipage. My horses and servants, trunks, mess-chest are all back. Indeed, I have nothing of my own, save the clothes on my back. When they will be here I do not know. I shall telegraph for them today.

I have almost been glad that my dear 42nd is not with me—there has been such terrible exposure of the soldiers here. But, Oh how I grieve at our separation.

Kiss our precious little Trot for me a hundred times. God bless you and her with the richest of his infinite love. Remember me to Father and Mother and all the family. Tell Harry & Almeda I wrote to them a short time before I reached Savannah.

My letters must be addressed to me "Care of 20th Brig. 6th Division Army of the Ohio—via Nashville—to follow the Brigade." This voluminous direction will Cause letters to reach me, and I hope a great number will come.

Ever & forever, your James

RUTHERFORD B. HAYES

TO

LUCY WEBB HAYES

---

*R*utherford and Lucy exchanged these letters around the time that he was wounded at the battle of South Mountain, Maryland, in the preliminaries to the Battle of Antietam. Lucy left for Maryland to care for her husband the day after she wrote her letter on September 18.

Maryland. Sept 13 1862 A.M.

Dearest: Frederick,
Yesterday was an exciting but very happy day. We retook this fine

town about 51/2 P.M. after a march of 14 miles and a good deal of Skirmishing, Cannon firing, and uproar and with but little fighting. We marched in just at sun down the 23d a good deal of the way in front. There was no mistaking the Union feeling and joy of the people—fine ladies, pretty girls, and children were in all the doors and windows waving flags and clapping hands—some "jumped up and down" with happiness—Joe enjoyed it and rode up the streets bowing most gratefully. The scene as we approached across the broad bottom lands in line of battle, with occasional cannon firing and musketry—the beautiful Blue Ridge Mts. in view & the fine town in front was very magnificent. It is pleasant to be so greeted. The enemy had held the City just a week, "the longest week of our lives," "We thought you were never coming", "this is the happiest hour of our lives" were the common expressions.

It was a most fatiguing day to the men. When we got the town before the formal entry, men laid down in the road, saying they Couldn't stir again. Some were pale, some red as if appoplectic—half an hour after they were marching erect and proud hurrahing for the ladies!

Col. Mohr 28th of Cinti. was wounded and taken prisoner in one of the skirmishes yesterday. The enemy treat our men well, very well. We have of sick & wounded 500 or 600 prisoners taken here.

Well Lucy dearest—Good Bye—Love to all—Kiss the boys. Affectionately Ever R

L U C Y W E B B H A Y E S

T O

R U T H E R F O R D B . H A Y E S

Willow Branch Sept. 18th [1862]

My dearest R.

My camping ground is again changed. I am now at the old Home place 8 miles from Chillicothe—at Uncle Will—all the cousins have gone to the war—so there seems to be some great change every where but when I try to think what makes the difference I find all as usual but the kind affectionate cousins just grown and retaining all the early love for Cousin Lucy and her boys—indeed Ruddy no one has ever met with more real heart felt kindness than I. You will say—why want is the matter that I should feel it so much—you do not know how changed your absence makes me feel—a sadness—and oh dearest a fear which I try to banish—that it may be a long parting. How anxiously we watch the papers—and last Tuesday the announcement that Major R. B. Hayes was wounded sent the blood to my heart—but I took the paper and read it again of the Ohio Cavalry. As yet I feel you are preserved to us—and now dearest—just here—let me say to you again—if anything should happen to you or my brothers we can come without little Joe. Aunt Lu has said and wished me to write— that should anything happen—she will Keep our children while we go to you. I feared you might hesitate to send for us—knowing how young Joe is—but brighter days are coming—the three boys are with Grand ma at Elmwood—have been there two weeks. Uncle Scott disliked to part with them and Aunt Ellen said they were no trouble that they were the best children—there little Joe has tumbled over on the floor and is now expressing his feelings. Cousin Mag M'Kell is carrying and soothing him. He is such a dear little one—you cant realize And he is sitting alone—but then we think he is a red head—that will comfort brother Joe.

The whole Country is dried up—the grass dried and yellow— and yet no rain. Last night the wind blew hard and this morning a Little drizzling rain—gving the promise of an approaching rain. The fruit is drying up—and every thing looks yellow and wearied and foot-sore—will it never end from how many bleeding hearts—the cry is heard. I have now given up seeing you at the head of the 49th but probably in a day or two it will be announced that you are coming for two or three weeks past. I have been afraid to leave town for fear you might come and it would be a few hours before I would see you. When the Rebels first threatened Cincinnati I thought of your Library—it is so closely connected with you all the books selected by you and read with interest and you loved them and I though not the intellectual wife—that would have done you credit yet loved them because you did. As we are in the Country and no boys now to send to town I must close this for a neighbor. Write to me when ever you can—it is a strange feeling but I can hardly write when I do not know where you are. Mother is improving so fast—in three weeks she gained nine pounds. Dearest I wrote you asking advice about sending Birchie to school—when we return to it—you may not have received my letter—where shall I send him. All send love. I heard a man on the street the other day advising one who was going to war to all his old womans letters when he received them, probably the same advice would be good to R .B.

Good bye again my dearest R. Yours L. W. H.

MARY LINCOLN
TO
ABRAHAM LINCOLN

---

*M*ary Lincoln was in New York when she wrote this letter to her husband, urging him to replace General McClellan with "a fighting General."

Nov 2d [1862]

My Dear Husband
I have waited in vain to hear from you, yet as you are not given to letter writing, will be charitable enough to impute your silence to the right Cause. Strangers come up from W– & tell me you are well—which satisfies me very much. Your name is on every lip and many prayers and good wishes are hourly Sent up for your welfare—And McClellan & his Slowness are as vehemently discussed, Allowing this beautiful weather to pass away, is disheartening the North—

Dear little Taddie is well & enjoying himself very much. Gen & Mrs. Anderson & myself called on yesterday to See Gen Scott. He looks well, although complaining of Rheumatism. A day or two since, I had one of my Severe attacks, if it had not been for Lizzie Heckley, I do not know what I should have done. Some of these <u>periods</u> will launch me away. All the distinguished in the land, have tried how polite & attentive they could be to me Since I Came up here. Many say, they would almost worship you, if you would put a fighting General in the place of McClellan. This would be splendid weather, for an engagement. I have had two suits of

FIRST LADY MARY ANN TODD LINCOLN FREELY OFFERED ADVICE TO HER HUSBAND ON POLITICAL AND MILITARY MATTERS DURING THE CIVIL WAR.

clothes made for Taddie which will come to 26 dollars. Have to get Some fur outside wrappings for the Coachman's Carriage trappings. Lizzie Heckley wants me to loan her thirty dollars—So I will have to ask for a check of $100—which will soon be made use of, for these articles. I must Send you, Taddie's tooth—I want to leave here for Boston, on Thursday & if you will send the check by Tuesday, will be much obliged.

One line to say that we are occasionally remembered will be gratefully received by yours very truly M. L.

[P.S.] I enclose you a note from Mr. Stewart, he appears very Solicitous about his young friend. Mr. S. is so strong a union Man & asks so few favors—if it came in your way, perhaps it would not be amiss to oblige.

ANDREW JOHNSON BECAME PRESIDENT UPON THE ASSASSINATION
OF ABRAHAM LINCOLN IN 1865 AND PREVAILED BY A NARROW
MARGIN IN AN IMPEACHMENT TRIAL IN 1868.

ANDREW JOHNSON
TO
ELIZA JOHNSON

*A*ndrew Johnson, military governor of Tennessee and its former governor under the Union, was drumming up support for the war effort when he wrote his only surviving letter to his wife, who was living in Louisville, Kentucky.

Washington City March 27th 1863.

My dear Eliza,

It is so difficult for me to write I am almost detered from now trying after having commenced

I Desire to know how your health is I am kept in suspence all the time in reference to Some one of the family—Col Stover telegraphed that your health is about the same and that Mary is not well—I have heard nothing from Robert & Charles since I left Nashville. I hope all is right with them. Martha and children I fear I shall never see them again. I feel sometimes like givg all up in dispare! But this will not do we must hold out to the end, this rebelion is wrong and must be put down let cost what it may in the life and treasure. I intend to appropriate the remainder of my life to the redemption of my adopted home East Tenessee and you & Mary must not be weary, It is our fate and we Should be willing to bear it cheerfully. Impatience and dissatisfaction will not better it or shorten the time of our Suffering. I expected to have been back some time ago, but have been detaind here by the Govmt. In the event Genls Rosecrans & Burnside fails to redeem East Tennessee this spring or summer I making aragments to have a force raised to go there this fall. My matters are now nearly arranged and will leave in a day or so for Louisville. Things do not look in Tennessee at this time as would like to see them; but must take them as they are. I would like to see the confederate Army back before you and Mary goes to Nashville, but by the time I reach there we will see more about it. You have no doubt seen that there are more troops being sent into Ky and the intention is to send them from there into Tennessee unless they are beaten back by the Rebels which I do not think will be the case. However we must wait and See the result. Washington is about as usual as far as I have seen, nothing more than common. The weather since I left you has been unin-teruptedly bad. I have scarcely had a well day since reaching the north; aboniable cold, with horseness, sore throat and a bad cough. I have been speaking and exposed to some extent which has kept it up. I hope you are gaing strength and some flesh. I trust there is nothing serious the matter with Mary and that she will soon be well again. Tell Mary she must devote much of her time and atten-tion to the instruction and traing of her children and say to them that the're grand father thinks of them every day and prays for their future happiness. You must tell Andrew that his father's hopes rest upon him now and that he must make a man of himself he learn to do it if he will and I expect it of him. If he will only edu-cate him Self he has a destiny of no ordinry Character. When I get to Louisville I Shall expect to find that he has made considerable progress in writing as well as in his books. If he will be a good boy and learn as he can there is nothing that he wants that I can pro-cure for him but what he shall have. Say to Col. Stover that I receivd his despatch and will try and have it attend to &c. I hope he is fill-ing up his Regimnt.

Give my love to all and accept for yourself the best wishes of a devoted husband's heart.

Andrew Johnson

BENJAMIN HARRISON

TO

CAROLINE HARRISON

Benjamin Harrison pulled no punches in this vivid description of the carnage in a typical Civil War fight, addressed to his wife. In a later letter, he declared to her that he had "no more relish for a fight than for a good breakfast."

Camp 70 Ind. Vol. Infty
New Kenesaw Mountain
June 18th 1864

My dear Wife

Though in a bad plight for letter writing sitting shivering in the mud & rain I want send you a short line if only to let you Know that God still keeps me in safety. We had quite a hard fight at Golgotha Church about 2 miles from here on the 15th & lost killed & wounded 50 men. Sgt. J. Kutzel, Segt H. Olds, Ezra E Ross are among the killed & several have since died. My Regt. was advanced without any support to within 300 yards of a strong rebel breastwork where they had 8 pieces of artillery in position & nicely covered. We being entirely exposed. We stood there fighting an unseen foe for an hour & _ without flinching while the enemy shells & grapes fell like hail in our ranks tearing down large trees & filling the air with splinters. Two or three of my men had their heads torn off close down to the shoulders & others had fearful wounds. We were ordered to be there till night when we would be relieved & we did, though I think few veteran regts. would have done so. After dark we were relieved by a Regt of Coburns Brigade but they didn't stay there long & the position was not held. The 23 Corps should have occupied it but instead of that they fortified about 3/4 of a mile to the rear. After we were relieved we fell back in perfect order to the support of our four Batteries taking our Killed & wounded with us. Our Surgeons had got separated from us & putting our wounded in a deserted house I stripped my arms to dress their wounds myself. Poor fellows. I was but an awkward surgeon, but I hope I gave them some relief. There were some ghastly wounds. I pulled out of one poor fellows arm a splinter 5 or six inches long & as thick as my three fingers. Maj. Reagan was struck twice once with a musket ball which was turned aside by his spy-glass & once by a piece of a shell which bruised him badly in the side. I sent him from the field & hear now that he is getting along well & is not dangerously hurt. Capt. Heath & H. Lowes were slightly hurt with shell but on with the Regt again. The woods were literally torn into Splinters & in looking over the ground it seems marvellous that so few were hurt. Yesterday morning the Rebs evacuated that line & we have now run upon them again over Kenesaw Mountain & while I write the peltening of the stones mingling with the fire of artillery & skirmish. We are in reserve today for the first time & right glad of it. God does indeed most mercifully preserve my unworthy life. May it continue to be His Care not mine to Keep it. We lost one man killed (Kirsh) on the 16th in the entrenchments. The enemy will probably fall back on the River without much more fighting.

Love & Kisses to my dear children & to all who will admit of that familiarity among my <u>female</u> friends. As to <u>finances</u> I have a friend here (Capt. Heraig) who will loan me all I want. I hope Uncle Sam will make some arrangement to support our families if he don't give us any money.

I got a letter from you yesterday. Do write me more often & longer letters, telling me everything that is going on.

My health is good. Col. Merrill has returned to the Regt. improved in health. He was not in the fight of the 15th. My Regt was the only one that suffered much. My loss was equal to that of the other four.

But must close. I cant tell when I can get to go home. I would not like to leave my Regt to the command of another in a fight. I have got to love them for their bravery & for dangers we have shared together. I have heard many similar expressions from the men toward me.

When I can leave them & the Service you will be sure I shall come with swift feet to the wife & home of my heart. Your devoted Husband. Benj. Harrison

---

A B R A H A M L I N C O L N
T O
M A R Y L I N C O L N

---

*T*he Civil War was nearing its climactic conclusion when President Lincoln sent this excited telegram to his wife, who had been more than willing to offer him advice on military operations during the war.

Washington, D.C. City Point,
April 2. 7/45 1865

Mrs. A. Lincoln,

Last night Gen. Grant telegraphed that Sheridan with his Cavalry and the 5th Corps had captured three brigades of Infantry, a train of wagons, and several batteries, prisoners amounting to several thousands. This morning Gen. Grant, having ordered an attack along the whole line telegraphs as follows.

"Both Wright and Parke got through the enemies lines. The battle now rages furiously. Sheridan with his Cavalry, the 5th. Corps & Miles Division of the 2nd. Corps, which was sent to him since 1. This a.m. is now sweeping down from the West. All now looks highly favorable. Ord is engaged, but I have not yet heard the result in his front."

Robert yesterday wrote a little cheerful note to Capt. Penrose, which is all I have heard of him since you left. Copy to Secretary of War. A Lincoln

---

ULYSSES S. GRANT

T O

JULIA GRANT

---

*U*lysses S. Grant's Army of the Potomac had just driven the Confederate Army from Richmond, Virginia, when he sent this triumphant letter back home to his wife.

Apl. 2d 1865

Dear Julia

I am now writing from far inside of what was the rebel fortifications this morning but what are ours now. They are exceeding strong and I wonder at the success of our troops carrying them by storm. But they did do it and without any great loss. We have captured about 12,000 prisoners and 50 pieces of Artillery. As I write this news comes of the capture of 1000 more prisoners. Altogether this has been one of the greatest victories of the war. Greatest because it is over what the rebels have always regarded as their most invincable Army and the one used for the defince of their capitol. We may have some more hard work but I hope not.

Love and kisses for you and Jess. Ulys.

FRANKLIN D. ROOSEVELT

TO

ELEANOR ROOSEVELT

𝒫resident Roosevelt had sailed to Oran onboard the USS *Iowa* and then on to Tunis and Cairo to meet with Winston Churchill and Chiang Kai-shek. They were to discuss the Burma Theater and the "second front" in Europe, and to meet with his sons and son-in-law who were fighting with the Allies in Africa.

Tunis, Nov. 21 [1943]

Dearest Babs

We landed safely yesterday and came through to Tunis where I am safely ensconced in a very nice villa overlooking the sea and just beyond the ruins of Carthage. Elliot and F. Jr. met me when we left the ship—and are well, tho' F. Jr. has the trouble he wrote of. He finally decided he had best go back with the ship and I think he is right to want to see her safely to Charleston. He and I will probably get back about the same time.

This p.m. I reviewed Elliott's whole outfit. He is in top command of all the Reconnaissance Air—U.S.—Brit.—So. African and N. Zealand—5,000 men and 250 planes. He flies to Italy tomorrow and joins me in Cairo. By the way all this is secret. The press will say nothing for 5 or 6 days after it happens.

Cairo—Nov. 26th. The 1st meetings are in full swing. The Generalissimo and Mme. Chiang are here. Things have gone <u>pretty</u> well. We all have villas way out of town and about 1/4 mile apart.

I've visited the pyramids and been fortified by the Sphinx. I'll give free transportation to any Senator or Congressman who will go over and look at her for a long long time.

Last night I had a very nice Thanksgiving dinner. Elliott and John B. arrived in the a.m. and J. is O.K. I will keep them both with me from now on—also Winston and his daughter Sarah and A. Eden and old Lord Leathers and Tommy Thompson and my personal staff–19 in all.

We are off on the next leg tomorrow. All well but awful busy. Harry is standing it all right.

Ever so much love. Devotedly, F.

GEORGE H. W. BUSH

TO

BARBARA PIERCE

---

*G*eorge was awaiting his departure on a U.S. Navy aircraft carrier during World War II as he wrote this sole surviving wartime letter to his just "public fiancé."

Dec. 12. 1943

My darling Bar,

This should be a very easy letter to write—words should come easily and in short it should be simple for me to tell you how desperately happy I was to open the paper and see the announcement of our engagement, but somehow I can't possibly say all in a letter I should like to.

I love you, precious, with all my heart and to know that you love me means my life. How often I have thought about the immeasurable joy that will be ours some day. How lucky our children will be to have a mother like you.

As the days go by the time of our departure draws nearer. For a long time I had anxiously looked forward to the day when we would go abroad and set to sea. It seemed that obtaining that goal would be all I could desire for some time, but, Bar, you have changed all that. I cannot say that I do not want to go—for that would be a lie. We have been working for a long time with a single purpose in mind, to be so equipped that we could meet and defeat our enemy. I do want to go because it is my part, but now leaving presents itself not as an adventure but as a job which I hope will be over before long. Even now, with a good while between us and the sea, I am thinking of getting back. This may sound melodramatic, but if it does it is only inadequacy to say what I mean. Bar, you have made my life full of everything I could ever dream of—my complete happiness should be a token of my love for you.

Wednesday is definitely the commissioning and I do hope you'll be there. I'll call Mom tomorrow about my plan. A lot of fellows put down their parents or wives and they aren't going so you could pass as a Mrs.—Just say you lost the invite and give your name. They'll check the list and you'll be in. How proud I'll be if you can come.

I'll tell you all about the latest flying developments later. We have so much to do and so little time to do it in. It is frightening at times. The seriousness of this thing is beginning to strike home. I have been made asst. gunnery officer and when Lt. Houle leaves I will be the gunnery officer. I'm afraid I know very little about it but I am excited at having such a job. I'll tell you all about this later too.

The wind of late has been blowing like mad and our flying has been cut to a minimum. My plane, #2 now, is up at Quonset, having a camera installed. It is Bar #2 but purely in spirit since the Atlantic fleet won't let us have names on our planes.

Good nite my beautiful. Everytime I say beautiful you about kill me but you'll have to accept it.

I hope to get Thursday off—there's still a chance. All my love darling—

Poppy public fiancé as of 12/12/43

DWIGHT D. EISENHOWER
TO
MAMIE EISENHOWER

*J*ust days after D-Day, the Allied invasion at Normandy, General Dwight Eisenhower
wrote this upbeat letter to his wife.

Portsmouth, June 9, 1944

My darling:

I just sent you a teletype. As always when I go through these
intense periods of strain and effort I think of you, want you here,
and try to write to you—but I'm afraid that even my short notes
are rather incoherent!

Anyway, we've started. Only time will tell how great our success will be. But all that can be done by human effort, intense
devotion to duty, and courageous execution, all by thousands and

PRESIDENT EISENHOWER AND HIS WIFE MAMIE
POSE BEFORE A WHITE HOUSE ADDRESS.

thousands of individuals, will be done by this force. The soldiers, sailors, and airman are indescribable in their elan, courage, determination and fortitude. They inspire me.

How I look forward to seeing Johnny. It will be odd to see him as an <u>officer of the Army</u>! I'll burst with pride!

My goodness, I must run. Take care of yourself & loads & loads of love to you!

Always your Ike

DWIGHT D. EISENHOWER
TO
MAMIE EISENHOWER

On the eve of the formal German surrender at Rheims, France, Ike sent Mamie this matter-of-fact but insightful letter.

May 6, 1945

Darling

These are trying times. The enemy's armed forces are disintegrating, but in the tangled skein of European politics nothing can be done, except with the utmost care and caution, where the interests of more than one country are involved. How glad I'll be when this is all over, even though some of our worst headaches will come after all the shooting is over. Oh well—certainly by this time I should be used to "problems."

Had a recent note from Johnny. He seems to be in the best of health and looking for more work to do. He is a funny kid—half the time I cannot make out just what he does want to do.

Yesterday I forwarded to him the note you enclosed with one to me.

Last night I really expected some definite developments and went to bed early in anticipation of being waked up at 1,2,3 or 4 a.m. Nothing happened and as a result I was wide awake, very early—with nothing decent to read. The Wild Wests I have just now are terrible—I could write better ones, left-handed.

Well—here are the papers. Now I'll see what every office, all over the world, has to tell me. In times such as these, everybody and his brother have to have their say.

Loads of love & my best to Danny. Always your Ike

HARRY S. TRUMAN

TO

BESS TRUMAN

$\mathcal{T}$he president had received word just the night before that North Korea had invaded South Korea and had already determined on war, when he wrote this letter to Bess, two days before their wedding anniversary.

June 26, 1950

Dear Bess:

We had a grand trip back after we were in the air. Col. Williams was fooling around waiting for Landry to show up. Landry had gone to some golf course, after asking me if it would be all right for him to play Sunday afternoon. But he should have left the name of the club where he intended to play at the hotel. Evidently he arrived at the airport shortly after we were in the air and reported to us abut the time we were over St. Louis that he was fifteen minutes behind us. I told the communications officer to tell him to go back to K.C., get in touch with Gen. Vaughan and Ted Marks and bring them in tomorrow.

The crowd at the Washington Airport was made up of the Secs. of State and Defense and Army, Navy and Air.

Had them all to dinner at 8 and the dinner was good and well served. Fred and Rufus ate up in the parlor on the 2nd floor of the Lee House. We put them over there because those two rooms are air conditioned, and the others in the Blair House were very hot.

HARRY S. TRUMAN MAKES HIS FIRST PRESIDENTIAL ADDRESS
TO A JOINT SESSION OF CONGRESS AT THE U.S. CAPITOL ON APRIL 16,
1945, AFTER ASSUMING THE PRESIDENCY UPON THE DEATH
OF FRANKLIN D. ROOSEVELT.

My conference was a most successful one, and there is a chance that things may work out without the necessity of mobilization. Haven't been so badly upset since Greece & Turkey fell into our lap. Let's hope for the best.

Hope your mother is better. She seemed to me to be better Sunday at noon than she was the day before.

I've canceled my sailing trip. Don't want to be too far away. The reason I suggested Gen. Landry call Margie, I am afraid of the R.R. strike.

Lots & lots of love and many happy returns for the 31st year of your ordeal with me. It's been <u>all</u> pleasure for me. Harry

NEWLY RE-ELECTED PRESIDENT HARRY
S. TRUMAN IS CLEARLY AMUSED BY AN EDITION OF
THE CHICAGO DAILY TRIBUNE MISTAKENLY
PROCLAIMING HIS DEFEAT

CHAPTER 3

POLITICS

~⁀

"I would hate for you to go into politics."
—Claudia Alta (Lady Bird) Taylor to Lyndon Johnson,
October 22, 1934

*"My feeling is that we
have to get going and going quickly."*
—Eleanor Roosevelt to Franklin D. Roosevelt,
July 16, 1936

*"She wants you for a 3rd term
and I thought this most unwise."*
—Eleanor Roosevelt to Franklin D. Roosevelt,
August 1938

POLITICS is the focal point for most of the lives and letters of presidents and their wives. Even during peacetime, a president's political life could involve toil, trouble, strategy, and triumph, as these letters and messages between first spouses demonstrate.

he Continental Congress was about to debate American independence and the formation of a national government, when Abigail Adams wrote a series of remarkable letters to her husband, criticizing slave owners while urging him to "Remember the Ladies" and chastising him for proclaiming freedom while "retaining an absolute power over Wives."

Braintree, March 31 1776

I wish you would ever write me a Letter half as long as I write you; and tell me if you may where your Fleet are gone? What sort of Defence Virginia can make against our common Enemy? Whether it is so situated as to make an able Defence? Are not the Gentery Lords and the common people vassals, are they not like the uncivilized Natives Britain represents us to be ? I hope the Riffel Men who have shewen themselves very savage and even Blood thirsty; are not a specimen of the Generality of the people.

I am willing to allow the Colony great merit for having produced a Washington but they have been shamefully duped by a Dunmore.

I have sometimes been ready to think that the passion for Liberty cannot be Eaquelly Strong in the Breasts of those who have been accustomed to deprive their fellow Creatures of theirs. Of this I am certain that it is not founded upon that generous and christian principal of doing to others as we would that others should do unto us.

Do not you want to see Boston; I am fearfull of the small pox, or I should have been in before this time. I got Mr. Crane to go to our House and see what state it was in. I find it has been occupied by one of the Doctors of a Regiment, very dirty, but no other damage has been done to it. The few things which were left in it are all gone. Cranch has the key which he never deliverd up. I have wrote to him for it and am determined to get it cleand as soon as possible and shut it up. I look upon it a new acquisition of property, a property which one month ago I did not value at a single Shilling, and could with pleasure have seen it in flames.

The Town in General is left in a better state than we expected, more oweing to a percipitate flight than any Regard to the inhabitants, tho some individuals discoverd a sense of honour and justice and have left the rent of the Houses in which they were, for the owners and the furniture unhurt, or if damaged sufficient to make it good.

Others have committed abominable Ravages. The Mansion House of your President is safe and the furniture unhurt whilst both the House and Furniture of the Solisiter General have fallen prey to their own merciless party. Surely the very Fiends feel a Reverential awe for Virtue and patriotism, whilst they Detest the paricide and traitor.

I feel very differently at the approach of spring to what I did a month ago. We knew not then whether we could plant or sow with safety, whether when we had toild we could reap the fruits of our own industery, whether we could rest in our own Cottages, or whether we should not be driven from the sea coasts to seek shelter in the wilderness, but now we feel as if we might sit under our own vine and eat the good of the land.

I feel a gaieti de Coar to which before I was a stranger. I think the Sun looks brighter, the Birds sing more melodiously, and Nature puts on a more chearfull countanance. We feel a temporary peace, and the poor fugitives are returning to their deserted habitations.

Tho we felicitate ourselves, we sympathize with those who are trembling least the Lot of Boston should be theirs. But they cannot be in similar circumstances unless pusilanimity and cowardise should take possession of them. They have time and warning given them to see the Evil and shun it. I long to hear that you have declared an independancy—and by the way in the new Code of Laws which I suppose it will be necessary for you to make I desire you would Remember the Ladies, and be more generous and favourable to them than your own ancestors. Do not put such unlimited power into the hands of the Husbands. Remember all men would be tyrants if they could. If perticular care and attention is not paid to the Ladies, we are determined to foment a Rebellion, and will not hold ourselves bound by any Laws in which we have no voice, or Representation.

That your Sex are Naturally Tyrannical is a Truth so thoroughly established as to admit of no dispute, but such of you as wish to be happy unwillingly give up the harsh title of Master for the more tender and endearing one of Friend. Why then, not put it out of the power of the vicious and the Lawless to use us with cruelty and indignity with impunity. Men of Sense in all Ages abhor those customs which treat us only as the vassals of your Sex. Regard us then as Beings placed by providence under your protection and in immitation of the Supreem Being make use of that power only for our happiness.

ABIGAIL ADAMS FREELY ADVISED HER HUSBAND DURING
HIS POLITICAL CAREER, WHILE ALSO MANAGING THE
FAMILY FARMS AND RAISING A LARGE FAMILY.

Be May 7 1776

How many solitary hours I spend, ruminating upon the past, and anticipating the future, whilst you overwhelmd with the cares of State, have but few moments you can devote to any individual. All domestick pleasures and injoyments are absorbed in the great and important duty you owe your Country "for our Country is as it were a secondary God, and the First and greatest parent. It is to be preferred to Parents, wives, Children, Friends and all things the Gods only except. For if our Country perishes it is as impossible to save an Individual, as to preserve one of the fingers of a Mortified Hand." thus do I supress every wish, and silence every Murmer, acquiesceing in a painfull Seperation from the companion of my youth, and the Friend of my Heart.

I believe tis near ten days since I wrote you a line. I have not felt in a humour to entertain you. If I had taken up my pen perhaps some invective might have fallen from it; the Eyes of our Rulers have been closed and a lethargy has seazd almost every member. I fear a fatal Security has taken possession of them. Whilst the Building is on flame they tremble at the expence of water to quench it, in short two months has elapsed since the evacuation of Boston, and very little has been done in that time to secure it, or the Harbour from future invasion till the people are all in flame; and no one among us that I have heard of even mentions expence, they think universally that there has been an amaizing neglect some where. Many have turnd out as volunteers to work upon Nodles Island, and many more would go upon Nastaskit if it was once set on foot. "Tis a Maxim of state That power and Liberty are like Heat and moisture; where they are well mixt every thing prospers, where they are single, they are destructive."

A Government of more Stability is much wanted in this colony, and they are ready to receive it from the Hands of the Congress, and since I have begun with Maxims of State I will add an other viz. That a people may let a king fall, yet still remain a people, but if a king let his people slip from him, he is no longer a king. And as this is most certainly our case, why not proclaim to the world in decisive terms your own importance?

Shall we not be dispiced by foreign powers for hesitateing so long at a word?

I can not say that I think you very generous to the Ladies, for whilst you are proclaiming peace and good will to Men, Emancipating all Nations, you insist upon retaining an absolute power over Wives. But you must remember that Arbitrary power is like most other things which are very hard, very liable to be broken— and notwithstanding all your wise Laws and Maxims we have it in our power not only to free ourselves but to subdue our Masters, and without violence throw both your natural and legal authority at our feet.

> "Charm by accepting, by submitting sway
> Yet have our Humour most when we obey."

I thank you for several Letters which I have received since I wrote Last. They alleviate a tedious absence, and I long earnestly for a Saturday evening, and experience a similar pleasure to that which I used to find in the return of my Friend upon that day after a weeks absence. The Idea of a year dissolves all my Phylosophy.

Our Little ones whom you so often recommend to my care and instruction shall not be deficient in virtue or probity if the precepts of a Mother have their desired Effect, but they would be doubly inforced could they be indulged with the example of a Father constantly before them; I often point them to their Sire

> "engaged in a corrupted State
> Wrestling with vice and faction."

[P.S.] May 9

I designd to have finished the sheet, but an opportunity offering I close only just inform you that May the 7 our privateers took two prises in the Bay in fair sight of the Man of war, one a Brig from Irland the other from fyall loaded with wine Brandy and the other Beef &c. The wind was East and a flood tide, so that the tenders could not get out tho they tried several times, the Light house fired Signal guns, but all would not do, they took them in triumph and carried them into Lyn.

Johny and Charls have the Mumps, a bad disorder, but they are not very bad. Pray be kind enough to remember me at all times and write as often as you possibly can to your Portia.

JOHN ADAMS

TO

ABIGAIL ADAMS

---

*C*ongress had voted for independence the previous day, when John Adams wrote this euphorically triumphant letter to Abigail. The next day, Congress would approve the Declaration of Independence, declaring the equality of "all men."

JOHN ADAMS HAD BEEN MARRIED TO ABIGAIL SMITH ADAMS FOR MORE THAN FIFTY YEARS WHEN THIS LITHOGRAPH WAS MADE.

Had a Declaration of Independency been made seven Months ago, it would have been attended with many great and glorious Effects. We might before this Hour, have formed Alliances with foreign States. We should have mastered Quebec and been in Possession of Canada. You will perhaps wonder, how such a Declaration would have influenced our Affairs, in Canada, but if I could write with Freedom I could easily convince you that it would, and explain to you the manner how. Many Gentlemen in high Stations and of great Influence have been duped, by the ministerial Bubble of Commissioners to treat. And in real, sincere Expectation of this Event, which they so fondly wished, they have been slow and languid, in promoting Measures for the Reduction of that Province. Others there are in the Colonies who really wished that our Enterprise in Canada would be defeated, that the Colonies might be brought into Danger and Distress between two Fires, and be thus induced to submit. Others really wished to defeat the Expedition to Canada, lest the Conquest of it, should elevate the Minds of the People too much to hearken to those Terms of Reconciliation which they believed would be offered Us. These jarring Views, Wishes and Designs, occasioned an opposition to many salutary Measures, which were proposed for the Support of that Expedition, and caused Obstructions, Embarrassments and studied Delays, which have finally, lost Us the Province.

All these Causes however in Conjunction would not have disappointed Us, if it had not been for a Misfortune, which could not be foreseen, and perhaps could not have been prevented, I mean the Prevalence of the small Pox among our troops. This fatal Pestilence compleated our Destruction. It is a Frown of providence upon Us, which We ought to lay to heart.

But on the other Hand, the delay of this Declaration to this Time, has many great Advantages attending to it. The Hopes of Reconciliation, which were fondly entertained by Multitudes of honest and well meaning tho weak and mistaken people, have been gradually and at last totally extinguished. Time has been given for the whole People, maturely to consider the great

Question of Independence and to ripen their Judgments, dissipate their Fears, and allure their Hopes by discussing it in News Papers and Pamphletts, by debating it, in Assemblies, Conventions. Committees of Safety and Inspection, in Town and County Meetings, as well as in private Conversations, so that the whole People in every Colony of the 13, have now adopted it, as their own Act. This will cement the Union, and avoid those Heats and perhaps Convulsions which might have been occasioned, by such a Declaration Six Months ago.

But the Day is past. The Second Day of July 1776, will be the most memorable Epocha, in the History of America. I am apt to believe that it will be celebrated by succeeding Generations, as the great anniversary Festival. It ought to be commemorated, as the Day of Deliverance by solemn Acts of Devotion to God Almighty. It ought to be solemnized with Pomp and Parade, with Shews , Games, Sports, Guns, Bells, Bonfires and Illuminations from one End of this Continent to the other from this Time forward forever more.

You will think me transported with Enthusiasm but I am not. I am well aware of the Toil and Blood and Treasure, that it will cost Us to maintain this Declaration, and support and defend these States. Yet through all the Gloom I can see the Rays of ravishing Light and Glory. I can see that the End is more than worth all the Means. And that Posterity will tryumph in that Days Transaction, even althou We should rue it, which I trust in God We shall not.

ABIGAIL ADAMS

TO

JOHN ADAMS

---

*A*bigail wrote this angry and defiant letter to her husband on her return to Massachusetts from Washington, after John's defeat by Thomas Jefferson.

[Philadelphia. February 21, 1801]

My dear Sir

I write you once more from this City, the Trenton River is impassable and has prevented my Sitting out. We hope however that the rain may clear it. I Sent Townsend off to day; I have heard Some of the democratic rejoicing Such as ringing Bells & fireing cannon; what an inconsistancy Said a Lady to me to day, the Bells of Christ Church ringing of peals of rejoicing for an Infidel president! The people of this city have evidently been in terror; least their Swineish Herd Should rise in rebellion and Seige upon their property & Share the plunder amongst them; they have permitted them really to overawe them; I foresee some day or other that NEngland will be obliged to march their militia to preserve this very State from destruction.

There is great uneasiness with the Merchants, they Say the senate by rejecting the article in the convention to which they have excepted, have plunged them into great difficultys. That they know not what to do—that a better convention as it respects Commerce could not have been made and why it should be hazarded by the Senate they cannot conceive. The difference Mr Breche told me it would make to this Country in one Year, would be nine millions of dollars. The Chamber of Commerce meet this Evening and send off an express to morrow to the Senators of this State, Urgeing that Something may yet be done; that the president may be requested to return the Convention to the Senate with his reasons, and by this means give the Senate an other opportunity of accepting it. Mr. Breche Says that he wrote the Sentiments of the merchants of this city to Mr. Secretary Otis requesting him to communicate them to Mr. Bingham & others. Whilst the convention was before the Senate; they regret that they did not exert themselves before.

I could not help smiling when Mr. Breche told me he had conversed with Mr. Wolcott, but could get no satisfaction, pray Mr. Wolcott Said that there was no faith to be placed in French promise, treaties or conventions.

I shall leave this City tomorrow I believe there is Scarcely a Lady who ever came to the drawing room but has visited me either old or young and very many Gentlemen; as to a return of their visits, they cannot expect it; I believe they have made a point of it; who published my arrival in the papers I know not; but the next morning by ten oclock rainy as it was, they began to come and have continued to by throngs ever since. I thank them for their attentions & politeness, tho I shall never see them again.

Adieu by dear Friend I wish you well through the remainder of your political journey. I want to see the list of judges.

With Love to William, Yours affectionately AA

JOHN QUINCY ADAMS
TO
LOUISA CATHERINE ADAMS

*J*ohn Quincy Adams was a U.S. senator from Massachusetts when he wrote this letter about the conspiracy of former vice president Aaron Burr to lead an armed expedition to carve out an independent empire in what is now the American southwest, and other political and personal news.

Washington 1 February 1807

My dear Louisa.

The Potomac Bridge question is at last postponed untill the next Session of Congress after seven days of as warm and close debate as I ever witness'd in the Senate. The postponement was carried by a single vote 17 to 16, and in all probability had the question on the Bill itself been taken, it would have prevailed. I have been so constantly engaged upon it, that I could not find time for writing even to you, more than two very short letters, in the last fortnight, and my letters from my mother and father yet remain unanswered.

The Bridge is for the present dismiss'd; but king Burr furnishes a topic of no less interest and agitation in its stead. Two of his agents, <u>Bollman and Swortout</u>, who were employed to seduce

General Wilkinson and the army and whom the General seized and sent here have been committed upon a charge of high Treason; but I suppose they must be sent back to New Orleans for trial. At least they cannot as I believe be tried here.

I am much obliged to you for the copy you sent me of Mr. Osgood's estimate of the expence which it would cost to build the place I contemplated in Court Street. The amount is so much higher than I had expected, that I shall be obliged at least to postpone the Execution of the Plan. For although I might possibly borrow money to pay the bills, yet the chance of making it a profitable undertaking is so much lessened by the amount of the sum to be expended that I think it best not to embarrass myself with a heavy debt upon a prospect of remuneration which at best must be uncertain. I shall therefore not abandon the design, but reserve it for an opportunity if it should ever present itself when I can engage in it with safety and without getting too much involved. I have received in one of your late Letters Rigg's Bill, which together with the other you mention shall cheerfully be discharged. I am sorry that any thing in this matter has given you pain, and once more assure you that so long as I have a dollar in the world it shall always readily be devoted to anything which in your own Judgment can contribute to your comforts.

I rejoyce to learn that upon speaking to Mr. G. You have been better accommodated in the Article of diet. I was indeed much mortified and chagrined at hearing that you had any reason to complain in that respect and hope it will not happen again. The time is now fast approaching when I hope to return, and to go into our own house. I presume Mr. Shaw has informed Mr. Bradford that we shall want it at the expiration of his present quarter. You mentioned sometime since that you had a boy with you, who you thought would answer our purpose there. If you still continue of this opinion I wish you to engage him And also to procure in Season if you can a woman as Cook; for after what we hear of Sally, we must not think of taking her. Mrs. Bradford's quarter expires I think the 17th of March by which day I hope to be in Boston; and I would have you be ready to move without the loss of a day, as soon as the house shall be empty.

The inconveniences of the neighbourhood mentioned to you by Mrs. Sargent are to be regretted and certainly I shall use my best endeavours to have them removed.

I thank you sincerely my dearest friend for mentioning the pew for sale at Mr. Emerson's; if it can be purchased at <u>a reasonable</u> price, I wish Shaw would bespeak it for me. My personal friendship for Mr. Emerson concurring with other impressions on my mind induce me to be desirous of not leaving him, when I reside in Boston, though as a temporary object the pew which Mrs. Davenport now holds in the Brattle Street Church would suit me sufficiently.

Within the last fortnight I have dined both at Mr. Erskine's and Genl. Turneau's and have pass'd Evening's at Miss Lee's Georgetown and Mrs. Erskine's & Mr. Madison's in the City. Mrs. Lenox and Miss Keene are here. The latter a beauty of the most dazzling pretensions. We heard her perform the other Evening on the Tambourine, with all the confidence and all the graces of a gypsy. Her dress is as much admired as her person and manners, and in the practical view of Dr. Thornton:

> On her breast she wears a dart
> Which I warrant will make the heart
> Of many a fine Gentleman smart.

This morning as I was going to the Treasury to hear Mr. Laurie I met Mr. Hopkinson and Mr. Hare, who told me that he saw you about three weeks ago, though he did not say where. They are here to attend the Supreme Court which is to sit to morrow.

I called at Mr. Boyd's and gave Caroline's letter to Eliza. They were all at Breakfast so that we had the anecdote of Dr. Spring & his patient without going through the indirect cause of Mr. and Mrs. Boyd before it came to me. I am going there again to dinner, which obliges me to shorten this letter, that I should else certainly carry through the other page. Mrs. Boyd's child continues at intervals very ill—but is this day more easy. What his name is I never told you because I have not understood that it was finally fixed upon. I heard of its being called by my name, but never either from its father or mother. Be it called what it may, I pray God it may recover and do well. Your's affectionately. J.Q. Adams

[P.S.] Kiss my dear John for his remembrance of Papa and George too if he has returned.

DOLLEY MADISON
TO
JAMES MADISON

---

*D*olley Madison was in Philadelphia recovering from a knee injury when she wrote this letter to her husband, then Secretary of State, characteristically understating her political acumen—a classic example of a woman's diffidence in politics.

JAMES MADISON IS BEST KNOWN AS THE FATHER OF THE U.S.
CONSTITUTION, BUT HE HAD A LONG CAREER IN CONGRESS AND AS
THOMAS JEFFERSON'S SECRETARY OF STATE BEFORE
BECOMING PRESIDENT IN 1809.

Philadelphia Novr. 1st. [1805]

I have great pleasure, my beloved in repeating to you what the Doctor has just now said, that the knee would be well in one day more and in two or three I might begin to ride—so that I may reasonably hope that a fortnight more will be the extent of my stay in Philadelphia. I am so impatient to be restored to you.

I wish you would indulge me with some information respecting the war with Spain and disagreement with England, as it is so generally expected here that I am at a loss what to surmise—you know I am not much of a politician but I am extremely anxious to hear (as far as you may think proper) what is going forward in the Cabinet—on this subject, I believe you would not desire your wife the active partizan, such as her neighbor Mrs. L, nor will there be the slightest danger whilst she is conscious of her want of talents, and her diffidence in expressing her opinions always imperfectly understood by her sex—in my last I told you every thing the state of my finances &c &c. I have sent Peter to the office for letters and I hope to hear from you and to receive some account of Anna. I expect to see her every day.

Kiss my child for me and remember me to my friends. Could you speak a word to General Dearborn in favor of poor Mrs. Jackson—the Doctor's widow who used to supply so well the soldiers—adieu, my dear husband, Peter brings me no letters which really unfits me for writing more to any one, your ever affectionate. D.

ANDREW JACKSON
TO
RACHEL JACKSON

---

*C*ongress was debating a resolution censuring Andrew Jackson for the 1818 execution of two British citizens, Alexander Arbuthnot and Robert Ambrister, during his invasion of Florida in the First Seminole War, when he wrote this letter to his wife.

City of Washington
Janry [February] 6th. 1819.

My Love

I recd. Your kind & affectionate letter of the 20th ult. & I sincerely regret to learn that you are indisposed—my health thank my god continues, probably the excitement of mind since I have been here, has kept me up. The Seminole war is still before the house, when a question may be taken I know not as I never have been in congress Hall since I have been here, nor do I mix with the members, determined that my enemies shall not have it to say that I attempted to influence their vote—the voic of the people begins to its eff here—I am told that there will be a great majority in my favour— and the insidious Mr. Clay will sink into that insignficance, that all those who abandon principle & Justice & would sacrafice their country for self agrandizement ought & will experience.

I have bought a Negro girl recommended to me by Mrs. Peal of Philadelphia as honest & a good servant I send her to day to you by the mail stage—she carries a small quantity of wheat presented to me by a gentleman of this country that I wish carefully sown the instant it arrives—I send by the girl whose name is Sally a few carricatures, for the children—& to shew you the spirit of the times—& how Mr. Richey conduct is appreciated—let Stokely Hays have one of them—I shall return as soon as I can, in the mean time I have only to say to you take care of your health, & recollect that all earthly things are but baubles, compared to health—accept a reiteration of my sincere affection & believe me to be yr affectionate Husband Andrew Jackson

---

J O H N   T Y L E R
T O
L E T I T I A   T Y L E R

---

*W*hile he was a senator from Virginia, John Tyler wrote this detailed letter to his first wife, about an attempted assassination of President Andrew Jackson.

Washington, February 1, 1835.

My Dear Wife:

We had a most extraordinary scene at the capitol on Friday last.

Warren R. Davis, of South Carolina, had died two nights before, and his funeral ceremonies were performed in the House of Representatives. The body was then moved in procession to the east porch of the capitol, from whence it was to be taken to the burial ground. The members of the House went first, the Senate second, and the president and executive officers third. I was one of the last of the senators who reached the portico, and being unwell resolved not to go to the grave, and there stepped out of the line of procession to the right. The President followed on, some six or eight paces behind me.

While I stood contemplating the scene around me, I heard a sharp noise like that proceeding from the explosion of a cracker. I turned around to see from whence the noise proceeded, when I saw, but a few steps off, and some what in front of the President, who was advancing with his cabinet officers, and who, but a moment before, had entered the porch, a man presenting a pocket pistol at the President, which, in a moment, caused an explosion similar to that I had before heard. The President immediately raised his cane and put at him; but the crowd seized the man in an instant, threw him down, disarmed him, and handed him over to the marshal, who carried him before the civil authority. He is now in jail to await his trial at a future day.

The fact was that he had two pistols with percussion locks. The caps exploded as finely as ever caps did, but for some cause, possibly the dampness of the day, the pistols did not go off. If they had the President must have been killed, and I almost trembled to think what might have been the consequences. The pistols, it is said, were afterwards examined and found to be properly loaded. The man is ascertained to be a madman—a painter by trade, and an Englishman by birth, and to have been here about three years. It is said that he made an effort not long since to kill his sister, and afterwards to kill himself. I stood near by and saw the whole affair. The old general sprung at him like a tiger, and manifested as much fearlessness as one could possibly have done; but he got into a furious rage, and said some thing very unnecessarily. However, many allowances should be made for his situation at the moment.

If I had not heard from those who have used the percussion locks that they will not fire well in damp weather, I should either ascribe his safety to divine interposition, or the whole affair to a mere trick for political effect. Certain it is that there would be but one person benefited by his death, and that is the Vice-President, who by the Constitution would succeed him. The thing produced an immense sensation. Yesterday I called to see and to congratulate him on his escape. He was highly pleased at my laughing and saying to him: "Why, Mr. President, when I looked at you yesterday while springing on that man with your cane, I could have taken you for a young man of twenty-five."

Well, Leigh is elected and Daniel turned out. Brown, of Petersburg, Willcox's son-in-law, is said to have made a tremendous speech. I suppose that Ritchie & co., are to keep the State agitated for another twelve months. Rives appealed to the people; they decided against him; then he appealed to the Legislature, which has also decided against him; and now he takes another appeal to the people; but I think he will again be disappointed. Do not apprehend anything between Benton and myself. I shall avoid a quarrel if it be possible; and I rather think that he is no more inclined for one than myself. I will not, however, allow him to encroach upon me too far; but of this I have no expectation. I have not received a letter from Mary or Robert for some time. Mary wrote me that she would be here on the 10th; Robert was directed by me to purchase such clothes as he might want. You had better get jackets for Burwell and William at Harwood's or Daniel's. I have written regularly, and your not receiving my letters is a proof that it would be unsafe to send money by the mail. Peas ought to be sowed the first open good weather; but instead of stopping Burwell from the waggon Mr. Pearman had better make the other hands manure a square and spade it up. Burwell can then stop a few days to sow peas.

Well, this is the first day of February, and four more weeks will soon run by. Tell Alice that she must hem a handkerchief for me, and to learn her book; that father will soon be at home now. I hope the weather will continue good; but I fear we shall have a wet month. Since writing thus far, I have received a letter from Robert, in which he speaks of parties without end. Miss Mary Cook Smith seems now to be his flame. He tells me of his bidding her farewell on her quitting Williamsburg, and of her inviting him to Doctor Chamberlayne's whenever he should happen to visit Richmond. He is a curious fellow.

I cannot conclude without mentioning a rumor, which is that the President said in the midst of affairs on Friday, that Poindexter had set the ruffian on. What a charge! I am sure that it is wholly false. P. has I learn, written to him upon the subject; and if he is governed by proper feelings, the President will either deny the charge or apologize for having made it. What will be the sequel I cannot tell; perhaps the matter will be brought before the Senate to-day.

Yours affectionately, J. Tyler

SARAH POLK
TO
JAMES POLK

---

*S*arah Polk, who consistently provided political advice and information to her husband, here advised him following the death of President William Henry Harrison and during his unsuccessful campaign for reelection as governor of Tennessee.

Nashville April 14th 1841.

Dear Husband

I inclose you a communication given me this morning by Mr. Walker, from David Dobbins. Mr. Walker said he retained a copy and requested me to send you this. There is nothing since I last wrote you that is worth writing. The <u>Whigs</u> I am told are in a good deal of concern since the death of their President, not Knowing what <u>Tyler</u> will do &c. &c. according to my judgement the same powers will controul. <u>Clay</u> &c. The Banner is still harping on your two addresses. In their articles now, they award to you, what they never did before that you are able talented and a great leader and that the Whigs are in danger of another defeat. I am told that they have become here, very uneasy fearing that there will be a Democratic Legislature. They say in their articles you are a <u>Wily and a dangerous foe</u> so I think that they will level all their artilery against you. Their are more respectful towards you, than they were in former times. They make no new charges, and all they have said does not amount to much in my judgement.

I have felt some uneasiness, since you wrote me from <u>Jasper</u> that you were not well, and seeing in the papers that you declined speaking on some occasion because you were unwell. I hope to hear from you tomorrow and hear that you are well again. Success is not worth the trouble, much less ruining ones health by it and do take care of yourself.

<u>Thursday</u> April 15th. I was much disappointed that I did not hear from you to day. If I do not hear in a day or two I shall be uneasy, as the last I heard that you were sick. I have a letter from the Overseer in Miss. dated the first of April. All was well. He had planted corn and commenced planting cotton on that day. Nothing more at present.

Your affectionate wife Sarah Polk

SARAH CHILDRESS POLK RAN THE FAMILY PLANTATIONS AND
BUSINESS INTERESTS IN THE ABSENCE OF HER HUSBAND, WHILE ALSO
PROVIDING HIM WITH COUNSEL ESSENTIAL TO POLITICAL SUCCESS
IN TENNESSEE AND LATER ON THE NATIONAL SCENE.

ABRAHAM LINCOLN
TO
MARY LINCOLN

*A*braham Lincoln was in the midst of an extensive campaign tour for the Republican presidential nomination when he wrote this letter of frustration to Mary. It was exactly a year before he would be sworn in as president.

[Exeter, N.H. March 4, 1860]

I have been unable to escape this toil. If I had foreseen it, I think I would not have come east at all. The speech at New York, being within my calculation before I started, went off passably well and gave me no trouble whatever. The difficulty was to make nine others, before reading audiences who had already seen all my ideas in print.

LUCY WEBB HAYES
TO
RUTHERFORD B. HAYES

*L*ucy offered her insight on President Lincoln and General McClellan in this letter to her husband, on the eve of the battle of Antietam.

Chillicothe Sept [1862]

My dearest R.

It has been almost impossible for me to composedly sit down and write—although you were constantly in my mind—Our anxiety has been of the most intense and yet with all I felt you were protected I wonder sometimes that I can endure this suspense—to us here away from the scenes of Conflict—every thing looks dark. Since the late disaster—there is no ray of hope—the curse is upon us all—the protection of slavery is costing many many precious lives. My feeling toward Mr. Lincoln—has day by day changed—until now when he calmly sees our young men hurried into eternity—for the protection of this cause—my feelings are of the most bitter kind. What does he care—oh is it to continue so till our noble army is completely cut to pieces. I do not speak as I write—and try to guard that unruly member.

The good people of Cincinnati are in great alarm—they have so strong a force now—that I doubt whether the rebels will attack—but all the new Regt. are officered by men who know nothing—the one raised here commanded by Col. Marshal in which our cousins are—the Col is totally inefficient and also drinks. Isaac Welson and Allison Brown are the only ones that know anything of the drill—it is now camped beyond Covington. Yesterdays paper says that from direct and positive information—you are to return and take the 79th while I want so much to see you—I did hope that the tried and proved 23rd would be your lot—with the different rumors I am constantly hoping to see you I wish you would say to me what you think of Gen McClellan—do you think he is responsible for our defeat or great loss. I am neither for or against either Pope or McClellan—but wish you would give me a little resting spot—this is a queer mixture—don't feel annoyed at what I have written. I have the greatest desire to be at home. I might be able to do something. I have written enough with out speaking of our boys. Grand ma and her three boys are now at Aunt Marret's—Uncle Scott and Aunt Ellen did not want to give up Birch and Webb and had started them to school with their little ones but they wanted to see them at Aunt M's and Mother felt she would be better satisfied to have them with her—they have been at Uncle Scotts ever since we came up yesterday he said he missed Webb so much that I must come out and bring Joe—they are not tired of your wife and babies yet. Uncle S sometimes gets low spirited about our beloved country his health is very poor—and I fear that not many years will pass over him. I know the high estimation in which you are held and know also that he would enjoy a letter from you—so if you have time and feeling prompts you—why I should be delighted. Little Joe is on your mind—you call him the "little favorite"—well he is the dearest smart little one—and yet a bad one too—the Colic has not left him—so at night he insists upon nursing—which is not agreable for two reasons—it wearies me so much and will cause your spouse to fail much faster in appearance than she desires. Well darling this is all foolishness but the love for you is deep and true and constant.

I have not heard from any of the Columbus friends for along time—neither from Uncle b. I think they are in my debt. Your letters are such happiness the loving one from Flat Top—is engraven on my mind—know dearest that every thought and prayer for you is love. Write me as often as you have leisure—even a few lines are precious. We are all well and all join in best wishes.

Jim McKell is in the Hospital at Alexandria Fairfax St. Hospital—tell Joe where he is.

Once more good bye dear dear one. God bless you—and protect you. Yours Affc. L. W. H.

ULYSSES S. GRANT
TO
JULIA GRANT

---

*A*ndrew Johnson had just succeeded as president the assassinated Abraham Lincoln when Ulysses wrote this letter to Julia about the situation in Washington and the Confederate plot.

Washington Apl. 16th 1865

Dear Julia,

I got back here about 1 p.m. yesterday and was called immediately into the presence of our new President, who had already been qualified, and the Cabinet. I telegraphed you from Baltimore and

told Beckwith to do the same thing from here. You no doubt received the dispatches. All seems very quiet here. There is but little doubt but that the plot contemplated the distruction of more than the President and Sec. of State. I think now however it has expended itself and there is but little to fear. For the present I shall occupy a room in the office which is well guarded and will be occupied by Bowers and probably two or three others. I shall only go to the Hotel twice a day for my meals and will stay indoors of evenings. The change which has come upon the country so suddenly will make it necessary for me to remain in the City for several days yet. Gen. Halleck will go to Richmond to command there and Ord to Charleston. Other changes which will have to be made, and the apparent feeling that I should remain here until everything gets into working order under the new régime will probably detain me here until next Saturday. If I can get home sooner I will do so. I hope you will be in your house in Phila. when I go home. The inconvenience of getting from the Phila. depot to Burlington is about equal to the balance of the trip.

Love and kisses for you and the children. Ulys.

ULYSSES S. GRANT
TO
JULIA GRANT

*G*rant was certainly a reluctant participant in Lincoln's successor's national tour to drum up support for his Reconstruction Policy, as can be seen in this letter.

St. Louis, Mo. Sept. 9th/66

Dear Julia,

To-morrow morning the party starts on its Course East and will reach Washington on Saturday. I will be glad enough to get there. I never have been so tired of anything before as I have been with the political stump speeches of Mr. Johnson.—from Washington to this place. I look upon them as a National disgrace. Of course you will not shew this letter to anyone for as long as Mr. Johnson is President. I must respect him as such and it is the country's interest that I should also have his confidence.

This is Sunday morning and it is raining very hard. If it stops before 1 O'Clock Fred and I will drive out to see Anna. Lewis Dent has gone South.

Love and Kisses to you and the Children. Ulys.

RUTHERFORD B. HAYES
TO
LUCY WEBB HAYES

*P*resident Rutherford Hayes had just vetoed a bill prohibiting Chinese immigration, in direct violation of Burlingame Treaty of 1868, when he wrote this letter to Lucy.

Executive Mansion Washington. 25 May 1879

My Darling:

We have had cool and beautiful weather. The Home never was more attractive. Yesterday evening the Marine Band drew a larger audience than I have seen before on the lawn. Judge, and Mrs. Key and a fine daughter with Mrs. McKinley occupied the blue room portico—also Webb, Wm Henry Smith & Wm Penn Nixon, Scott and Joe Potter who is visiting Scott, amused the crowd with his goat rig under direction of Mr. Gustin.

The number of nice people from all quarters who are disappointed not to meet you is a daily reminder of your absence, and of your hold on the people both "plain" and "cultured."

My veto message is printed—not a "ringing" document—but well enough as a plain statement for the "plain people" of this branch of the controversy.

Mrs. Felton called and talked politics in a warm and encouraging way. I hear a good deal of this. Yet the rules of the House, requiring a two thirds vote to get a measure before the House for action, unless by the consent of a Committee, makes it difficult if not impossible to pass appropriations, pure and simple, even with a majority in favor of them.

I feel more anxious to get out to the House early, on account of the throwing up of fresh earth in such great quantities in our front. If Congress adjourns before the usual time of going out, I shall want to go out at once.

Mrs. McKinley goes to Canton this evening. The Major will attend the Convention at Cinti the 28th.

Monday 26th.

All well. Joe Potter made yesterday a busy day for Scott, and a happy one. The rains improved the lawn and trees. I hope Ohio has its share of the needed showers. We expect Dr. and Mrs. Bushnell tomorrow. Enjoy yourself with the Uncles and Aunts and Cousins—the dear kindred and return to your lovely household and Your Affectionate husband R.

JAMES GARFIELD
TO
LUCRETIA GARFIELD

*A*fter a long and arduous but successful convention struggle to secure the Republican nomination for the presidency in 1880, James Garfield sent these brief but triumphant telegrams to his wife.

[June 8, 1880]

Mrs. Ja. Garfield
I am unanimously nominated. Ja Garfield

[Chicago, June 8, 1880]

Dear Wife: If the result meets your approval, I shall be content. Love to all the household.

J. A. Garfield

HELEN TAFT
TO
WILLIAM HOWARD TAFT

*H*elen Taft and her husband were seeking President Roosevelt's support for Taft's presidential bid when Helen wrote this letter about a private meeting with the president, who thought she had an "inordinate" desire for the presidency.

1603 K. Oct 27 [1906]

My darling Will
I thought of you many times during the Evening and wondered how your Speech was coming on. I do hope you wont mind so

much when you get started as you did when you left. This morning I got a telephone from the White House inviting me to lunch so I went to find the Mexican Minister of War and a German Professor in Harvard whose name I forget, Secretary & Mrs. Root & the Metcalfs. Mrs. Roosevelt was not there having taken Ethel on the river. It was rather slower & more forced that usual, I thought. After lunch the President said he wanted to talk to me and drew me off to sit down in the window. As usual it was about you, but on a new tack. He seems to think that I am consumed with an inordinate ambition to be President and that he must constantly warn me that you may never get there-And he now says that while you are his first Choice, that in case you are not persona grata to the powers that be, it may become necessary for him to support some one Else, like Hughes, for instance should he win in New York. I felt like saying, "D–you, support whom you want for All I care." But suffice it to say I did not. He began by saying that his Kentucky friends had come to him to say that you had turned them down by saying Coldly that you were not a Candidate. He had told them to go ahead, as you would not decline, but he could not always do that for various reasons, and that you must be more Energizing. He mentioned Scotty being for Shaw. I should not wonder if your dragging the tariff into that Maine Speech would cost you the nomination. Mr. Root sat on my other side at lunch but as he is perfectly uninterested in me, I can never talk to him. Metcalf was more calfy than ever.

Charles went to a party at Joe Humphrey's so I drove out after him and found them all at a table with Halloween decorations which delighted them much. Mrs. Humphrey arrayed herself like a Chinaman and passed refreshments. They had a pie with presents in it. I had my hair curled today and try to feel festive, but it is very lonely without you and Tim Barry had the cheek to send me a schedule by which you don't return until the 19th. I have the rest of the family to write to so must stop. Carpenter dropped in to see me, but had not news. With dearest love. Helen

*H*elen Taft sent this simple, triumphant message after her husband's victory in the 1908 presidential election.

Cincinnati Nov. 3, 1908

Hon. Wm Taft Personal

Heartiest congratulations I was never so happy in my life. Helen

PRESIDENT WILLIAM HOWARD TAFT AND HIS WIFE HELEN
MAKE THEIR WAY TO THE WHITE HOUSE IN A HORSE-DRAWN
CARRIAGE AFTER HIS INAUGURATION IN 1909.

WOODROW   WILSON

TO

ELLEN   WILSON

*W*oodrow Wilson, then governor of New Jersey, was campaigning for the 1912 presidential nomination when he wrote these two brief notes from the road to Ellen, reporting on the public nature of the trip and his brief meeting with William Jennings Bryan.

My precious one,

Don't be surprised to see me follow this letter soon! I am having a good time, full of interest and pleasure,—but with no <u>rest</u> in it at all. I am not left to myself at all. Publicity (my own dear, pet Publicity) has closed about me like a prison. I am freer at home than anywhere else—and <u>you</u> are there, my pet, my darling. I think I will come back and put my vacation into taking you to the theatre.

I am perfectly well—and, strangely enough, do not feel fagged. I am snatching a moment before going to Church, father's old church. Even there I am to be made a public man of! But what I am most <u>conscious</u> of being is Your own Woodrow

[P.S.] Deep love to all.

[Lincoln, Neb. Oct. 6, 1912]

Fine Sunday rest after strenuous day yesterday. Am perfectly well and feeling quite equal to the task. Enjoyed my visit with Mr. Bryan very much indeed. Dearest love to all.

EDITH BOLLING GALT
TO
WOODROW WILSON

---

*W*hen William Jennings Bryan threatened to resign as Secretary of State in protest of President Wilson's strongly worded diplomatic notes to Germany over the sinking of the *Lusitania*, Edith Galt wrote Woodrow, then her ardent suitor, this stinging rebuke of the Secretary. A confirmed pacifist, Bryan resigned within days of this letter.

May [June] 5th & 6th. 1915

My precious One:

The clock is just tolling out the midnight hour and, at last, I can feel I am alone with you, away from that deadly telephone, which has kept up a continual ringing ever since I got home.

First it was Dr. Grayson, who sounded really sick, and who poured out his heartache to me, as much in his <u>tone</u> as in what he said. I do feel so sorry for him, and the long agony of uncertainty he has been through. Unless you really need him, Sweetheart, make him stay away next week, and take a few days complete rest. After talking to him, and to Helen (who was sweet enough to call and ask me if I was safe and sound) my sister telephoned, and asked a thousand questions about you—<u>what we talked about</u>, if I thought you really liked her, and if I enjoyed being there! I answered these as well as I could, and now I instinctively turn to you before I go to sleep: @ Do you know what that round thing stands for? Well, it is a bad word, for I had to stop again to answer the telephone, and it is now nearly one oclock and it does not seem quite proper to be talking to a gentleman at such an hour. However at this long distance I will disregard conventions and go on talking to you because—I can't help it!

What great fun it is to be together, and just the content that fills my heart keeps me from talking, or telling you so many things I think of when I am away.

I am so pleased that you "worked for <u>me</u> on the German reply." I am more than honored, and wish I could have heard the finished document. Then I did want to ask you more about the resignation of "W.J.B." but saw the subject troubled you so would not let myself discuss it. I think it will be a blessing to get rid of him and might as well frankly say I would like to be appointed in his place, for then I should have to have daily conferences with you. And I faithfully promise not to interfere in any way with your continuing to do all the work!

I know how you feel about being loyal to this person, but if he deserts you now he is entitled to small courtesy or consideration, and I would not hesitate to put myself on record if he does so scurvy a thing.

Remember, when you are sitting silent and with Presidential, Presbyterian air in church tomorrow, that just a few squares away there is someone who loves you, who says a fervent amen to the prayer for "all those in authority," and who longs to have you with her where she can turn to find, in your dear eyes, the answer to so much that is in her heart.

I think I will go to lunch at Mother's tomorrow, so am afraid I will be out if you send me a note. But I will try to get this to you before the day is over.

I have had such a happy evening, dearest one, and please forget all I said that troubled you. Goodnight, and "God bless you all the day, and God keep you all the night." Always Edith

---

WARREN G. HARDING
TO
FLORENCE M. HARDING

---

*W*arren G. Harding, while a U.S. senator from Ohio, was campaigning for the Republican Party in the 1916 election when he wrote this letter to his wife, commenting on the power of the women's vote in the western states. Florence was an ardent collector of newspaper clippings.

Ogden, Utah. Oct. 6 [1916]

Dear Florence:

You will be amused to note enclosed telegram which arrived this morning. Am also enclosing a "phiz" which I never saw before—taken from the paper at Great Falls, Mont.

I can not send clippings because I am usually gone before the papers are out with reports. I am at Evanston, Wy., tonight and must leave there at 9:50 tonight to get to Cheyenne for meeting on Saturday night. The two Wyoming towns are over 400 miles apart.

Had a good meeting here last night and Sutherland was immensely pleased over what I said of him. Women vote here as they do in Idaho and Montana and they seem to be very friendly to Wilson, because he has Kept us out of war, so they think, any way.

Must hustle and pack in order to catch my train. Hastely W. G.

WARREN G. HARDING AND HIS WIFE FLORENCE GREET PHOTOGRAPHERS DURING THEIR SUCCESSFUL 1920 CAMPAIGN FOR THE PRESIDENCY.

ady Bird and Lyndon had known each other only weeks when she voiced her displeasure with Lyndon's plans for a future in politics.

Monday nite [October 22, 1934]

Dearest beloved-

Were you anxious to get this letter—to hear what I would have to say? Your letter written Saturday morning just came—I think its funny nobody has noticed that I look different. I <u>feel</u> different.

And so, my dearest, something has happened which precludes all possibility of our marriage for four or five years? I believe it is something which will involve a much lower salary for a number of years and then chances of a much greater advancement. It is something of a gamble but you think it will be better in the long run, don't you? Whatever will be better for you, Lyndon, I am <u>for</u>! And now, as for me—I shall keep right on loving you. I shall not feel dismissed, I shall not even have forebodings! A few years— are not so long. And, too, you probably over-estimate the amount you would have to be making.

Of course there is the problem that in the meantime one of us may meet someone he or she likes better. I think, Lyndon, if we do it will probably be you. In all these twenty-one <u>lovely</u> adventurous years you are the only person I've ever considered marrying. Besides you are in a position to meet attractive and intelligent and charming young women. And I—am rather "on cold storage." So it is you, not I, who will be more likely to forget.

And as for telling Vic. The fact that we can't be married for sometime doesn't alter my feeling toward you. I love you. And that affects the way I feel toward all other men.

What of your coming to Texas, Love? (For you are coming to Texas before long, aren't you?) When and where? But you will tell

me all that in your explanatory letter, won't you? I, too, <u>hate</u> your giving up your law course—like the very <u>deuce</u> I do! Shall you be close enough to any law school to go?

Lyndon, my dear, do you want me to keep on loving you? Shall we keep on writing each other every day? Shall you (perhaps, <u>sometimes</u>) call me? And are you going to keep on loving me, with an eye to the new somewhat-more distant future? I want to know. As for me—I shall keep on writing you. I shall keep on loving you. I do not want anything to come between us.

You won't be in Washington in January, will you? But, then, perhaps you'll be in Texas a great deal sooner! Which will be even better! Because, what's Washington to seeing you?!! The only thing I hate is not getting to take Gene—I <u>did</u> want her to have a lovely vacation.

Lyndon, please tell me as soon as you can what the deal is. I am <u>afraid</u> its politics. Oh! I know I haven't any business—nor any "propriety interest"—but I would hate for you to go into politics. Don't let me get things any more muddled for you than they are though dearest!

You haven't yet told me all about the New York deal. What was it—please tell me sometimes.

Thanks for the <u>proof</u>—only I didn't know it was a proof. I thought it was a real picture! I'm having it framed tomorro—But I believe I told you that in the letter which I began Sunday afternoon and did not finish and mail until this morning.

Well darling, I believe I've said all there is for the moment. You understand, don't you, that I shall be in a jitter to hear from you after this letter. It will be a Saturday or Sunday one, won't it? I'm counting the closest time. I shall be wanting to know all about the business, when and if you'll be coming to Texas (I <u>must</u> see you as soon as you do), and how you plan to feel about me now.

I still love you, Lyndon—I want to say it over and over—Goodnight, <u>not</u> goodbye, Bird

---

ELEANOR ROOSEVELT
TO
FRANKLIN D. ROOSEVELT

A brief note from Franklin to Eleanor, followed by two of the few extant letters from Eleanor Roosevelt to her husband, illustrate their working relationship in the political realm.

The White House,
June 16, 1936

Memorandum for Mrs. Roosevelt:
I wish you would read this. It seems to show that the figures which interested you and me so much were almost wholly incorrect.

From E. R.
It seems to me the Chamber of Commerce of Youngstown from whom the former figures were obtained should either have more accurate figures or not give them to anyone! Also I wonder if any figures are accurate; everyone colors to please themselves. Perhaps the Chamber of Commerce did not want to say anything was <u>nearly</u> as good as in 1929!

The White House,
July 16, 1936

To the President and James Farley

I spent part of Tuesday afternoon and the morning of Wednesday at Democratic Headquarters. I had a conference with Miss Dewson and Mr. Farley; a conference with Mrs. Owen and Miss Dewson; and a conference with Mr. Michelson.

My impression is that the women are further along in their organization and more ready to go than any other unit as yet. I hear from outside sources that the Landon headquarters are set up and ready to work full time. They have continuity people writing for the radio, they have employed advertising people to do their copy, and the whole spirit of a crusade.

My feeling is that we have to get going and going quickly, as I stated yesterday. I sat down and analyzed things which I thought necessary to organization. Some of the things I had in mind Mr. Michelson answered, a few things Mr. Farley answered for me at the time of the conference. I am putting them down again simply as a matter of record to get the answers in black and white.

I hope the answers will be mailed to reach us at Eastport, Maine, on the 27th or 28th of July, when the President expects to be there.

1. At the meeting in Washington, the President said that Mr. Michelson, Steve Early, Stanley High and Henry Suydam would constitute the publicity steering committee, and I take it this must include radio, speeches, movies, pamphlets, fliers, news releases and trucks or whatever news goes out to the public. This committee is extremely important.

Because of the importance of this committee, I hope a meeting will be held immediately for organizing and defining the duties of the members and that you will have the minutes kept at every meeting in order that a copy may go to the President and if the committee is willing, one to me as well so that I may know just what is done each time also.

2. Who is responsible for studying news reports and suggesting answers to charges, etc.?

3. Who is responsible, not for the mechanics of radio contracts for I understand you have a good man, but for the planning of a

radio campaign, getting the speakers through the speakers' bureau, making the arrangements in the states for people to listen and getting in touch with Chester Davis, for instance on agriculture or any other people appointed as particular advisors on special subjects? In other words, who is making decisions under your committee on the above questions?

4. Who is in charge of research? Have we a department with complete information concerning all activities of the New Deal, and also concerning Landon and his supporters? If Miss Blackburn is in charge of this department as she was in the last campaign, have the heads of all campaign departments, men, women and young Democrats been notified as to where to apply for information? This information should go to the state committees also.

I gather if the President ok's it, the aggressive campaign against Landon's record will begin before Landon's acceptance speech. Who is to collect and maintain the complete data up to date and to check on all inconsistencies in Landon's pronouncements or those of his campaign managers as they relate to his former statements or record? Is there adequate material on this now at hand?

5. What definite plans have we made for tying in the other publicity organizations, both of men and women with the national publicity organization? I feel that anything of importance should go directly from a member of your committee and from the women in charge of national publicity to every publicity person in charge in the states.

6. Have you mapped out continuous publicity steps which will be taken between now and November? Is there any way at least of charting a tentative plan of strategy for the whole campaign, changing course, as new things occur?

7. In the doubtful and Republican states what special attention do you plan to give and have you collected any data as yet on these states?

8. Who is handling news reels and will it be a committee or just one person and will your committee direct the activities?

9. Has your committee assigned as yet to each member definite fields for supervision?

10. How many people are now working on campaign speech-

es, both for men, women and young Democrats? Who is going over them for criticism so they cover all the necessary subjects?

11. Who is your man making contacts with news papers all over the country?

12. Who is responsible for sending regular news to friendly newspapers? By this I mean feature stories, pictures, mats, boiler plate etc.

I feel Mr. Rayburn should come at once to plan the policy and mechanics of the speakers' bureau. Then he could leave for a time.

I think it would be well to start some Negro speakers, like Mrs. Bethune to speak at church meetings and that type of Negro organization.

More and more my reports indicate that this is a close election and that we need very excellent organization. That is why I am trying to clarify in my own mind the functions at headquarters and have the President see a picture of the organization as clearly as possible in order that he may make any suggestions that he thinks necessary. Eleanor Roosevelt

---

FRANKLIN D. ROOSEVELT
TO
ELEANOR ROOSEVELT

---

*W*hether to run for a third presidential term, breaking the unofficial rule established by George Washington, and Eleanor's opposition to this third term, were the topics of these letters between Franklin and Eleanor.

The White House, Aug. 12, 1938

Memorandum for E. R

I hope you will definitely persuade our good friend Mrs. Meloney to have no discussion of third term at the Herald-Tribune Forum.

If such a discussion is held in any form I will, of course, take no part in the Forum and I hope you will not either.

It is a simple fact that any President of the United States is cursed in the last two years of his first term by constant publicity about whether he will be renominated or if renominated can win. Any President is doubly cursed in his second term by discussion of the possibility of a third term. Such discussion in either term—and this discussion is fomented by newspapers—keeps any President from doing his best work. You can make it perfectly clear that in 1938 I am considering only the problems of 1938—and throughout 1939, I will be considering only the problems of 1939.

In other words, any discussion would hamper my efficiency as the existing President of the United States and I, therefore, consider that any discussion would be contrary to the public interest.

The White House [August 1938]

F. D. R.

She wants you for a 3rd term and I thought this most unwise. You know I do <u>not</u> believe in it, however I think you should say Murphy is the man. E. R.

H A R R Y   S .   T R U M A N
T O
B E S S   T R U M A N

---

*T*he end of the 1944 campaign for the presidency had nearly arrived, when vice-presidential candidate Harry Truman wrote this determined letter to Bess. Because of President Roosevelt's health and the demands of war, Harry had been forced into the role of chief traveling candidate.

Saturday Oct 21 '44 Butte Mont.

Dear Bess:

You don't Know how badly I felt when I didn't get to talk to you from Seattle. They simply had me so full of appointments and time was so short there that I couldn't even eat any dinner. It was so necessary to help Mon all I could that I didn't dare take a chance of insulting anyone.

The letters were sure a treat. There were two good ones and the one to John Stigal which I'm returning.

We had quite a day yesterday. Everywhere the train stops for a minute there are big crowds and back platform appearances are in order. At two Idaho towns they dismissed the schools and all the Kids were at the station. I am very popular, at least with the Kids in those towns. I've made 26 speeches since leaving New Orleans and I was only supposed to make three up to this point. But we knocked 'em over in Los Angeles and San Francisco, and even <u>Time</u> is coming out with a special edition with me on the cover Nov. 6. "Ain't that sompin." It's a satisfaction to make 'em like it.

Had a nice visit with G. Watter. He's a very pleasant fellow. Seemed interested in all the family. Asked about Mother Wallace, Fred, Geo, Frank, Gates and Margaret & you. Had a fine meeting here. Murray present but no Burton K. I'm, glad I didn't have to see him. Here is the new schedule. It's a dinger. They seem to think I'm cast iron, and I am in a campaign I guess.

Kiss my baby. Love. Lots of it. Harry

[P.S.] read the schedule to the office. It is your business too to tell me what goes on at the office. Very much I'd say.

DWIGHT D. EISENHOWER
TO
MAMIE EISENHOWER

---

*P*resident Eisenhower was finishing his second term when he asked his wife to pinch-hit for him at a political dinner during the Kennedy-Nixon campaign (which she did not, due to the death of her mother, Elivera Doud).

August 22, 1960

Memorandum For M. D. E.:

Republicans are having a closed circuit television dinner on September 29th. Its purpose is to raise money for the campaign.

I rather think that I may have to go to Boston for a quick trip, and to make a speech that evening—leaving here in the late afternoon and returning the following morning.

Chairman Morton hopes that you will attend the Washington dinner. He further submits a request that you, during a contrived break in the proceedings, make an appearance with these words:

"I have never made a political speech. This is my first. It is very short and factual.

I am going to vote for Pat and Dick on November eighth."

They think this would be a ten-strike, particularly because it would be natural for you to include Pat in your statement. They want to emphasize the difference between the wives of the two candidates as potential First Ladies.

I send you this in memorandum form because I have been forgetting it for the past three days when I am home.

LADY BIRD JOHNSON
TO
LYNDON B. JOHNSON

---

*O*n the eve of the 1964 Democratic National Convention, Lady Bird wrote this letter of encouragement to her husband.

[August 1964]

Beloved—

You are as brave as Harry Truman—or FDR—or Lincoln. You can go on to find some peace, some achievement amidst all the pain. You have been strong, patient, determined beyond any words of mine to express.

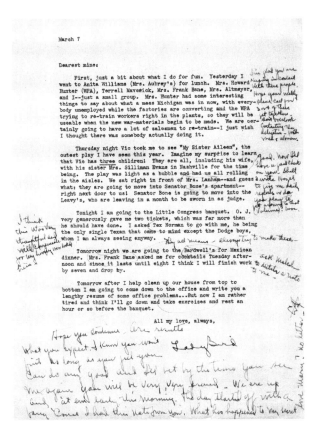

March 7

Dearest mine:

First, just a bit about what I do for fun. Yesterday I went to Anita Williams (Mrs. Aubrey's) for lunch. Mrs. Howard Hunter (WPA), Terrell Maverick, Mrs. Frank Bane, Mrs. Altmeyer, and I—just a small group. Mrs. Hunter had some interesting things to say about what a mess Michigan was in now, with everybody unemployed while the factories are converting and the WPA trying to re-train workers right in the plants, so they will be useable when the new war-materials begin to be made. We are certainly going to have a lot of salesmen to re-train—I just wish I thought there was somebody actually doing it.

Thursday night Vic took me to see "My Sister Aileen", the cutest play I have seen this year. Imagine my surprise to learn that Vic has three children! They are all, including his wife, with his sister Mrs. Silliman Evans in Nashville for the time being. The play was light as a bubble and had us all rolling in the aisles. We sat right in front of Mrs. Lanham—and guess what: they are going to move into Senator Bone's apartment— right next door to us! Senator Bone is going to move into the Leavy's, who are leaving in a month to be sworn in as judge.

Tonight I am going to the Little Congress banquet. O. J. very generously gave me two tickets, which was far more than he should have done. I asked Tex Norman to go with me, he being the only single Texan that came to mind except the Dodge boys, whom I am always seeing anyway.

Tomorrow night we are going to the Bardwell's for Mexican dinner. Mrs. Frank Bane asked me for cocktails Tuesday after- noon and since it lasts until eight I think I will finish work by seven and drop by.

Tomorrow after I help clean up our house from top to bottom I am going to come down to the office and write you a lengthy resumé of some office problems...But now I am rather tired and think I'll go down and take exercises and rest an hour or so before the banquet.

All my love, always,

THE CLOSE WORKING RELATIONSHIP BETWEEN LYNDON B. JOHNSON AND HIS WIFE IS CLEARLY EVIDENT IN LADY BIRD'S LETTER TO LYNDON DURING WORLD WAR II, WHICH WAS HEAVILY ANNOTATED BY THE ABSENT CONGRESSMAN.

I honor you for it. So does most of the country.

To step out now would be wrong for your country, and I can see nothing but a lonely waste land for your future. Your friends would be frozen in embarassed silence and your enemies jeering.

I am not afraid of Time or lies or losing money or defeat.

In the final analysis I can't carry any of the burdens you talked of—so I know its only <u>your</u> choice. But I know you are as brave as any of the thirty-five.

I love you always. Bird

*R*onald Reagan, who disliked flying, was making one of many trips speaking on behalf of Republican candidates around the country when he wrote this letter to Nancy from Milwaukee, Wisconsin.

Tues. Night [1966]

Dear Little Mommie

Knowing you (in addition to loving you) I think it's time to put something on the record. I've always known that someday my ground hog days would end, and now these political shenanigans have made "someday" come around. No one talked me into this so no one should have any feeling of responsibility.

I have to write this because of all our talks about flying and because you'd try to take the blame personally if ever something did happen. That would be wrong. God has a plan and it isn't for us to understand, only to know that He had his reasons and because He is all merciful and all loving we can depend on it that there is purpose in whatever He does and it is for our own good. What you must understand without any question or doubt is that I believe this and trust him and you must, too.

What you must believe is that I love you more and more each day and it grows more bright and shining all the time.

Good night, middle size muffin, who is all the rest of me I need. I love you Poppa.

PAT NIXON
TO
RICHARD NIXON

*A*ccording to her husband's memoir, at a family dinner during which Nixon announced his intention to run for president, Pat responded dutifully:

January 15, 1968

"I know what you are asking us to do, and what you are asking of yourself. Now that the decision is made, I will go along with it."

GERALD R. FORD
TO
BETTY ANN FORD

*O*n the eve of President Nixon's resignation from the presidency, the vice president and his wife talked over Gerald's impending rise in unprecedented circumstances, as reported in Ford's autobiography, *A Time to Heal.*

PRESIDENT GERALD FORD AND HIS WIFE BETTY RELAX IN THE
PRESIDENTIAL LIVING QUARTERS OF THE WHITE HOUSE IN 1975.

"After dinner, we returned home, sat in the family room downstairs, and talked about what had happened that day. As I described my two meetings with Haig, her eyes widened in disbelief. She had long shared my view that everything we'd been told by the White House was the truth. Now the story was falling apart, and she was dumbfounded.

"'My God,' she replied, 'this is going to change our whole life.'...

"'I just can't tell you what's going to happen,' I said. 'We could be going to the White House next week, maybe even sooner, or we could be dangling for the next six months while the impeachment process winds through the House and the trial concludes in the Senate. It all depends on what Nixon decides to do.'

"Next we discussed the options that Haig had said were still available to the President. Betty was very firm in her view that because of the peculiar position I was in, I shouldn't get involved in making any recommendations at all. Not to Haig, not to Nixon, not to anybody. I concurred fully. Finally we talked about her pending trip to New York. Things were moving so fast, we agreed, that the proper thing to do would be to postpone it until we had a better idea of what was going to happen."

JAMES E. CARTER AND ELEANOR ROSALYNN SMITH BEAM WITH JOY ON THE WAY TO THEIR WEDDING IN PLAINS, GEORGIA, ON JULY 7, 1946.

ROSALYNN CARTER
TO
JAMES E. CARTER

*T*he Iranian hostage crisis was a pivotal event in the administration of President Carter and in the political campaign of 1980. These telephone conversations reported by Rosalynn Carter reveal the tension of the times.

April 24 [1980]

"As soon as he answered the telephone I knew something was wrong. 'The news is bad,' he said in a voice that sounded as sad as I had ever heard it, 'but I can't talk to you about it now. This is an open telephone line.' While my heart went out to him, my mind raced.' 'Have the children moved?' I asked, quickly inventing a code. 'No, they haven't moved,' Jimmy replied. 'But I can't talk about it on the telephone.' Numbly I hung up, not knowing what had gone wrong....

"He told me to call him from Texas, even though he still might not be able to tell me anything.

"It was close to midnight when I arrived in Austin, but there was still no definitive news from Jimmy. 'Everything is going to be all right,' he told me quickly. 'Go to bed and get some sleep, and I'll call you as soon as I can tell you anything. But I want you to come home. You won't be able to campaign tomorrow, but don't say anything about leaving until I call you back.'

"...I still have the note I wrote that night as he talked. It reads: 'U.S. aircraft preparing for a possible rescue mission. accident on ground in a remote desert area of Iran...8 casualties no hostile action no Iranian casualties.'

"'I'm sorry,' was all I could think of to say to Jimmy as I listened to the suffering in his voice. 'I'll fly home as soon as I can.'"

"I felt a surge of hope, a feeling I hadn't allowed myself since the failure of our rescue mission. But Jimmy quickly tempered it. 'I want you to be prepared,' he said over the phone. 'This means it could go either way.'

"'What could? The release of the hostages or the election?'

"'Both,' he said quietly....

"It was the first inkling I'd had that Jimmy thought he might lose—and the first time I had considered the possibility either. 'Don't worry,' Jimmy said. 'We've done our best. Go out and campaign, and I'll handle this as well as I can.'"

GEORGE H. W. BUSH
TO
BARBARA BUSH

---

*I*n 1988, George Bush was in the midst of his successful presidential campaign against Michael Dukakis, noted for his outward affection to his wife, when he wrote this humorous note to his wife, Barbara.

BARBARA PIERCE BUSH JOINED ABIGAIL ADAMS AS BOTH A WIFE AND A MOTHER OF PRESIDENTS WHEN HER SON GEORGE W. BUSH ASCENDED TO THE ROLE IN 2001.

Sweetsie:

Please look at how Mike and Kitty do it.

Try to be closer in, more—well er romantic—on camera.

I am practicing the loving look, and the creeping hand.

Yours for better TV and more demonstrable affection.

Your sweetie-pie-coo-coo.

Love 'ya GB

WILLIAM J. CLINTON
TO
HILLARY RODHAM CLINTON

---

*B*ill Clinton was in his first term when he and his wife had these conversations about two critical issues, as reported by Hillary Clinton: the appointment of a health-care task force (ultimately chaired by Mrs. Clinton) and the appointment of a special prosecutor to conduct an independent investigation of Whitewater.

[At a meeting in the White House]
January 25, 1993

"We had been encouraged by the electoral success of Harris Wofford, the new Democratic Senator from Pennsylvania who had campaigned on a health care platform... But Ira [Magaziner] was getting a different message.

"'They think we're gonna get killed,' said Ira, who hadn't touched his sandwich. 'We'll need at least four to five years to put together a package that will pass Congress.'

"'That's what some of my friends are saying too,' I said...on this day, it was Bill's boundless optimism and his determination that kept me in my chair.

"'I'm hearing the same thing,' Bill said. 'But we have to try. We just have to make it work.'"

PRESIDENT AND MRS. WILLIAM J. CLINTON DANCE AT ONE
OF SEVERAL INAUGURAL BALLS ON JANUARY 20, 1993.

[On a telephone conference call]
January 11, 1994

"I felt sorry for him and wished that he didn't have to deal with such a crucial decision under these circumstances. He was terribly hoarse, and we had to lean in close to the black, batwing-shaped conference phone to hear his voice.

"'I don't know how much longer I can take this,' he said, frustrated that the press didn't want to talk about the historic expansion of NATO that would soon open the door to the former Warsaw Pact nations. "All they want to talk about is why we're ducking an independent investigation.'

"...After several heated rounds back and forth, Bill, exhausted, had heard enough. I wrapped up the meeting, asking only David Kendall to remain for a few more words with the President.

" The room was quiet for a moment, and then Bill spoke.

"'Look, I think we've just got to do it,' he said. 'We've got nothing to hide, and if this keeps up, it's going to drown out our agenda.'

"It was time to fold my cards. 'I know that we've got to move past this,' I said. 'But it's up to you.'

"...David left the room, and I picked up the phone to talk to Bill alone.

"'Why don't you sleep on the decision,' I said. 'If you're still willing to do it, we'll send a request to the Attorney General in the morning.'

"'No,' he said, 'let's get it over with.'"

GENL. GARFIELDS BUSINESS OFFIC

PRESIDENT-ELECT JAMES GARFIELD WORKS AT HIS
HOME OFFICE IN MENTOR, OHIO, IN 1881, BEFORE LEAVING
FOR HIS INAUGURATION IN WASHINGTON, D.C.

CHAPTER 4

HOME AND FAMILY

~ɔ

*"My Child is a Model...and is not
to be the prize, I hope of any, even reformed Rake."*
—John Adams to Abigail Adams,
January 22, 1783

"He must be given a chance to be on his own."
—Dwight Eisenhower to Mamie Eisenhower,
June 22, 1944

WHETHER at home or away, presidents and their first ladies still had to maintain their families and their homes (in some cases, several houses or farms). Presidential couples also had to work their way through issues with their children, finances, and property, the latter of which, for nearly half our history, sometimes included slaves. These letters reveal that presidential couples, despite their celebrity and political power, faced the same domestic issues as did most Americans of their time.

*W*hile one of America's ministers in France, John wrote this sharp letter to Abigail, criticizing the courtship of their daughter by Royall Tyler, and, by implication, his wife for allowing the relationship to develop.

Paris Jan. 22. 1783

My dearest Friend

The Preliminaries of Peace and an Armistice, were Signed at Versailles on the 20 and on the 21. We went again to pay our Respects to the King and Royal Family upon the Occasion. Mr. Jay was gone upon a little Excursion to Normandie and Mr. Laurens was gone to Bath; both for their health, so that the signature was made by Mr. Franklin and me. I want an Excursion too.

Thus drops the Curtain upon this mighty Trajedy. It has unravelled itself happily for Us. And Heaven be praised. Some of our dearest Interests have been saved, thro many dangers. I have no News from my son, Since the 8th December, when he was at Stockholm, but hope every hour to hear of his Arrival at the Hague.

I hope to receive the Acceptance of my Resignation So as to come home in the Spring Ships.

I had written thus far when yours of 23 decr. was brought in. Its Contents have awakened all my sensibility, and shew in a stronger Light than ever the Necessity of my coming home. I confess I don't like the Subject at all. My Child is too young for such Thoughts, and I don't like your Word "Dissipation" at all. I don't know what it means, it may mean every Thing. There is not modesty and Diffidence enough in the Traits you Send me. My Child is a Model, as you represent her and as I know her, and is not to be the prize, I hope of any, even reformed Rake. A Lawyer would be my Choice, but it must be a Lawyer who spends his Midnights as well as Evenings at his Age over his Books not at any Ladys Fire side. I Should have thought you had seen enough to be more upon your Guard than to write Billets upon such a subject to such a youth. A Youth who has been giddy enough to Spend his Fortune or half his Fortune in Gaieties, is not the Youth for me, let his Person, Family, Connections and Taste for Poetry be what they will. I am not looking out for a Poet, nor a Professor of belle Letters.

In the Name of all that is tender don't criticise Your Daughter for those qualities which are her greatest Glory her Reserve, and her Prudence which I am amazed to hear you call Want of Sensibility. The more Silent She is in Company, the better for me in exact Proportion and I would have this observed as a Rule by the Mother as well as the Daughter.

You know moreover or ought to know my utter Inability to do any thing for my Children, and you know the long dependence of young Gentlemen of the most promising Talents and obstinate Industry, at the Bar. My Children will have nothing but their Liberty and the Right to catch Fish, on the Banks of Newfoundland. This is all the Fortune that I have been able to make for myself or them.

I know not however, enough of this subject to decide any Thing. Is he a Speaker at the Bar? If not he will never be any Thing. But above all I positively forbid, any Connection between my Daughter and any Youth upon Earth, who does not totally eradicate every Taste for Gaiety and Expence. I never knew one who had it and indulged it, but what was made a Rascall by it, sooner or later. This Youth has had a Brother in Europe, and a detestible Specimen he exhibited. Their Father had not all those nice sentiments which I wish, although an Honourable Man.

I think he and you have both advanced too fast, and I should advise both to retreat. Your Family as well as mine have had too much Cause to rue, the Qualities which by your own Account have been in him. And if they were ever in him they are not yet out.

This is too serious a Subject, to equivocate about. I don't like this method of Courting Mothers. There is something too fantastical and affected in all this Business for me. It is not nature, modest, virtuous, noble nature. The Simplicity of Nature is the best Rule with me to Judge of every Thing, in Love as well as State and War.

This is all between you and me.

I would give the World to be with you Tomorrow. But there is a vast Ocean. No Ennemies. But I have not yet Leave from my Masters. I don't love to go home in a Miff, Pet or Passion nor with an ill Grace, but I hope Soon to have leave. I can never Stay in Holland—the Air of that Country chills every drop of Blood in My veins. If I were to stay in Europe another Year I would insist upon your coming with your daughter but this is not to be and I will come home to you.

Adieu ah ah Adieu.

JAMES MONROE
TO
ELIZABETH MONROE

The Monroes had been married barely a year when James wrote to Elizabeth detailing his plans for dividing their time between their new home in Fredericksburg, Virginia, and Richmond, while he attended the courts.

ELIZABETH KORTRIGHT MONROE, THE BEAUTIFUL DAUGHTER OF FORMER BRITISH OFFICER AND NEW YORK MERCHANT LAWRENCE KORTRIGHT, MARRIED JAMES MONROE WHEN HE WAS A VIRGINIA DELEGATE TO THE CONTINENTAL CONGRESS IN NEW YORK IN 1786.

Richmond April 13. 1787.

I arriv'd here the evening aftr you left me and have since been in health. I lodge & dine with Mr. Jones. I hope to hear from you by the post this evening. I have the utmost anxiety to know that yourself & our little Eliza are well. that you are well recd. & kindly treated by Mrs. Lewis. of this I have no doubt but shall be happy to hear it from yrself. has she grown any and is there any perceptible alteration in her?

Mr. Madison writes me some time will yet elapse before our furniture will reach Fredricksbg. on the 1st of this month it had not left N. York. it is finish'd & will be forwarded by the first opportunity. I have been disappointed in the rect. of money here for my carriage. Mr. Jones[...] to have furnish'd me with 100_ but doubt whether he will so many dollrs. you are [...] our little establishment in Fredricksburg than myself. have you heard how Peter proceeds in the garden & what the state of every thing there? I hope they are safe. I was sorry you had not with you one article you mention'd as necessary for the little monkey. I hope she suffers no inconvenience from it. I have engag'd Lucy of Mr. Jones and shall upon our return home dismiss Priss & her family. I shod. be happy as you prefer her to keep her, provided it cod. be done with propriety. but as it cannot be done for reasons that I an persuaded will be satisfactory to you, we had better dismiss her. It is however as you please. I hope you use much exercise. I am satisfied the pain you often complain of in your breast arises from this source. Let me intreat you not to neglect it—it will also contribute much to secure you from the disease of this country, the ague & fever. Quarvier has engag'd to begin another carriage for us. he objects to making it perfectly flat or straight before. he says it will sink & be apt to leak. that they are also out of fashion—be so kind as inform in what style you wish it and the color you prefer. I find it impossible to make arrangments for your reception here during the present term of the ct. Mr. Randolph hath not mention'd it & I have no money. I have partly arrang'd the affr. with Mr. Carrington that we shall get an house together this fall & bring yrself & his lady [...] Lady will be content to live on very little during the court, & his pay during the assembly. and I have assur'd him you will be as easily satisfied. Such difficulties as are insurmountable shod. be submitted to with fortitude and patience, however painful or afflicting they may be. In future I trust we shall have little occasion to exercise this kind of fortitude for I hope, we shall be able so far to surmount those difficulties which the severities of fortune had impos'd on us in our commenc'ment, as to avoid a seperation for such length of time. I cannot yet determine whether I shall be up before the end of the court, which will be the 6th of May or abt. that time. It is essential to my character here and of course to my prospect of extricating ourselves from our present embarrasments, that I shew the publick I can attend to business. if I travell about they will think otherwise. It is necessary not only that I be faithful & honest but that they shod. think that so. this they will not do if there is the least ground to suspect the contrary. suspicion often destroys (without the smallest foundation for it) the best characters & disturbs the peace & tranquility of the most upright & amiable. That I have attended to my duty in other stations is of little consequence. I am but

OUR FIFTH PRESIDENT, JAMES MONROE, IS DEPICTED WORKING AT HIS DESK IN THIS ENGRAVING FROM THE "AMERICAN KINGS" SERIES.

a new character here, & must cultivate all the forms & circumstances that wod. Be necessary, if I had just set out in the world;
otherwise I fail. Mr. Jones will have this on tuesday next. by him
I will write you again. Let [...] by every opportunity to write [...]
if possible but if none offer by post—forward yr. letters to Mr.
Brooke he will send them on here. Believe me my dear Eliza most
affectionately yours

Jas. Monroe

[P.S.] Kiss the little babe for me & take care of yourself & of her—
make my respects to Mrs. Lewis & Mrs. Lightfoot. you need not
mention that Mr. R hath not press'd your coming down.

JAMES POLK
TO
SARAH POLK

---

*J*ames Polk sent this now-startling letter to Sarah about plantation affairs, including the buying and selling of slaves and his plans to send them "to the South" in order
"to make more money."

At the plantation Sept 26th 1834

Dear Sarah

Within an hour after I wrote to you on yesterday, I sold my land
to Mr Booker for $6,000—one half down at Christmas and the
other half upon a year's credit. To day I have bought <u>Mariah's</u> husband, and have some expectation that I may be able to get <u>Caesar's</u>
wife. My crop is better than I expected. There is a fair prospect
that it will yield me including corn & cotton both, about $2,500.
<u>Beanland</u> has done well—considering the trouble he has had with
the negroes. <u>Old Jack</u> is now gone, without any known reason and
has been away for near three weeks. No account can be had of
him. I fear he has taken another trip to the Mississippi River.

I will send up <u>Jim & Ben</u> with old Mr. Moore (George's father) who will start on monday. I will give them a letter to <u>Mr. Harris</u> requesting him to deliver them to their owners. I find negro clothing very high here, and will write by them to Mr <u>Harris</u>—requesting him to buy for me, their clothing and send it down with Old Mr Moore who will be returning with a waggon. I am resolved to send my hands to the South, have given money to <u>James Brown</u> to buy a place & employed <u>Beanland</u> as an overseer. I am determined to make more money or loose more one. I have been kept exceedingly busy since I got here, have not been off the plantation except to a neighbour's house on business. I have received no letter from home, and have seen no newspaper, and of course know nothing of the character of the publications, which the Editor of the Republican had promised to make before I left home. I determined not to perplex myself about it, until I had done my business. I hope to be able to get off on tomorrow evening or the next day; and I think I may have an opportunity to sell my land near Boliver, and will probably be detained there for a day or two, and will then come directly home. I bought Mariah's husband a very likely boy—about 22 years old for $600. and paid for him with the notes I held on his master for land which I sold him several years ago.

Your affectionate Husband James K. Polk

P.S. I will write to Mr. Harris giving him a statement of the articles I wish sent down for the plantation when Old Mr Moore returns. If he is not at home will you see to it, and get <u>Saml. Walker</u> to buy them for me upon the lowest terms he can. I have written for enough to make two suits round. The nigrars have no idea that they are going to be sent to the South and I do not wish them to know it, and therefore it would be best to say nothing about it at home, for it might be conveyed back to them. Yrs. Truely J .K. P. N.B. Since my writing it occurs to me, that I will have to go a day or two out of my way, with the hope of getting a negro in payment of a debt due me by Silliman to whom I sold land.

Yrs. &c   J. K. P. Sept. 27. 1834.

*I*n this, the only surviving—though nearly illegible—letter written by Jane Pierce to her husband, the care of their son Benjamin ("Benny") is the focal point.

Saturday Morng. Just after breakfast
[ante January 6, 1853]

My beloved husband.

I write a line on business tho the writing books without and with the recollection that your letter received last evening giving good accounts of precious Benny, and at the solicitation of sister.. and the rest who come and says "give my...to Mr. Pierce and tell him that your are...at any rate." Still I should put getting rest until I have the promised...by the afternoon mail and good account of you and may...Benny. I send those clothes home that Mary may

JANE PIERCE WAS A RELUCTANT FIRST LADY, BUT A STAUNCH
SUPPORTER OF HER HUSBAND IN HIS RUN FOR THE PRESIDENCY.

have them on Monday morning. I shall take the...car on Monday I earnestly hope and pray that all may be well with you until that time. I know how watchful you and Pamela...are in regard to that dear child. She must not relax in her care but see that his feet do not get cold that he is well coverd at night, in regard to his diet &c. I send a little book which Aunt Mary took up and told me to send to Benny. it will amuse him when he finds his Mother does not come. he will be the...little "Farmer Boy" I see in it.... Your always aff. Jane

---

MARY LINCOLN
TO
ABRAHAM LINCOLN

---

*M*ary Lincoln had gone to her father's house in Lexington, Kentucky, leaving her husband in Washington, D.C., seeing to his congressional duties, when she wrote this letter about their family affairs and separation.

Lexington-May-48–

My Dear Husband-

You will think indeed, that <u>old age</u>, had set <u>its seal</u>, upon my humble self, that in few or none of my letters, I can remember the day of the month, I must confess it as one of my peculiarities; I feel wearied & tired enough to know, that this is <u>Saturday night</u>, our <u>babies</u> are asleep, and as Aunt Maria B. is coming in for me tomorrow morning, I think the chances will be rather dull that I should answer your last letter tomorrow. I have just received a letter from Frances W, it related in an <u>especial</u> manner to <u>the box</u>, I had desired her to send, she thinks with you (as good persons generally agree) that it would cost more than it would come to, and it might be lost on the road, I rather expect she has examined the specified articles, and thinks as <u>Levi</u> says, they are <u>hard bargains</u>—But it takes so many changes to do children, particularly in summer, that I thought it might save me a few stitches. I think I will write her a few lines this evening, directing her not to send them. She says Willie is just recovering from another spell of Sickness, Mary or none of them were well. Springfield she reports as dull as usual. Uncle S was to leave there on yesterday for Ky. Our little Eddy, has recovered from his little spell of sickness—Dear boy, I must tell you a story about him—Roby in his wanderings to day, came across in a yard, a little kitten, your hobby, he says he asked a man for it, he brought it triumphantly to the house, so soon as Eddy, spied it—his tenderness, broke forth, he made them bring it water, fed it with bread himself, with his own dear hands, he was a delighted little creature over it, in the midst of his happiness Ma came in, she you must know dislikes the whole cat race, I thought in a very unfeeling manner, she ordered the servant near, to throw it out, which of course, was done, Ed screaming & protesting loudly against the proceeding, she never appeared to mind his screams, which were long & loud I assure you—Tis unusual for her now a days to do something quite so striking, she is very obliging & accommodating, but if she thought any of us, were on her hands again, I believe she would be worse than ever. In the next moment she appeared in a good humor, I know she did not intend to offend me. By the way, she has just sent me up a glass of ice cream for which this warm evening, I am duly grateful. The country is so delightful I am going to spend two or three weeks out there, it will doubtless benefit the children—Grandma has received a letter from Uncle James Parker of Miss. saying he & his family would be up by the twenty sixth of June, would remain here some little time & go on to Philadelphia to take their oldest daughter there to school, I believe it would be a good chance for me to pack up & accompany them. You know I am so fond of sight-seeing, & I did not get to New York or Boston, or travel the lake route. But perhaps dear husband, like the irresistible Col. Mc, cannot do without his wife next winter, and must needs take her with him again—I expect you would cry aloud against it—How much, I wish instead of writing we were together this evening, I feel very sad away from you. Ma & myself rode out to Mr. Bell's splendid place this afternoon, to return a call, the house and grounds are magnificent, Frances M would <u>have died</u> over their rare exotics. It is growing late, these summer eves are short, I expect my long <u>scrawls</u>, for truly such they are, weary you greatly—if you come on, in July or August I will take you to the springs. <u>Patty Webbs</u> school in S—closes the first of July, I expect <u>Mr Webb</u> will come on for here, I must go down about that time & carry on quite a flirtation, you know we always had a <u>penchant</u> that way. With Love I must bid you good night. Do not fear the children, have forgotten you, I was only jesting—Even E—eyes brighten at the mention of your name. My love to all—Truly yours M L—

ULYSSES S. GRANT
TO
JULIA GRANT

$\mathcal{A}$s General Grant's Union Army tightened the noose around the Confederate capital of Richmond, Ulysses took time to offer Julia advice on relocating the family home from Illinois to Princeton, New Jersey.

City Point, Va. Aug 1st 1864.

Dear Julia,

Since writing to you before about going to Princeton N.J. I have made further enquiries. I find they have as fine schools there as is to be found in the country. It is one of the nicest places to live, the best society, and near to every place in the East. It is close to Long Branch, a favorite Summer resort, near to New York, near Philadelphia, within seven or eight hours of Washington City and within a day, nearly, of here. If you leave for me to decide I say emphatically you will go to Princeton. As soon as I have your say in this matter I will send Col. Porter of my Staff (he was sent to Princeton to school before he went to West Point) to secure you a house. I will leave it to you whether to keep house or board. In my opinion it will be better, if you go there, to keep house. By having a good trusty house keeper you can all ways leave home for a few days and whilst in the East I can always get home, if not in a few hours, in a day at furthest. You would bring Little Rebel with you for the children to ride and I would send you Egypt for you to drive. I know with these, and Jess to <u>escort</u>, you would be happy. I could not send you the black pony Jeff Davis. He has got to be one of the most beautiful horses you ever saw, very fleet, and he always was just as easy as a rocking chair. I have been offered $1,000 for him and $1,200 for the horse given to me by Mr. Grant of Cincinnati. Of course, I could not sell them but it shows how fine they are regarded.

Love to all and kisses for you and the children. I write, as usual, after every body else is in bed, and with full twelve hours constant wrighting to do, which I must do, before me. Tell Dr. Barrett I rec'd his letter this evening. He must not be disappointed if I do not answer him. Ulys

---

LUCRETIA GARFIELD
TO
JAMES GARFIELD

---

*I*n preparation for James Garfield's inauguration as president, Lucretia went incognito to New York City for a shopping trip, leaving the president-elect home to manage the house and family. The missives reveal the difficulties of their new celebrity and the continuing demands of parenting.

New York Tribune New York Jan. 20th. 1881

My Darling—

No word from home yet! Yesterday we made effective by making some decisions—final in regard to two Suits at least. The prices seem extravagant still I have not made very large inroad into the amount you sent. Mr. Reid says tell you that we have not been betrayed yet. And shall not unless Mrs. Sheldon forgets to address me as "Mrs. Greenfield" at some unguarded moment. The carriage is at the door again, so I must be excused for the delightful work again. I will write you again this evening and tell you some things you will be very glad to know.

With kisses and love to yourself and the little boys, Yours Forever, Crete

---

Mentor O. Jany 20. 1881

My Darling.

Your first letter came this morning and filled the house with gladness. It must have required great skill to ride in the same car to N.Y. with two prominent friends and Escape their notice. You are developing fine diplomatic qualities. Our life here is the usual monopoly of Eventfulness—but the house is very empty and cannot be filled until you return.

A letter came from Hal this morning addressed to "Dear Lawnfield," which would delight Mr. Cowles—the Godfather of the place. Hal has a chance to join Lulu's musical class, all girls but him. He asks permission to join it, & I have telegraphed him permission, subject to Col. Rockwells approval. I called on Grandma Aldrich this morning. She has broken her thigh bone at the hip joint, & is suffering greatly. Mother will go to see her Soon. I leave the clothes question wholly with you—but with this suggestion. It would be rather embarrassing to me, to quit Carson and take up any other Merchant tailor at Cleveland. By the way, I noticed a touch of ancestral Spelling in the word "taylor"—Perhaps you were momentarily attracted to the present occupant of my old seat in the House.

If you send a tailor from N.Y. have Mr. Reid telegraph me in time that I may not be away. This little Sheet is too small to record Even a tithe of the love which Lawnfield wishes to send. As Ever and all your own James

*T*heodore Roosevelt was serving as a New York State legislator when he wrote this charming letter to Alice, who was expecting the couple's first child.

Albany, January 28, 1884

Darling Wifie,

All of the men were perfectly enchanted with their visit to our house; they admired the rooms, the hall, the hunting trophies (Elliott's), and more especially the hosts. They could hardly believe that mother was really our mother; and above all they praised my sweet little wife. I was very much amused by Welch, who said that he had never seen any one look so pretty as you did when you were asking me not to tell the "shaved lion," story; he said "I would have felt just as badly as she would have if you had gone on to tell it." So I felt very glad we had entertained the three "pollys."

Tonight I dine at the Newbolds; tomorrow with Owe; I am afraid I can not be down till late Thursday.

With warmest love for my hearts dearest I am <u>Ever Your Fond</u>.

ELLEN WILSON
TO
WOODROW WILSON

*M*argaret Woodrow Wilson, the first child of Woodrow and Ellen, had been born on April 16, 1886, in Gainsville, Georgia, five days before Ellen was allowed to write to her husband.

I am allowed to write, my darling, just long enough to say that I love, love, love you & to tell you how my heart aches to see you, & to have you see the baby. It is a little beauty, darling. Everyone says the prettiest little baby they ever saw, & so plump & healthy; so perfectly well. Ah how good our Heavenly Father is to us! How tenderly He has cared for me!

I am just as well as can be,—"have never been sick yet" the nurse says. Both baby & I are considered perfect phenomenons in the way of "doing well." Every danger is over & I am quite myself again. So you must put aside all anxiety about me & celebrate my recovery by having a "grand old time" in Boston. Am so glad you can carry a light heart this trip. Goodbye my darling, my love, my life, my dear dear husband.

Your own little wife Ellen.

[P.S.] They wont let write again until the regular day, Monday. I got out a special license for this I love you sweetheart.

CALVIN COOLIDGE
TO
GRACE COOLIDGE

$\mathcal{P}$resident Calvin Coolidge wrote this brief letter about domestic issues to Grace, who was in Northampton, Massachusetts, caring for her ill mother.

December 21, 1928

My dear Grace:

The opossum has been sent to the zoo to be fattened up, so it will be nice to eat when you get home. We also have three nice turkeys. I do not think much of anything has come in for you except a shoe case holding 18 pairs for use when you go traveling.

I got along better with the dogs last night. It is quite cold here today. I have not heard from you since you went away, so I suppose you did not find anything new to report on your mother. Mr. Morrow has gone home. I am having a portrait done by a Mr. Crafton for the Chicago Stock Yards. The Englishman, Salisbury, will attend on me at Sapeloe Island to make the portrait. With love.

FRANKLIN D. ROOSEVELT
TO
ELEANOR ROOSEVELT

---

*C*oncerned about their rising income taxes, even though president, Franklin Roosevelt urged the first lady to economize on food.

The White House, Oct. 7, 1942.

Memorandum for E .R.

In view of the new income tax law, it will, of course, result in such a cut in the net I receive from the Government that we shall have to take some steps to reduce the White House food bill, to which I pay $2,000 a month, or $24,000 a year. Next year the taxes on $75,000 will leave me only about $30,000 net and SOMETHING HAS TO BE DONE! I do not think I can contribute more than $1,500 a month—leaving a total of $18,000 for Mrs. Nesbitt for the year.

The only thing I can think of is to reduce the number of servants whom we feed. Because they have a Civil Service status we should, of course, see that they get employment elsewhere in the Government. We must remember, too, that I am away on an average of about ten days out of each month, not counting the more extended trips like the last, which I take at least once a year. When you are away my entertaining very rarely amounts to more than a dinner party of four or five people.

I do realize that the cost of food has gone up. However, I would suggest that something drastic be done about the size of portions served.

For instance, for my luncheons I have pleaded—when it is an egg dish—for only one egg apiece, yet four eggs for two people constantly appear. In the same way in the evenings, vegetables and meat keep coming up to the Study when night after night more than half of the dish goes back to the pantry. I know of no instance where anybody has taken a second help—except occasionally when I do—and it would be much better if I did not take a second help anyway. F. D. R.

*R*ichard Nixon, then a naval officer, and Pat wrote about some of their favorite domestic activities.

[c. June 1944]

I always like to hear of your get togethers too—you always make people have a good time. Our parties have always been your successes. Remember the time you even made the chop suey!!! When I think of all the wonderfulnesses for me—didn't I take advantage? But dearest, it was appreciated then and now. I never shall forget how sweet you were the night Margaret and I had the teachers for a wiener roast—You carted, helped with the salad, bought the pies, went to LA for Mary's gift, etc.

VICE-PRESIDENT ELECT RICHARD NIXON AND HIS WIFE EXAMINE
RETURNS AFTER THEIR 1952 VICTORY WITH DWIGHT D. EISENHOWER.

RICHARD NIXON
TO
PAT NIXON

[c. July 1944]

Dear One

I have nothing to spend money on here and for that reason I want
you to make up for me there. Get good dinners, see lots of shows,
buy nice clothes, have your hair fixed—and anything else you
want or need. It will make me feel swell to think of you having
some enjoyment.

DWIGHT EISENHOWER
TO
MAMIE EISENHOWER

*S*hortly after D-Day and their son John's visit to England, General Eisenhower wrote
to his wife wondering about John's future and cautioning Mamie about being overpro-
tective of their only surviving son.

Bushy Park, London, June 22, 1944

My darling

Tomorrow is two years since I left Washington!

It has been lots of fun, being with Johnny and trying to catch his
viewpoint—his ideas, ambitions and general outlook. He is certainly approaching his army work with great seriousness, but is apparently
a bit puzzled as to what he wants to do with his personal life. This
is a natural thing, at his age, the only unusual thing being the amount
of thought he gives such things. Most youngsters just rollick along
in a healthy fashion, letting adventure and problem alike come up
as they please—and meeting them on the spur of the moment.

He says you are going to visit him in Benning. I think that's fine, as it will be nice for you to know how he is living, etc. etc., But I think it would be unwise to stay too long. Undoubtedly he has some feeling (at least subconsciously) that he has always been carefully watched over. He is wondering how he will do "on his own." So he must be given a chance to be on his own before he comes up against really critical problems. I know how you feel about him—and how desperately you want him by your side as long as possible. But I think brief visits to him are more advisable than any long stay.

I am so glad he will be able to tell you about us here—all we do—how we live, etc. I think it will help a lot.

We both talk of you all the time. I love you deeper. Don't forget me, because I'm looking forward only to the day I rejoin you permanently. Always your Ike

[P.S.] Love to Min & Papah & Auntie.

HARRY S. TRUMAN

TO

BESS TRUMAN

---

*W*orld events and politics are never far away in presidential families. President Harry S. Truman wanted to discuss his daughter Mary Margaret in this letter to Bess, but world events, such as his March 12 speech outlining aid for Greece and Turkey (the Truman Doctrine), soon crowded out his familial concerns.

Key West, Fla. March 14, 1947

Dear Bess:

I sent Margie a long letter last night and hoped to get this off at the same time but failed to make it. I had no idea I was so tired. I have been asleep most of the time. Didn't get up until 8 o'clock yesterday and 7:30 today so you know I'm rather all in. Even drove to the beach instead of walking as I did before. Had a forty-minute sun-bath at eleven o'clock and will have another one this morning of one hour.

I am very much in favor of Margie's coming back to Washington next Monday. Then we can take stock and decide what's best to do. I hope she shows you my letter to her.

They are running a special wire in here from New York so I can listen to her without interruption, so I guess I'll stay over a day or two beyond Sunday if it is all right with you.

Stelman and Clifford were as nearly all in as I was so it is a good arrangement all around. Hope the result of the message will be for world peace. It was a terrific step to take and one I've been worrying about since Marshall took over the State Dept. Our very first conversation was what to do about Russia in China, Korea, and the Near East.

As far as I've seen the papers, there has been a favorable reception except by the crackpots headed by Henry and his crowd. I don't believe they can get a following. It was pleasing the way the Congress reacted—didn't you think it was nearly unanimous.

How I wish you and Margie and your mother were here. The ship is tied up right in front of the house—just a block away. Maybe I'll come home aboard it if it doesn't take too long.

I'm looking for a letter! <u>Lots & lots of Love</u> Harry

JACQUELINE KENNEDY

TO

JOHN F. KENNEDY

---

*J*ackie Kennedy reported this exchange with her husband, made in an attempt to get him to participate in decisions about home and hearth, which he usually left to his wife.

JACQUELINE BOUVIER KENNEDY EMPLOYED HER UNIQUE ELEGANCE AND
BEAUTY TO FURTHER HER HUSBAND'S POLITICAL CAREER.

"When I start to ask him silly little insignificant questions about whether Caroline should appear at some reception, or whether I should wear a short or long dress, he just snaps his fingers and says 'That's your province.' And I say, 'Yes, but you're the great decision-maker. Why should everyone but me get the benefit of your decisions?'"

RONALD REAGAN
TO
NANCY REAGAN

---

*R*onald and Nancy were trying to cope with the trials of raising teenagers when he wrote this letter to his wife.

Thurs. Pacific Palisades [May 24, 1963]

My Darling

Last night we had our double telephone call and all day (I didn't work) I've been re-writing the story of my life as done by Richard Hubler. Tomorrow I'll do my last day of location and then I'll call you and I'll tell you I love you and I'll mean it but somehow because of the inhibitions we all have I won't feel that I've expressed all that you really mean to me.

Whether Mike helps buy his first car or spends the money on sports coats isn't really important. We both want to get him started on a road that will lead to his being able to provide for himself. In x number of years we'll face the same problem with The Skipper and somehow we'll probably find right answers. (Patti is another kind of problem and we'll do all we can to make that one right, too.) But what is really important is that having fulfilled our responsibilities to our offspring we haven't been careless with the treasure that is ours—namely what we are to each other.

Do you know that when you sleep you curl your fists up under your chin and many mornings when it is barely dawn I lie facing you and looking at you until finally I have to touch you ever so lightly so you won't wake up—but touch you I must or I'll burst?

Just think: I've discovered I can be fond of Ann Blyth because she and her Dr. seem to have something of what we have. Of course it can't really be as wonderful for them because she isn't you but still it helps to know there are others who might just possibly know a little about what it's like to love someone so much that it seems as if I have my hand stretched clear across the mountains & desert until it's holding your hand there in our room in front of the fireplace.

Probably this letter will reach you only a few hours before I arrive myself but not really because right now as I try to say what is in my heart I think my thoughts must be reaching you without waiting for paper and ink and stamps and such. If I ache, it's because we are apart and yet that can't be because you are inside and part of me, so we aren't really apart at all. Yet I ache but wouldn't be without the ache, because that would mean being without you and that I can't be because I love you. Your Husband

A CHRONICALLY ILL ELIZA MCCARDLE
JOHNSON NOT ONLY TUTORED HER HUSBAND
ANDREW BUT PROVIDED THE NECESSARY DOMESTIC
SUPPORT FOR HIS POLITICAL CAREER.

CHAPTER 5

EDUCATION

~ﾑ

"Teach the Elements of those
Sciences to my little Girl and Boys."
—John Adams to Abigail Adams,
September 26, 1775

"He thinks all we are made for is to work,
and as for the accomplishments, it is a sin even to think of."
—Lucretia Rudolph to James Garfield,
April 1, 1855

THEIR own educations and that of their children were always
major concerns of presidents and their spouses. Professional choices were paramount topics for discussion. Over time, the focus of
education for women shifted from home and family management
to outside careers. Although the presidential wives have tradition-
ally been portrayed as "stay at home," some, including Lucretia
Garfield, Eleanor Roosevelt, and Hillary Clinton, only reluctantly accepted—and often avoided—the general rule.

*W*hile attending the Continental Congress during the American Revolution, John Adams wrote this letter to his wife, urging her to teach "my little Girl and Boys" geometry and geography.

Philadelphia Septr. 26. 1775

My Dear

I have not written the usual Compliment of Letters since I left Braintree; nor have I received one Scratch of a Pen from any Body, till the last Evening, when the Post brought me a Line from Mrs. Warren, in which she informs me that you had been ill, but was better. I shall be unhappy till I hear farther from you, tho I hope for the best.

I have enjoyed better Health, this session than the last, and have suffered less from certain Fidgets, Pidlings, and Irritabilities which have become so famous. A more serious Spirit prevails than heretofore. We shall soon be in Earnest. I begin to think We are so. Our Injunctions of Secrecy are so much insisted on, that I must be excused from disclosing one Iota of any Thing that comes to my Knowledge as a Member of the Congress. Our Journal of the last session however, I conjecture will be speedily printed and then I will inclose it to you.

I want to be informed from Hour to Hour, of any Thing which passes in Boston—whether our Friends come out—what Property they bring? How they fare in Town? How the Tories subsist &c. &c. &c. Whether the Troops are healthy or sickly?

I also want to know every Thing which passes in our Army. The Feats and Exploits of our little Naval Armaments would be very agreable.

Tudor is made easy. He must keep a Clerk, or there will be Jealousies. Indeed it is his Duty for it is impossible he can do the

Business himself, and if that is not done, Injustice to the public will be done.

I have seen the Utility of Geometry, Geography, and the Art of drawing so much of late, that I must intreat you, my dear, to teach the Elements of those Sciences to my little Girl and Boys. It is as pretty an Amusement, as Dancing or Skaiting, or Fencing, after they have once acquired a Taste for them. No doubt you are well qualified for a school Mistress in these Studies, for Stephen Collins tells me that English Gentleman, in Company with him, when he visited Braintree, pronounced you the most accomplished Lady, he had seen since he left England. You see a Quaker can flatter, but don't you be proud.

My best Wishes and most fervent Prayers attend our little Family. I have been banished from them, the greatest Part of the last Eighteen Months but I hope to be with them more, in Time to come. I hope to be excused from attending at Philadelphia, after the Expiration of the Year. I hope that Dr. Winthrop, Mr. Sever, Mr. Greenleaf, Coll. Warren, Mr. Hawley, Mr. Gerry, some or all of them will take their Turns, in the States—and suffer me, at least to share with my Family, a little more than I have done, the Pleasures and Pains of this Life, and that I may attend a little more to my private Affairs that I may not be involved in total Ruin, unless my Country should be so and then I should choose to share its Fate.

JOHN QUINCY ADAMS
TO
LOUISA CATHERINE ADAMS

---

*J*ohn Quincy Adams was about to become the Boylston Professor of Rhetoric and Oratory at Harvard College when he wrote this informative, somewhat jocular, letter to his wife.

Boston 10 May 1806.

My dearest Louisa,

I wrote you last Sunday, the day after my arrival at Quincy and gave you an account of the progress and termination of my Journey from New York. On Tuesday I went with my father to Cambridge to attend the inauguration of the new President of the College, Mr. Webber. The ceremonies of the day were sufficiently dull. The performances mostly in Latin, with a comfortable proportion of English in the Idiom to make it intelligible. There was however a young Gentleman just out of College, who knew more about making Latin, as they call it at school than the rest, and pronounced a sort of complimentary Oration, which would have pleased me very well, but for a little prophetical fancy in which he told them what wonders of Eloquence they were to perform when the new Professor should come. My turn will be next, and as there is no installation without a Speech, I have asked the privilege of pronouncing it in a language which I can write and the hearers can understand. I expect to be indulged, though some of the adherents to the Old School are very tenacious of the immemorial usage and abhorrent of innovation. I suppose my induction to Office will be the week after next.

On Thursday I came to this Town and am lodged for the present at Whitcomb's. I dined yesterday at Mr. T.C. Amory's and this day at Mr. G. Green's. I am seeking for a place to lodge and board for the Summer, but know not yet whether I shall fix in Boston or in Cambridge. At Mr. Amory's I met Sir Isaac Coffin, a British admiral who has just arrived from England and is going to take the naval Command at Halifax. He tells me that Mr. Merry is recalled and a Lord Selkirk appointed in his stead. This Lord Selkirk is said to be a great philosopher and perhaps may be of great use to you know whom, in helping to make a Moon.

There are two boxes of things for which you had written waiting for a passage, and I see in the newspaper a vessel up for Alexandria to sail in a few days. Her name I think is the rambler— I have desired Mr. Shaw to open one of the boxes, and put in the Cotton, which according to your order I procured for you at Providence and which I hope you will find such as you wanted. It was compared with the two specimens you gave me and purchased at the same Shop where I went with you before—By the way, I found on opening my trunk a piece of Silk which you put up with my clothes; but either you forgot to tell me the purpose of sending it, or I have forgotten what you told me. I conjecture your object was to have it dyed, but for better certainty will thank you to write me word.

I have this day received with great pleasure your kind letter of the 5th instt: And although you tell nothing of your health, I flatter myself from your early attention to the Thermometer, that it is at least tolerable. I hope however that neither for the thermometer, nor for any other consideration, you will let it suffer by depriving yourself of your rest. The observation at 8 or 9 in the morning will answer the purpose quite as well as at 6—The Book which I made for you must have got somewhere mislaid, for I do not find on looking over my trunk of papers, that I took it with me. I did indeed in the hurry of departure take the case of the thermometer with me so that if you should remove to another house it will be necessary to take it in the hand. I have not yet commenced my observations here, but intend to, as soon as I get settled; I find upon the comparison for the twenty days that my brother kept the register at Quincy, untill his instrument got broken, with the same dates and hours at Washington a very good commencement for an estimate of the difference between the two climates.

The 150 dollars which I left with you for Mr. Hallen was for the purpose of settling with him on account of our Expences from the time of the last payment I had made him untill I came away. The other 80 dollars for my part of Cookendorfer's bill. In both these instances, as in all the former, as Mr. Hallen has always declined mentioning any precise sum I have been obliged to measure it by an estimate or guess of what would be proper & Satisfactory to him. As an indemnity for all positive expence—but not for that invariable kindness and attention both from him and Mrs. Hallen to you and to me, for which I shall always feel and acknowledge the obligation.

I suppose the Notes from Mr. Maitland will be important to the Administrators in England, to shew the nature of his connection in business with your father, and much of the subsequent correspondence to shew the State of Accounts between them. Maitland's answer to the Bill in Chancery must be given upon Oath. If he gives it with <u>truth</u> it appears to me there must be a large balance for which he will be compelled to Account. If he should prevaricate the notes Accounts and especially the ratification of the heavy charges of payment to the Captain of the Indian Chief, which he never made, will be very important to the Administrators. Mr. Pinkney may safely be entrusted with the Notes, to make use of them if he should judge it expedient—And it does...probable they will even be of importance in this Country. If however your Mother...conclude to send them it will be prudent to keep copies well attested, to prevent accidents.

Our dear Children are both in perfect health and both anxious for Mama to come home. John especially talks of you continually, and is as charming as when we went away last November. He is not so far as we left him, but has grown in Stature, and his Countenance has lengthened a little, like George's. He is the Delight of all the family and my father thinks he has more ideas than any child of his age that he ever knew. I have abandoned the hope of having either of them with me, this summer and this deprivation sharpens the severity of that which I feel in the absence of their mother. The ensuing year will I hope be more propitious and bring a consolation for the necessary sacrifices of the present. I do not find that Sister T.B. would be under any such necessity of staying behind if he were called away, but I have not ventured to ask the question, and I am not Conniseur in Shapes enough to decide upon external inspection.

Dearest Louisa, I send you les plus tendres baiser da l'Amour.

The education of their adopted son, Andrew Jr., was discussed in this letter from Andrew Jackson to his wife Rachel, written while he was away on one of his many expeditions to arrange peace with the Creek and Chickasaw Indian tribes.

Chikesaw council house Sept. 18th. 1816

My Love

I have this moment recd. Your affectionate letter of the 8th. Instant, I rejoice that you are well & our little son. Tell him his sweet papa hears with pleasure that he has been a good boy & learns his Book, Tell him his sweet papa labours hard to get money to educate him, but when he learns & becomes a great man, his sweet papa will be amply rewarded for all his care, expence, & pains—how thankfull I am to you for taking poor little Lyncoya home & cloathing him—I have been much hurt to see him there with the negroes, like a lost sheep without a sheperd.

We had a long and disagreable time of it here, our servants have been all sick, Doctor Bronaugh very low, Jane had like to have went, but is on the mend—I hope we will get through our business tomorrow & leave here day after for Turkey town in the cherokee nation, I hope to reach home about the 5th or 6th of October we have made a conditional Treaty with the cherokee delegation and are to meet a full council at Turkey Town of the 28th Instant to have it fully ratified.—I have a sanguine hope, we will be fully successfull with the chikesaw and once more, regain by tribute, what I fairly, & hardly purchased with the sword, so much trouble & cost has been occassioned by the rashness, folly, & Ignorance of a great little man. But as successfull as I have reason to believe we will be at present, I shall be contented—I have truly noted the conduct of the overseer, & negroes, as soon as I return will take a satisfactory order on all—and you will charge him to sell nothing without your express orders—or I will make him more than answerable for the Vallue—with my sincere prayers for your health & happiness, and my little son & all the family believe me to be affectionately yours. Andrew Jackson

P.S. I thank you for your admonition I hope in all my acts & conduct through life they will measure with propriety and dignity, or at least with what I believe true dignity consists, that is to say honesty, propriety of conduct & honest independence— A J. Mr. James Jackson on your application will take order on Sampson if necessary, that family will sell any where, better below than in Nashville, but I suppose in Nashville for $14. or 1500—

L U C R E T I A   R U D O L P H
T O
J A M E S   G A R F I E L D

---

*D*uring their engagement, James Garfield returned to Williams College in Massachusetts to complete his undergraduate studies, while Lucretia remained at the Eclectic Institute in Hiram, Ohio, trying to decide what course of studies to pursue while teaching school. The letter intimates that even the faintest suggestion that women should pursue a career outside the home could be offensive.

Hiram, April 1. 1855.

My Dear James:

They call this "fools day"; but I will try and not fool you any worse than I always have, which I hope is not very badly, as I am sure you must know something of what I am by this time. Owing to the bad roads yesterday's mail did not reach here till this morning. Consequently, your letter was not received until then, and as my time is so fully occupied through the week that I shall be unable to answer before Friday evening next unless I write tonight, I have concluded so to do, trusting it will not be very wicked. I am engaged

LUCRETIA RUDOLPH GARFIELD WAS A VIGOROUS SUPPORTER
OF WOMEN'S EDUCATION (THOUGH NOT THEIR POLITICAL RIGHTS)
BOTH BEFORE AND AFTER HER HUSBAND'S PRESIDENCY,
WHICH ENDED IN HIS ASSASSINATION IN 1881.

in school again, reading Horace, and studying french, also teaching two classes. The same I taught last session, and today Bro Hayden spoke to me about taking a class commencing French. The class in Horace read it all last winter, and are now reading about 100 lines per lesson, which for me is a rather long pull. We will be through with it in a few weeks and then we read "Cicero" the remainder of the term. I am feeling much better than I did two weeks ago, though not entirely well yet, and presume I shall not be until the weather becomes more settled as I must of necessity expose myself a good deal. Your <u>whisker logic</u> is <u>doubtless</u> very good; but was it not a great blunder in dame Nature to furnish <u>man</u> with such a <u>necessary</u> protection for his lungs and leave poor frail woman's throat unprotected?

Bro. Crane and lady have left us—gone to take charge of Bro. Scott's school Covington, Ken. It was a good thing for them that they went when they did, for probably <u>he</u> would have been dismissed if he had staid here as a good number were quite determined he should be, and Bro. Mainvill and Bro. Damshee among them. <u>Who</u> recommended him to Bro. Scott I do not know. Mrs. Rhodes has three classes and as the number of students is less than usual they get along without engaging any other new teachers, <u>Your old room</u> is occupied entirely by Mrs. Rhodes and <u>myself</u> this session. <u>Can I</u> refuse Memay when she occasionally reminds me of <u>one year ago</u>? The school is starting very pleasantly and we are all hoping to have a fine session.

I saw Symond's mother at church to day and inquired after his health. She told me that he was better, still seemed to feel a good deal of anxiety about him yet.

"Uncle Symonds" gave the ladies a terrible dressing a week ago today, so they say. I did not hear it. I judge he thinks all we are made for is to work, and as for the accomplishments, it is a sin even to think of them. What an idea of life! Bake bread, wash dishes, scrub, iron, and mend, week in and week out, month after month, year after year—without a thought of anything else. True, those things must all be attended to, and each one should bear her part, but to make their thorough performances the end and aim of life, and the only object to receive any attention is most intolerable; and yet she must be an angel in goodness, mild as a summer morning and smiling as a moonbeam. Strange inconsistency! I do think Bro Rider, good as he is, is the most unreasonable man sometimes I ever knew. But I suppose we ought to bear with him patiently as he is getting to be an old man. Why has the God of Nature thrown all about us with such lavish hand beauty and grace if we are not to love it and cultivate it in our hearts and lives? Mrs. Stowe says, "Did not He who made the appetite for food make also that for beauty? And while the former will perish with the body is not the latter immortal? And is it not as much our <u>duty</u> to feed our higher nature with food sufficient for it, as our bodies? And as much, or even more, a sin to let it famish and die than leave our animal bodies to perish for lack of proper nourishment?

I am finished reading "Sunny memories" and am well pleased with them. Her travels in Germany interested me not a little, as she visited many places, the theaters of those nations which made upon the Romance of Paul Flemming–"Interlachen" where he met, loved and parted with crushed hopes for his Mary, "Strasbourg," "Heidelberg," and several other places.

I hear nothing from Philip and Marg and never expect to. Tuesday John and Ellen are married; and what to me seems very strange "O.P. Miller" has gone to perform the ceremony. I do think it such a droll idea. I should not feel as though the <u>knot was half tied</u>. He took "Lucy Baldwin" with him. I do believe the fellow is flattering himself that he can "shine" there; but he may as well "hang his harp on the willow."

Now, my dear, may I expect another letter in just two weeks? I don't like to wait after I expect one. With truest love, I am faithfully your own, Lucretia

The education of their children was always a priority for the Grants, even in the midst of the climactic struggle of the Civil War for the defeat of the Confederate Army of Virginia.

City Point, Va. July 7th 1864

Dear Julia,

I received two letters from you this evening, written after you had received mine stating that you could come to Fortress Monroe to spend the Summer. I am satisfied it is best you should not come. It would be expensive to furnish a house there and difficult supplying it afterwards. The camp life we are leading you would not be able to be where I am often and then only to come up and go immediately back, with an express boat that might be running at the time.

I wrote to you in my last why not make the same arrangement for the children as last year? Permanency is a great thing for children at school and you could not have a better home for them than with Louisa Boggs. If they were with her I should always feel easy for you to leave them for two or three months to stay with me if I was where you could possibly be with me. I want the children to prosecute their studies, and especially in languages. Speaking languages is a much greater accomplishment than the little paraphanalias of society such as music, dancing &c.I would have no objection to music being added to Nellies studies but with the boys I would never have it occupy one day of their time, or thought.

If you think it advisable to go some place where you can keep the children with you, and where they will be at a good school, I will not object. But I cannot settle for you where such a place would be, probably St. Louis would be as good as any other, for the present. Love and Kisses for yourself and the children. How much I wish I could see you all. Ulys

PRESIDENT RUTHERFORD B. HAYES AND HIS WIFE, LUCY WEBB HAYES,
MADE A FORMIDABLE POLITICAL TEAM, ALTHOUGH THE FIRST LADY
WAS A MORE RADICAL REPUBLICAN THAN HER HUSBAND WHEN IT
CAME TO THE RECONSTRUCTION OF THE SOUTH AFTER THE CIVIL WAR.

*L*ucy wrote about their newborn and school-age sons to her husband, who was fighting in the Union Army.

Chillicothe-Nov. 1st 64

Dearest R.

Your dear boy Webb has labored hard to print you a letter. All afternoon he was printing never discouraged but once when he said I don't believe papa can read—I read it for him—and told him you would prize it from him. He tells you we are going to Uncle Scotts Saturday—that he and Birch were there last Saturday—that he is doing well at school—was head of Spelling class five days. We are all well having most delightful weather.

Just heard from Ruddy—he is well sends me word he is burning leaves—Birchie is also writing you a letter—it has not been handed to me for perusal yet—do let us hear from you as often as you can—it is such a comfort to me. Mrs. Douglas and her little family are well—we see each other nearly every day.

I am so sorry to hear that Capt. Hastings wound is so serious—is his sister with him—Our poor dear baby has the Colic terribly—the boys are now home from school—and I have just got baby down. Mother had to go out—so I have been alone with him. I still hope he will get over it.

Remember me to all friends—What name do you propose for the boy—he will be a noble looking little fellow.

Your Own— L. W. H.

[P.S.] M stand for me—in Webb letter—Just received your letter of 25th—so glad to hear from you. Yesterday received Joes letters of 21st.

After the death of her father, Ellen made immediate plans to leave Rome, Georgia, and go to New York to study art at the Art Student's League. With the assistance of Woodrow, she soon carried out her plans.

Rome July 7, 1884.

My darling Woodrow,

If thoughts and words were one,—if as they say of pure spirits, the deed could always follow the wish to do, how many letters I would have written you since last Thursday! It seems strange that all my thinking since then has not proved an irrisistible power <u>forcing</u> me to write in spite of circumstances. All that I can say about it is that it was a case in which the spirit truly was willing but the flesh was weak. But now I am all right again, and the work, which at one time, owing to various back-sets, seemed likely to "go on forever" is actually <u>finished</u>; and I mean to do better as to my letter writing. I really must make a noble effort, and acquire the useful art of writing <u>short</u> letters, so that whether people are satisfied or not, they, at least, need not be anxious. I am so <u>very</u> sorry that you were made to suffer anxiety on my account. Am I <u>really</u> to believe that you not hearing has such an effect upon your spirits? Somehow I can't "take it in" that <u>my</u> letters <u>could</u> make such a difference to anyone! However, you are better, be the cause what it may, and I am so happy to hear it. If I could only be sure that it is a permanent improvement! If I could but know that you were <u>well</u> and likely to remain so! I don't know that I was ever more relieved than by those first words of your Saturday's letter–"<u>very much better</u>." you see instead of coming at dinner-time, as usual, it didn't reach me until night, which gave me time to get up a first class panic; for I knew that after your last letter, you would be sure to write soon again, if you were able.

So I must say what I think of the conclusion of the Arkansas matter! Must let you know whether or not I am "altogether gratified"? My darling, you have yourself answered the question—I <u>do</u> love you with my whole heart and I <u>do</u> wish what you wish! Won't that do? Or shall I say still more? Well, then I do miss you always—I <u>need</u> you always—and—I am <u>not</u> "altogether gratified"! And your arguments had <u>almost</u> persuaded me that you would gain more by going, than by staying in Baltimore, that you would really work to better advantage. I say I was almost persuaded, but not quite; for you know you would have relinquished a great deal in leaving just now. When I look at that side of the question, as of course I do <u>altogether</u> now, I am most <u>content</u>. I am sure that things have turned out for the best, and that it will simply end in your reaping the benefits of <u>both</u> plans,—those of Baltimore now, and of the smaller college a little later. That plan is not abandoned, but simply postponed; and though a year, or two, or three may seem very long now, we know how swiftly time flies; they will be gone before we dream of it. In short, it has been decided that you are to have the <u>whole</u> instead of a <u>part</u>, as you in your impatience would have chosen. And then you will always be spared the fear of having made a mistake. I think that fear would always have haunted me more or less; the pros and cons were so nicely balanced; the case was so difficult to decide, and at the same time of such serious consequence. But now it has been submitted to a judge who <u>never makes mistakes</u>, who can see the end from the beginning. "When we observe what mistakes we mortals make when we have our own way, it seems strange that we should be so fond of it."—I believe I am beginning at last to realize that, a little, to be somewhat less wise in my own conceit; for I don't seem to care half as much about my own way as I used to.

Yes, I suppose I will be going to New York now, beyond a peradventure. That is the present plan at any rate. The fall session at the <u>League</u>; (not <u>Cooper's</u>,—I wouldn't care to go there.) Begins the first Monday in Oct. Oh, dear me, <u>why</u> will you propose such delightful plans as that Wilmington visit, with the Northward journey at it's close? I am so tempted and tantalized by the thought of it, that it positively makes me unhappy. You can have no idea how hard it is for me to say "no"—hard, because I would, for some reasons so much like to do it; and harder still—much harder—because you wish it. And yet I <u>must</u> say it, because I gave Grandmother my solemn promise not to go. Even if I had not promised I couldn't think of going when she is so violently opposed to it. She talked and <u>talked</u> and <u>talked</u> to me about it, over and over again, none less earnestly and pleadingly because she met with no opposition; for I only laughed and said, "Why Grandmother I have no idea of going, I must admit, I would like to, but still—I can't." She was a wise old lady, she knew that whether I had the idea then or not, it might <u>possibly</u> be instilled into my mind. She knew, what I did not suspect then but now perceive, how all-powerful you are; that a few earnest words from you would make me not only yield my point, but literally change my mind. So she didn't rest until she made me promise, "upon my honour," not to go, under any circumstances. Her opposition is the <u>only</u> thing <u>now</u> which prevents my doing as you wish; but of course you see yourself that it would be impossible under the circumstances for me to go. Please give your dear mother my love, and tell her I thank her with all my heart both for her invitation and her desire to have me. I would be so glad to see her and your father as well as yourself. I am delighted to hear that she continues to improve. Good night, my dear one. Remember that I love you "with the smiles, tears, breath of all my life"—and that however much we may be separated I am always and altogether. Your own Ellie.

LOU HENRY

TO

HERBERT HOOVER

---

*L*ou Henry, a senior geology major at Stanford University, was soon to graduate and become engaged to a recent graduate, Herbert Hoover, then pursuing his engineering career in Australia.

Palo Alto Cal Apr 98

My dearest

I do not know how much a letter you will get, for I am up in Maymir room waiting for her to come from Gym, when we are going over to see the base ball practise. Only a few more days until baseball and track and debate are settled for this year.

We have been having a regular dead lock over the track and for a while it seemed we would have no field day,—all sorts of circuses came up, based, of course, upon Berkeley's characteristic obstinacy. I cant resist going into detail, even tho' boring you, for we are so thoroughly alive to it all here.

You know Charley is the Captain, and has the finest team we ever had—there is little doubt we can beat Berkeley. And the manager is as fine as the captain—Dave Brown—last year's mile runner—do you remember their telling of his running "the prettiest race ever seen" then he tired out Berkeley's man, then dropped back and brought in the other Stanford man second?

Well he carried everything thro' beautifully for Stanford. But he wanted the bicycle race held on another track (a safer one) than the one provided for in the written intercollegiate agreement, and tried for weeks in vain, to have the change. But finally had to give it up. There was no written agreement as to the counting of places, but of course it was expected to have them count 5, 2, 1 as they have here the last few years. At the very last just a couple of weeks ago UC decided the only chance of its winning was to have them counted 5,3,1—which would certainly be worse for Stanford. So there was a disagreement between the managers, and before they could get it settled, Berkeley's faculty appeared on the scene. At an informal meeting of the managers at which the UC faculty athletic committee, and Dr. Angell, representing our faculty athletic committee were present. Prof Bacon said substantially, "Since there is a very grave controversy between the management of the two track teams, the UC faculty have decided to take charge of affairs for Berkeley, as no doubt your faculty will for Stanford. For that reason we are here to see how matters can be arranged." Prof. Angell replied "it is the Stanford faculty's policy never to meddle with student affairs unless absolutely necessary. As we have full confidence in Mr. Browne's judgment and integrity, we see no need of interfering now." (How is that for typical Stanford spirit?) So Mr. Dave Brown Stanford student and the UC faculty athletic committee go into session with UC manager and Stanford's faculty representative in the background.

Prof Bacon "Well Mr. Brown, there seems a disagreement about the counting of places, we think it best to arbitrate the matter."

Mr. Brown "There is no agreement whatever governing the matter. I am perfectly willing to have it arbitrated." (Smart boy. He knew he had the only right side, if it came up before <u>anyone</u> for arbitration. I wont go into enough detail to explain why)

Prof. Bacon. "And I understand you do not agree about the bicycle race. It will be best to arbitrate that also."

Mr. Brown (with all Stanford behind him) tired of being a toy for Berkeley's whine. "The details of the bicycle race are in the intercollegiate agreement. I refuse to reconsider them at this late date, after arrangements have been so completed. I gave mr. Barnes

(Berkeley's manager) ample opportunity to have that changed weeks ago."

Prof. Bacon. "Very well then. I think it my duty to declare the field day off."

That is just about the length of the conference. I had a full report of it from Mr. Brown himself next day. You can imagine the effect. We were disappointed—but Berkeley! The Berkeley track men were wild! The faculty & students were at sword's points! Rebellion was rife in the land. All because "the faculty muddled." But of course Berkeley's faculty could not back down from any position. Mr. Brown could not do anything for he was representing Stanford, he could do nothing to compromise her dignity, and since he was right in the first place there was nothing for him to do. Berkeley's men intimated to him that the faculty were now ready to accept <u>any</u> proposition he would make. He told the faculty, unofficially, that since they had broken off negotiations, they would necessarily be the ones to reopen them. They assured him, also unofficially, that they had no proposition to offer. He told them if they would announce that they were ready to receive any statement from Stanford, he would then offer one. They would make no such an announcement, but told him, unofficially, if he would make <u>any</u> proposition, it would receive due consideration. What was to be done? Both student bodies were at fever heat—both sullen—UC at her own faculty. The only way apparently that the deadlock could be broken was for Stanford University to come down and humbly beg the University of California to reopen hostilities instead of preserving an armed reclusion.

Then it was that our Dave Brown proved the trust we put in him. The last possible day had arrived. A mass meeting was called, and on a two hours notice the chapel was jammed—and enthusiastic! Mr. Brown explained in detail what had already passed—we all knew it by heart—and said that he would not take the next step he deemed best without the approval of the student body. That our track men and Berkeley's had been at great expence of time, labor, & money, and both were anxious for the frays which unless settled that day (yesterday) could not take place. That it would be impossible for Stanford to recede from this position she had been forced into in defence and therefore could not offer to confer with Berkeley as to a settlement of the pending issues.

But, we are so anxious to meet Berkeley on the field, that we will agree to do so, under any conditions the Berkeley faculty may decide.

(I fear I can't make the distinction there very great—but it was. It was magnificent, magnanimous way almost anything, and calculated to make UC faculty & students see themselves thro' the small end of the magnifying glass.)

Everybody howled. Then Dr Angell was called for. Expressed his entire satisfaction with the way everything had gone, with the way Stanford's students could take care of themselves, particularly of the way Dave Brown could take care of them and approved of the present solution. (Interrupted with applause thro' out) Various others were called on for speeches. Fickert, Dole, etc. Then a motion was made approving of all Mr. Brown had done and was about to do. Zion of course opposed it, and wished to strike out the latter clause. But it was carried unanimously and enthusiastically—you have not an idea of it—(but of course you are a part of Stanford yet. A telegram was immediately sent to Berkeley—and—the joke—the faculty committee which had hitherto sat on its dignity and a—no one knows what else—proceeded to a thorough investigation, and decided Stanford had been right on both points!

That was Wednesday night. A big force of men have to get to work on the track, and in two days put it in the shape expected in a week. Saturday we meet, and before you read this, you will have seen by the papers that we have beaten.

That is a long rigmarole to write you. But you ought to be interested in it merely as an example of intercollegiate diplomacy, and I think that one good view of us at an exciting a critical moment, ought to make us nearer you than any amount of chit chat gossip.

Thats why I told it at such length dear. And I was right at the heart of it all, and you can imagine how concerned. If Mr. Winship had gotten a momentary glimpse of my state of mind he would have found it doing something more than "purring."

But it is "purry" time now, so come on and go to bed dearest.

After his reelection defeat in 1912, William Taft taught law at the Yale University Law School and traveled around the country giving lectures. In this letter to Helen, William reports on a trip to the "Negro" school, Hampton Normal and Agricultural Institute in Virginia.

Office of the Principal,
The Hampton Normal
and Agricultural Institute,
Hampton, Virginia April 24th 1914

My darling Nellie.

I spent a good night last night. The Fissells have made me very comfortable. They have a most comfortable house. There are a lot of bright women Bostonian and southern as well as interesting men. Kelsay is here but will not go back with me on the boat because he must be in Boston tomorrow morning. If I could be quiet I think this toe of mine would grow better. A colored trained nurse is waiting for me now to dress it. Mrs. Judge Lowell is here and so is Miss Paine a sister of that stiff clergyman in New Haven. They are both bright and taste of Cambridge and Boston. Dr. Peabody whom we heard preach a few weeks ago is here too. I like him.

I go back to Washington tonight. If my foot is better I shall stay on at the dinner tomorrow night. If not, I shall wait only a few hours and try to reach New Haven tomorrow night I'll telegraph.

I spoke last night on the Mexican War. I suppose I must say something at Commencement this afternoon at Commencement. I have just signed 200 diplomas. I was made Pres. of the Board yesterday. But the nurse.

Lovingly yours Will

*L*yndon Johnson was studying law at Georgetown University and working as an aide to a Texas congressman when he exchanged these letters with his future wife.

[September 17, 1934]

Dear Monday Nite

This time last week you and I were riding along on our way to Marshall. It seems <u>ages</u> and yet its so vividly remembered it seems only an hour ago.

The Delco has pftt (that's no word—only one of Mr. Winchell's expressions) so I'm sitting here by a kerosene lamp and a candle. And Feeling like one on the last outposts of civilization. When I come up the stairs the lamp makes the queerest shadows in the corners and I am very scared! (I wish for you more than ever then.)

Today I discovered two of Mother's old carved stone flower pots, muchly covered with dirt and accumulation of years of debris. So I scrubbed them up until they're nice and new and now I'm going to put soil in them and plant lavendar hyacinths and red tulips! Its more fun making things look prettier and renovating old things! Also I learn quite a lot.

What courses are you taking dear? And how long do you go to school? And whenever do you <u>play</u>, Lyndon? There isn't any time left for you to, you poor lamb. But I <u>adore</u> you for being so ambitious and dynamic!

Laura was there when I talked to you last night. I, of course, got there about a half hour ahead of time and we had a long talk–the first time I've seen anyone besides Dorris since getting home. She (Laura) was as thrilled as I over your call! (Nobody in Marshall knows you can talk that far over the phone—especially just for fun and not business).

It <u>was</u> so darling to hear your voice, right up close. Also it was nice because Saturday I was feeling quite low and then all of a sudden I'd remember I had something to look forward to Sunday night. And I would feel happy!

Daddy expressed himself about you the other night and <u>was</u> I surprised. I mean because he is so seldom enthusiastic about any of the young men I bring around. And he thinks very highly of you! I surely was glad. He made several complimentary remarks, quite of his own volition, and I just sat up there and grinned to myself.

I must write Gene. And do you likewise, love, when you've ever time! Goodnite, dear dear Lyndon. Bird

---

LYNDON B. JOHNSON
TO
LADY BIRD TAYLOR

House of Representatives.
Washington, D.C.
Saturday Noon [October 1934]

My dear

This morning in the early mail the postman brought me your letter written Wednesday Night. It made me very happy—but the gem was written Tuesday night. I stopped by the hotel on my way to school and it was waiting for me. I read it several times before I finally retired at two this morning.

Upon reflection I thought it best not to send you the long letter I referred to which outlined the problems which were giving me Concern. It had entirely too much in it about an unpleasant subject—at least unpleasant in l934. Then, too, later developments would make all I said sound very silly. I am about ready to conclude that my letters are not nearly as persuasive and appealing as they should be. Consequently it is frequently that I hesitate to write all I think or all that I want to say.

But when I think of our unsatisfactory telephone conversations, coupled with the expense that "person to person calls" involve, I'm reluctant to blame it all on my letters.

My Senators haven't written since I talked to them and I know very little that you would be interested in that I haven't told you. Welly may call tonight. A letter from the University today tells me that my credits have been approved and the schedule worked out for me is satisfactory to them. Evidently some of the courses I'm taking here are not offered at Texas the second semester but they state I can get them in the summer. I'm very, very anxious to hear something further before the end of another week. It appears that my entrance at Texas takes my first semester work here for granted, hence I probably won't leave here until late in January. If I can do the job, exist and finish as they have planned purely from the economical aspect it will be well worth the change. Only I want a lot of things more than <u>surplus cash</u>.

About the financial angle, dear, I'm sure the salary will be some less than I'm making here but much more when the buying power is taken into consideration. It isn't enough for the two of us tho' and the salary following graduation won't be. It is bad to fall in love with a girl who had had some comforts and advantages but it is worse than <u>bad</u> to attempt to make her happy with a nominal salary after marriage. I haven't learned that from marriage but took a few lessons from a good teacher when I was only a youngster. No, honey, I haven't over estimated what My Bird should have.

Now, dear, a minute on what I'm suppose to take back—'taken at the flood' etc. I'm sure we care just as much as we did a few weeks ago. What I meant to convey in that statement was not "that I was glad to have the golden opportunity gone and over with" but to explain in some way that our approaches to questions were very different, thus creating a question in our minds as to the possibility of a future <u>for each other</u>. That sentence is somewhat involved—this may make it easier—I see something <u>I know I want</u>. I <u>immediately exert efforts</u> to get it. I <u>do</u> or <u>don't</u> but I <u>try</u> and do my best. You see something you <u>might</u> want. You tear it to pieces in an effort to determine if you <u>should</u> want it. Then you wonder <u>why</u> you want it, and conclude that <u>maybe</u> the desire isn't an "everlasting" one and that the "sane" thing to do is to wait a year or so, and then if you still want it to decide at that time Whether or not you <u>should</u> make an effort to get it. It may be love—it may be a new job, or it might be the purchase of a new car. I try to be reasonably deliberate. I try to Keep my feet on the ground. I Keep from going off half-Cocked, because I realize the personal effect in all such decisions. "We can make our own floods and tides" but it wouldn't be best for me to decide the way out— then wait a year or two for you to <u>deliberate</u>, only to find we had been Caught in the meantime.

A letter from Mother and Josepa this Morning. Mothers says— "How is the lady-love? Have you heard from her this week? I am sure she writes clever and lovely letters; doesn't she? How old is she? All the details are of interest to your Mother who loves you so dearly." And I'm very glad she too loves you. Outside of your love I want no one to care for me—to admire and respect me quite as much as I do your father. He has done so much for you, that you couldn't disappoint him at this stage of life.

The show last night didn't get over with me. I was quite disgusted with it. We drove to the apartment about eleven and Helen talked until almost two. At my insistence she told me all about her father. He will retire next year from the N.Y. Court of Appeals— having reached the age limit. Roosevelt appointed him to this the highest court in N.Y. just before he finished his term as governor. Last year I met Helen's Mother and we spent several interesting evenings together. The Mother has now asked Helen to have me visit them 'Xmas and if I'm here I'm going by to spend a day or two. One should get an inspiration from just a few hours around such a scholar.

If I followed my natural impulses tonight I would stay in my room and read until it was time to Call you—then I would have a long sweet talk with my love—read some more—get anxious to leave immediately for Texas—then <u>go go</u>—go to bed—But I'll probably approach this question cautiously—with deliberation— think about the extravagance involved—and finally at the last minute run out to the Shoreham for a few hours dancing with an incident expenditure of several telephone calls—only to wake up late in the morning to start on our Sunday picnic in Va.

I shall be so anxious to receive the pictures and <u>thanks</u> for the cotton dress—I've almost forgotten how you look in one—'cause two months represents years to me.

Your Wednesday night letter tells me "If there isn't (a letter)—perhaps I'd better stop writing so <u>much</u> and <u>often.</u>" You of course Know what your letters mean to me, and altho' I live from one day to another for them, I realize such a course would only be followed after due reflection and a careful analysis upon the part of the sweetest most deliberate little girl in all the world.

All my love, Lyndon Baines

WOODROW WILSON AND HIS FIRST WIFE,
ELLEN LOUISE AXSON WILSON, DURING HIS CAMPAIGN
FOR GOVERNOR OF NEW JERSEY IN 1910.

CHAPTER 6

SORROW
AND CONSOLATION

"Our little one breathed out her life."
—Lucretia Garfield to James Garfield,
December 6, 1863

"My poor stricken darling!"
—Woodrow Wilson to Ellen Axson,
June 1, 1884

"The wound is a trivial one."
—Theodore Roosevelt to Edith Roosevelt,
October 14, 1912

DEATH and illness were no strangers to presidential families. Often, the emotional load was carried chiefly by the first lady, with both her sorrow and the consolation experienced chiefly in public. Fear, sorrow, anger, and yes, sometimes relief and joy are among the range of emotions displayed in this collection of letters and messages.

ABIGAIL ADAMS
TO
JOHN ADAMS

*A*bigail Adams and her husband, who was then in Philadelphia as a member of the Continental Congress, exchanged these frank, sorrowful letters shortly after the still-birth of a daughter.

July 16 1777

Join with me my dearest Friend in Gratitude to Heaven, that a life I know you value, has been spaired and carried into Distress and danger altho the dear Infant is numbered with its ancestors.

My apprehensions with regard to it were well founded. Tho my Friends would have fain perswaded me that the Spleen the Vapours had taken hold of me I was as perfectly sensible of its discease as I ever before was of its existence. I was also aware of the danger which awaited me; and which tho my suffering were great thanks be to Heaven I have been supported through, and would silently submit to its dispensations in the loss of a sweet daughter; it appeard to be a very fine Babe, and as it never opened its Eyes in this world it lookd as tho they were only closed for sleep. The circumstances which put an end to its existence, was evident upon its birth, but at this distance and in a Letter which may possibly fall into the Hands of some unfealing Ruffian I must omit particuliars. Suffice it to say that it was not oweing to any injury which I had sustaind, nor could any care of mine have prevented it.

My Heart was much set upon a Daughter. I had had a strong perswasion that my desire would be granted me. It was—but to shew me the uncertainty of all sublinary enjoyments cut of e'er I could call it mine. No one was so much affected with the loss of it as its Sister who mournd in tears for Hours. I have so much cause for thankfulness amidst my sorrow, that I would not entertain a repineing thought. So short sighted and so little a way can we look into futurity that we ought patiently to submit to the dispensation of Heaven.

I am so comfortable that I am amaizd at myself, after what I have suffrd I did not expect to rise from my Bed for many days. This is but the 5th day and I have set up some Hours.

I However feel myself weakend by this exertion, yet I could not refrain the temptation of writing with my own Hand to you.

Adieu dearest of Friends adieu. Yours most affectionately.

JOHN ADAMS
TO
ABIGAIL ADAMS

Philadelphia July 28. 1777

My dearest Friend

Never in my whole Life, was my Heart affected with such Emotions and Sensations, as were this Day occasioned by your Letters of the 9.10.11. and 16 July. Devoutly do I return Thanks to God, whose kind Providence has preserved to me a Life that is dearer to me than all other Blessings in this World. Most fervently do I pray, for a Continuance of his Goodness in the compleat Restoration of my best Friend to perfect Health.

Is it not unaccountable, that one should feel so strong an Affection for an Infant, that one has never seen, nor shall see? Yet I must confess to you, the Loss of this sweet little Girl, has most tenderly and sensibly affected me. I feel a Grief and Mortification, that is heightened tho it is not wholly occasioned, by my Sympathy with the Mother. My dear little Nabbys tears are sweetly becoming her generous Tenderness and sensibility of Nature. They are Arguments too of her good sense and Discretion.

THOMAS JEFFERSON, WHOSE WIFE MARTHA DIED IN 1782
AFTER HER SIXTH PREGNANCY IN TEN YEARS, STANDS HOLDING THE
DECLARATION OF INDEPENDENCE, WHICH HE DRAFTED IN 1776.

*L*ouisa had given birth to a stillborn son less than a week before she wrote this moving letter to her husband, who had returned to Boston from Washington to deliver a series of lectures at Harvard College.

Washington June 29 [1806]

My very best friend

My health continues to mend rappidly and the prospect of soon rejoining you and my little darlings supports my spirits and enables me to bear the dreadful stroke that has befallen me with more fortitude than otherwise I fear I should have done.

I can safely assure you that this misfortune was not caused by any imprudence on my part. Dr. Weem is satisfied that the Child had been subject to violent convulsions sometime before he died and had he lived the probability is that he woud have been all his life subject to fitts much as I suffer for the loss of this lovely Infant. I could not desire its life upon terms so painful.

I am in the greatest anxiety to hear from you two days have passed over the accustomed time and I feel a degree of terror lest some sickness or accident should have prevented your writing. Oh my best beloved friend should any thing have happen'd to you or the Children I do not think I could live over it my spirits are very weak and my frame more so they tell me it is fortunate I have no child to Nurse.

John Randolph has challenged T. M. Randolph for his speech in the house which was supposed to be made up and they are to fight shortly the P. has made such arrangements as to be able to quit Washington as soon as the duel takes place. We learn this from Mr. & Mrs. <u>Mad</u>. therefore you may rely on the truth of it.

A horrid circumstance took place here yesterday Mr. Mason sometime ago whipped one of his negroes whom he had the greatest confidence in the man more to be revenged and before day break yesterday morning when the family were all asleep at their house on the Island which you know to be of wood laid fire at each end of the roof of a sort of wide passage which forms the Centre of the building and communicates with each wing the Centre and one of the wings were entirely consumed and the whole family would have been destroyed had the wretch not been betrayed by one of the Women Servants, he was immediately secured by the Counstables his hands tied and put into a Boat to be convey'd to Prison he however threw himself overboard and was drown'd before any assistance could be obtain'd his body was found late in the evening.

Adieu my best friend Mr. & Mrs. Cranch have been to see me she looks very well and tells me Mrs. T. B. Adams expects to be confined every day. I most sincerely wish she may be more fortunate than I have been Carolina will accompany...and I shall take the opportunity...with Dr. May or Mrs. Winn who I understand are going shortly Kiss my lovely boy a hundred times for me and remember me to all the family and believe every thing that is tender and affection from her whose delight is to sign herself your grateful and sincerely attached Wife. L. C. Adams

---

JOHN   QUINCY   ADAMS

TO

LOUISA   CATHERINE   ADAMS

---

*J*ohn Quincy Adams wrote this reply to an unfound note of June 22 reporting the stillborn birth of a child to his wife, Louisa, who had remained in Washington because of her pregnancy.

Cambridge 2 July 1806.

My dearest Louisa

On going yesterday into Boston, I received Mrs. Hellen's letter of the 22d of last Month, with the few lines which I am afraid you must have cruelly suffered in writing; and also yours of the 24th which at least administered the consolation of knowing that you were as well as you could expect. My great concern is that in the tender effort you made when thus severely ill to write, was too great an exertion for your strength and I rejoyced in the determination express'd in your last of omitting to write again for several days. I have endeavoured to gather resignation under

JOHN QUINCY ADAMS TOOK TIME OUT FROM THE FIRST YEAR
OF HIS PRESIDENCY TO POSE FOR POSTERITY.

the hand of Heaven in this Calamity, and with you I turn my thoughts to the inexpressible blessings yet left us in our remaining children.

You will see by my last that I had first received yours of the 23rd which gave me the first Intelligence of our Misfortune. And that I had anticipated your idea of coming on as soon as your health and strength will permit. But let me conjure you not to hasten too much your departure. If by the beginning of August you are able to travel, you may reach this by the twentieth, and I will have a house here ready to receive you. If Dr. May or Mrs. Winn comes on you will have the advantage of a companion the whole way. But if only to New York, I will meet you there should it be possible to absent myself from this place.

Give my best thanks to Mr. Hellen for his kind letter, and his friendly consolations. Heaven bless all our friends for their affectionate attention to you in the day of your distress, and grant a speedy restoration of perfect health to you—and of you to the arms of your ever affectionate husband. John Quincy Adams

---

LUCRETIA GARFIELD
TO
JAMES GARFIELD

---

*J*ames Garfield, who had resigned as a Union Army general after being elected to the U.S. Congress, had just returned to Washington when he and his wife exchanged emotional letters about the death of their young daughter, Eliza (Trot) Garfield, just weeks after the birth of a son, Harry.

Hiram, December 6, 1863.

My Dear Precious Husband:

I have just come from kneeling beside the bed where our little one breathed out her life. I have asked of Our Father a more perfect resignation of spirit to this great sorrow which has fallen upon our lives so heavily, and I hope that He has given it to me—to us both. I hope, dear Jamie, that you are trying to look up, through tears though it be, to our Saviour's face and from His words of comfort, gathering peace to your soul, and a larger strength to do well the work of life.

These words have been much in my heart today: "The Father chastenth whom He loveth," and the thought has come to me that not only has He honored us in giving us to keep a while a little nature so pure and noble but that he also loves us so well that He will make surer our clinging to Him by taking our cherished one to Himself, that where our treasure is, there may our hearts be also. These have been, Oh, such sad strange days that I fear there have been in my heart questionings and doubts which were almost wrong; but I hope God is lifting my spirit out from the shadow and that I am gaining a hold on a larger truer life, and I trust it so with you, my dear one. Surely we can be thankful for this at least that we have come to be so much nearer and dearer to each other, that our love has been made so perfect through this great suffering. I feel that we need each other now as we have never before, and that we can the most truly live when near each other. Still I submit to whatever seems best and will try patiently and faithfully "to labor and to wait." My dear Jamie, you do not know the large place you won in my heart by your gentle care and attention when at home. It surprised me and made me love you so tenderly to see you taking care of our little girl, and watching beside her so gently; and so much dearer is our home now for the notice and care you took of it. I have almost feared that your heart was so saddened by the loss of our darling that you would dread to return here, and that our home would have little attraction for you now; but I hope it is not so. To me it is now a holy place, and I want it to be so to you. I do not feel like writing more now; but we will write to each other very often and live very near each. I did not write yesterday as I promised since a letter would not go until tomorrow.

That you may be blessed and kept good and noble and true is the prayer of your loving trusting little wife, Crete

P.S. Commencing with the 13th verse of 1st Thessalonians, 4th Chapt. Read through to the close of the Epistle. I find there much to comfort and strengthen my heart. Crete

---

J A M E S   G A R F I E L D
T O
L U C R E T I A   G A R F I E L D

Washington, Dec. 13, 1863

My Precious Crete:

Your dear noble letter of the 8th inst. came to me yesterday. It was balm to my heart, and it made me feel more than ever before how noble and true you are. Pray for me, dearest, that my heart may, like yours, become more resigned and see the hand of our good Father in this great sorrow. It is a lovely day, after a cold and cheerless morning of storm. I ought to be cheerful and happy as are the sun and the sky, and though your brave words have made me calmer and stronger, I still struggle with my grief and think of our precious darling with such a yearning agony of heartbreak that at times it seems as though I could not endure it. I have read twice over this morning the passage you told me of from Thessalonians. It is touchingly tender and hopeful. I would that my heart could rest upon it as I when a child rested in my mother's words. I pray that my faith may grow stronger. I try to be hopeful but Tennyson speaks for me when he says.

> "Yet in these ears till hearing dies,
> One set slow bell will ever toll
> The passing of the sweetest soul
> That ever looked with human eyes."

How her image and little nature has grown upon me since she is gone. "Death has made His darkness beautiful with her." you must read "In memoriam." it really seems as if it were written for us. Only a change of gender is needed to make it seem direct and real. I hope you have gotten my letters by this time. They have all been very hurried, but I know you will appreciate something of the amount of my work and will forgive my meagerness in what I write. Really, Dearest, I wish you would think whether you cannot manage to come back with me after the Holidays, if I return home then as I now hope to. It really does not seem as though I could stay here all this lonely winter. We will talk of it when I come. Do not fear that I will not love our home. It is more sacred to me than ever. I did for a little while think I could not live in it any more, but I think differently now. Tell me about the little boy. Is he well? How is your own health now? I hope you are being very careful and getting strong again. I sent you a draft the other day: did it reach you? Give my love to Mother and all the family. I am still stopping at the corner of N.Y. Avenue and 13th St. and logging away at the letters.

With all my heart, I am ever, your own James.

RUTHERFORD B. HAYES
TO
LUCY WEBB HAYES

---

*T*he assassination of President Lincoln was the subject of these two letters exchanged by Rutherford B. Hayes and his wife.

New Creek West Va.
16th April (Sunday) 1865

Dearest

When I heard first yesterday morning of the awful tragedy at Washington I was pained and shocked to a degree I have never before experienced. I got on to the cars, then just starting, and rode down to Cumberland. The probable consequences, or rather the possible results in their worst imaginable form, were presented to my mind one after the other, until I really began to feel that here was a calamity so extensive that in no direction could be found any, the slightest glimmer of consolation. The Nation's great joy turned suddenly to a still greater sorrow. A ruler tested and found in every way and in every way found equal to the occasion to be exchanged for a new man whose ill omened beginning made the Nation hang its head. Lincoln for Johnson. The work of reconstruction requiring so much statesmanship just begun. The calamity to Mr. Lincoln, in a personal point of view, so uncalled for, a fate so undeserved, so unprovoked. The probable effect upon the future of public men in this country, the necessity for guards, our ways to be assimilated to those of the despotism of the old world and I would find my mind filled only with images of evil and calamity until I felt a sinking of heart hardly equalled by that which oppressed us all when the defeat of our Army at Manassas almost crushed the Nation. But slowly, as in all cases of great affliction, one comes to feel that it is not all darkness—the catastrophe is so much less happening now than it would have been at any time before since Mr. Lincoln's election—at this period after his first inauguration—at any of the periods of great public depression—during the pendency of the last Presidential Election—at any time before the defeat of Lee—such a calamity might have sealed the Nation's doom. Now the march of events can't be stayed, probably can't be much changed. It is possible that a greater degree of severity in dealing with the Rebellion may be ordered, and <u>that</u> may be for the best. As to Mr. Lincoln's name and fame and memory, all is safe. His firmness, moderation, goodness of heart—his quaint humor, his perfect honesty and directness of purpose, his logic, his modesty, his sound judgment and great wisdom, the contrast between his obscure beginnings and the greatness of his subsequent position and achievements—his tragic death—giving him almost the crown of martyrdom—elevate him to a place in history second to none other of ancient or modern times. His success in his great office—his hold upon the confident and affections of his countrymen, we shall all <u>say</u>, are only second to Washington's. We shall probably <u>feel</u> and <u>think</u> that they are not <u>second</u> even to his.

My mountain expedition is at an end. If I go on any more campaigning, it will be an easy march to occupy some point on the Central Virginia Railroad—Staunton or Charlottesville. I anticipate however an early call of an extra session of Congress. In any event I shall probably not see any more active service.

I enclose my good-bye to my old First Brigade. I now regard the order separating us as not unfortunate. It must have been soon, and could not have been in a better Way.

Direct your letters to this point—2nd Brigade, 1st Division, Department West Virginia.

Love to all.
Affectionately, R

L U C Y   W E B B   H A Y E S
T O
R U T H E R F O R D   B .   H A Y E S

Chillicothe April 17th 1865

Dearest—

From such great joy how soon we were filled with sorrow and grief past utterance I do not know how you will feel—whether Mercy or Justice—will be nearest your heart. I am sick of the endless talk of Forgiveness—taking them back like brothers—we are not savages—that we want revenge—but excuse me for beginning a letter to you in this strain last evening I heard Wm. McClintick talk or speak to a crowded house altogether of Mercy and followed by another Mercy Man—that I felt as most in the house did—that Justice and Mercy should go together. Now don't say to me Ruddy that I ought not to write so—but I will come back to the dear little ones.

Birchie is devouring Gulliver—Webb looks at the pictures—and has bargained with me to read to him. I don't think it will tire you for me to say again that they are good boys at school "boys of good report"—even Webb—last month Birchie again got the

Reward for being best in recitation to his class—no need to speak of his conduct—it does seem to me strange the feeling of confidence I have in him. I would not trust impulsive little Webb—to go after Night to hear a speech from the Court House—but Birch is so much interested in public speaking—that he listens like a Man—and at the conclusion comes home happy and will tell much that has been said.

They are working in their garden it will be very pretty—many of the seeds are coming up—and oh such happy youngsters— that the little Banty hen is setting and so they have enough to make them glad—and withal they often say to me—papa will soon be home—then Webb goes off in some antic our "Pops" as he calls you. Young Rud is pursuing his studies under difficulties—he has been allowed to spade up some of the garden—and feels his importance—but last not least George Cis a splendid boy—I would not have you think it simply his "Mother's Vanity"—We are all well—Aunt Phebe is better than when I last wrote. Uncle Scott about as usual. I have not seen him since this terrible blow to the Nation. All are well at Uncle Moses. John has been home—he had called to see Mother Hayes—and would not forget to do so while he remained there—he has always had some old person to care for—so that I think it makes him feel more tenderly towards Age.

Birch is very happy with the Illustrated Magazine—at first we thought Uncle Birchard sent it—but after all it was papa thinking of his boys.

Write soon. Where is Joe. Love to him Yours Lu

[P.S.] Mother don't like to have a letter go off—without a special morsel of love sent.

JAMES GARFIELD
TO
LUCRETIA GARFIELD

*J*ames Garfield, then a U.S. congressman, was in New York on private business, when he heard the news of Lincoln's assassination. When he wrote of "our great sorrow" to Lucretia, there was no way that they could know that he would himself be assassinated in a little more than sixteen years.

> Metropolitan Hotel, New York.
> April 17, 1865.

Dearest Crete:

My heart is so broken with our great national loss that I can hardly think or write or speak. I reached here Friday night at midnight and in the morning heard the shocking news. Places of business have been closed. Nothing is in the heart of anyone but our great sorrow. Saturday night I went out to Lewisboro and spent Sunday at Rebecca's. Her Mother is just able to sit up part of the day, but I fear will never be well. I came back early this morning, but such is the deep grief and sorrow that no one seems capable of doing any business. The day is nearly gone and I have as yet done nothing. If I could see the men with whom I desire to transact in reference to land and other matters, I could leave for home In a day or two. When I can now leave I don't know. I may have to go to Washington tomorrow to attend the funeral. If so, it will very badly break in upon my plans. I am sick at heart and feel it to be almost like sacrilege to talk of money or business now. More than ever before in my life I want to be at home with you. Could I have you and our precious boy in my arms I could almost let the world and its work go without a thought or a care for them. From present appearances I shall not start for Cal. before the 1st of May. I want you to know that there are not the dangers attending the journey that you have supposed. Mr. Stanton tells me that the route is well guarded by troops, and Warren Leland, one of the proprietors of this Hotel, with whom I have talked an hour or two today, has lately come across the plains and says the route is very safe, and the journey a pleasant one. Your dear good letter was found awaiting me on my arrival here. It came close to my heart with its loving tenderness and found a formed quick and joyful response. I thank God every day for the tender love with which He has filled our hearts, and I trust we shall grow nearer and dearer to each other as we approach the confines of the silent land. Dearest wife, with all my heart I long to be with you now as the sun is setting and tell you in words and kisses of my love. I shall not fail, I think, to be home before the week closes. Kiss Darling Harry again and again for his papa. Your dream had no basis in reality. Ever your own James.

E L L E N   L O U I S E   A X S O N
T O
W O O D R O W   W I L S O N

---

*E*llen Axson wrote this emotional letter to Woodrow Wilson just after her father's death. In spite of her grief, she was clearly prepared to move on.

Rome June 2/84

My darling Woodrow,

I suppose you have, ere this, received Minnie's note of Thursday, and so know of the new sorrow which has fallen upon us. Yet, it is even so:—my dear father passed quickly away on Wednesday night. He seems to have sunk rapidly at the last; we had not warning whatever except that terrible letter to Uncle Will, which was indeed the best preparation for this which we could have had. God has been very merciful to him. He <u>has</u> "been pleased to deliver him." He has "made haste to help him." Yet I don't know that it made it much easier for me. One may think they have no hope but when death ends all they discover that they had. And it seems to me that the terrible sense of desolation—of emptiness of heart and hands,—of a part of one's self having been forever torn away, is all the greater when that which we have lost has been an ever-present, anxious, sorrowful thought, an all-engrossing care. And then it is so hard, so hard, that people should think and say—to me too—that "it is better so"! Oh my dear, dear, father, the best, the purest, truest man I ever knew: so useful too! One who lived so well, and did his work so faithfully and earnestly,—better that <u>he</u> should die than live! What an end to such a life! What a dreadful, hopeless tragedy it would seem, if we did not know that his true life has but begun; that the other is a probation, which, seen in God's light, is "but for a moment" and is followed by "a far more exceeding and eternal weight of glory."

June 3rd

You see, I am not as brave as I thought I was, dearest. I thought that I would heed the counsels of my friends, break through my old reserve on such matters, and to you, though to you alone, "give sorrow words"; but I could not bear it. I will not try again today.

I am so <u>glad</u>, so very glad, and <u>proud</u>, my darling, that you have taken the scholarship. No indeed, I won't scold about not having heard of it before, for it is too delightful to receive it as a complete surprise. What a <u>splendid</u> man, you are, to be sure! What an "extra-special" man! You bring forward such various proofs of that fact, and in such rapid succession, that you quite take my breath away. I am struck dumb with awe. How long do you stay at the University? How gratifying that you should have been the choice of both professors and students! Certainly, your year in Baltimore has been a complete triumph, or rather a series of triumphs. My darling, are you <u>very sure</u> that you are wise to think of going elsewhere next year? Of course I can't pretend to judge in the matter, since I can't know all the circumstances, but the first thought which strikes me, and outsiders too, in view of the honours you have won, is that it would be "<u>such</u> a pity" for you to give them all up so soon, before you have reaped the advantages. You have made a place for yourself there,—have gained distinction. Is it well for you to drop out of it <u>now</u>, and go so far away, where you would be no more a living <u>presence</u>, but only a <u>voice</u>?—not that even—only the echo of a voice. In short, won't you win your laurels sooner,—wont you find it easier to gain your proper place in the literary world, if you remain longer in that great centre of thought and work? Then you say that if you leave, you must resign your work with Dr. Ely; and it seems to me that <u>that too is a pity</u>. Would not that work be a great advantage to you?—a very valuable introduction to the general public? That is just the sort of fact, you know, by which it (the general public!) Is most easily influenced,—most profoundly impressed. And again if you remain, you will have <u>all</u> your time for study, and for the work you like best, and which is of the first importance, whereas if you went away, you would be for a time almost engrossed by other things, "getting into harness," adjusting yourself to your new position, to the duties of a professor. I fear you would find at first little time for your own special work,—unless you overdid it all and half killed yourself. And that would be another danger of the situation. I know what you have said, that you have or <u>may</u> have a good opening, and that if you let it pass, you may not find another just when you want it. But perhaps there is no great danger of that. And what if you are obliged to wait, you can <u>afford</u> to wait if you have scholarships, &c. and you will have all the more time for uninterruped work and study.

I hope you will pardon my saying so much on matters which I probably know nothing about; but then I <u>must</u> say how the situation strikes me. And I am <u>so</u> anxious that you should decide on that course which will be wisest "in the long run." And especially that you should be unbiased in your decision by any considerations in which I am involved. But I am sure it is unnecessary for me to say that. <u>Of course</u> you can't be so weak as to refuse to see what is <u>best</u> to be done and to <u>do</u> it, simply because there is something else which as it happens you would <u>like</u> to do, but which can <u>just as well</u> wait. Indeed you <u>must</u> leave me out, in forming your judgement, for I have now a positive offer of a place as art teacher which I must decide upon in a few days. And you know I told you how I felt about it, and that I wouldn't be justified in letting things drift.

I am <u>so</u> sorry, and disappointed, to learn that your dear mother is still not strong. I wish you could devise some change—some plan—that would build her up. Give my warm love to her, and to your father and Josie, and keep for yourself "just as much as you want." My darling! You are indeed now "all the world to me." As ever Your own Ellie

---

EDITH ROOSEVELT
TO
THEODORE ROOSEVELT

---

*P*resident William McKinley had been fatally wounded by Leon F. Czolgosz in Buffalo, New York, the day before Edith Roosevelt sent the first of these two telegrams to her husband, who was vacationing at Tahawus, New York, in the Adirondacks. He soon rushed to the president's bedside in Buffalo.

Tahawus, N.Y.
Sept. 7, 1901
Vice Prest.
Deeply grieve for president. Children all well and happy we leave here fourteenth.

Tahawus, N.Y.
Sept. 8th, 1901
Vice President Roosevelt:
Give Mrs McKinley my congratulations on good report of Presidents condition. Shall I go to you. Edith Roosevelt

THEODORE ROOSEVELT
TO
EDITH ROOSEVELT

*T*heodore Roosevelt was shot in Milwaukee by John N. Schrank during a campaign speech. He finished the speech before sending this telegram to his wife from the hospital emergency room. Although his message seems anything but overwrought, Edith, no doubt, had a much more emotional reaction.

October 14, 1912.
Milwaukee

Am in excellent shape. Made an hour and a half speech. The wound is a trivial one. I think they will find that it merely glanced on a rib and went somewhere into a cavity of the body; it certainly did not touch a lung and isn't a particle more serious than one of the injuries any of the boys used continually to be having. Am at the Emergency Hospital at the moment, but anticipate going right on with my engagements. My voice seems to be in good shape. Best love to Ethel.

FIRST LADY GRACE ANNA GOODHUE COOLIDGE, A
STAUNCH SUPPORTER OF THE RED CROSS, ENROLLS HER
HUSBAND IN THE ORGANIZATION ON OCTOBER 29, 1925.

CHAPTER 7

HEALTH AND
CONCERN

~◡

"Quiet is what I need."
—William H. Taft to Helen Taft,
April 30, 1924

"Please don't think I am sick."
—Dwight Eisenhower to Mamie Eisenhower,
September 8, 1943

ALTHOUGH health is normally considered a personal matter, it has always been a public issue for presidents and their wives, from public concern over George Washington's anthrax-infected leg to today's public bulletins about the president's annual check-up. Like all people who are frequently separated, health—good or bad—is a major topic of concern in these messages, which express a broad range of emotions.

DOLLEY MADISON
TO
JAMES MADISON

𝓗ere, Dolley Madison explained an injury to her knee that had prevented her from accompanying the Secretary of State back to Washington, D.C., from Philadelphia, where they had gone to visit her relatives and friends.

23d; October 1805

A few hours only have passed since you left me my beloved, and I find nothing can releave the oppression of my mind but speaking to you in this only way.

The Doctor called before you had gone far and with an air of sympathy wished you could see how much better the knee appeared—I could only speak to assure him it felt better—Betsey Pemberton and Amy are sitting beside me and seem to respect the grief they know I feel, at even a short seperation from one who is all to me—I shall be better when Peter returns, not that any length of time could lessen my just regret, but an assurance that you are well and easy will contribute to make me so. I have sent the books and note to Mrs. Dallas—B. Pemberton puts on your hat to divert me, but I cannot look at her.

24th: of October. What a sad day! The watchman announced a cloudy morning at one o'clock, and from that moment I found myself unable to sleep from anxiety for thee my dearest husband—detention cold and accident seem to menace thee! B. Pemberton who lay beside me administered three or four drops of Laudinum, it had some effect before the Dr. came, who pronouced a favorable opinion on the knee.

Yesterday the Miss Gibbons called upon me, in the evening Mrs. Dallas and daughter with Mrs. Stuart and Nancy Pemberton. Every one is kind and attentive.

25th: This clear cold morning will favour your journey and

enliven the feelings of my darling! I have nothing new to tell you—Betsey and myself sleep quietly together and the knee is mending. I eat very little and sit precisely as you left me. The doctor during his very short visits, talks of you, he says he regards you more than any man he ever knew and nothing could please him so much as passing his life near you—sentiments so congenial with one's own, and in <u>such cases</u>, like dew drops on flowers, exhilarate as they fall! The Governor, I hear, has arrived and is elated with his good fortune. General Moreau is expected in town in a few days, to partake of a grand dinner the citizens are about to give him.

Adieu, my beloved, our hearts understand each other. In fond affection thine

Dolley P. Madison

LOUISA CATHERINE ADAMS
TO
JOHN QUINCY ADAMS

---

*I*n April 1814, Louisa Adams had been left in St. Petersburg, Russia, when her husband was recalled to the Netherlands to negotiate the treaty to end the war with Great Britain. She soon suffered a severe attack of "fainting fits."

St. Petersburg May 8. 1814

Yesterday morning I received a few lines from you dated from Heglecht. I am extremely happy the accident was so trifling, and hope your servant was successful in his search.

I wrote you the day after you left us, but I fear you will not receive my letter at Reval. Since your departure there has arrived a large number of dispatches among which was one brought by Mr. Lewis's brother who came in the Frigate which conveyed the Ministers to Gottenburg. they arrived on the 11th of April. Mr. Hall enclosed several packages the covers of which were very much

worn in coming by the Mail. I took the liberty of opening the out-side imagining they might contain <u>letters for me</u> but was entirely disappointed. I immediately put them into the hands of Mr. Smith and can assure you that I did not read one word of the letters which were enclosed unsealed. you will I am sure pardon the lib-erty, and make allowance for my great anxiety to hear from my family and Children. Mr. Smith intends serving partly by Mr. Per-son and partly by Mr. Norman as there are too many to trouble one Gentleman with. We have heard of the appointment of Mr. Hughes but not a word of Mr. Harris excepting that he went to England with the Grand Dutchess.

I have been very sick. I had been very unwell from the day you left us and on Thursday last I was siezed almost instantaneously with one of those deadly fainting fits, which I used to be subject to when I was first married it left me so weak I was confined to my bed untile to day owing to its having produced my old com-plaint to a great degree. I am however much better and hope to be quite well in a few days.

I am endeavouring to prevail on Charles to write you but he has got the toothache so bad that I fear I shall not prove successful.

I enclose this for Mr. Spyer at Stockholm. we are rejoiced at the reappointment of Mr. Galatin to whom I beg you will pres-ent my best respects. We all unite in affectionate wishes for your welfare and success on which you are almost <u>too well</u> assured hangs the soul of your affectionate wife. L. C. Adams

*L*ucy wrote this humorous account of an illness-disrupted celebration of Thanksgiving, followed by a long litany of family illnesses.

Cincinnati Dec. 10th 65

My dearest R

Last night I received your loving letter written on Thanksgiving day—that day we were to have been invited out—but sickness of the cook prevented—so late Wednesday evening I got a turkey and thought we would have a little quiet dinner—at eleven o'clock the girl announced Col Scott and Lady—Will and his new wife—imagine the consternation of your <u>spouse</u>—never capital at getting up a dinner—and then to think no pumpkin or mince pies—no real Thanksgiving doings—but fortunately Aunttie Warren decided on sending a mince pie to the boys. I flatter myself you would not have discovered that she was at all discomposed—a little Strategy made the pie ample. We had a pleasant day—they left on the four o'clock boat—all much pleased with Wills wife.

Mother has been quite sick—but that was before you left—but she has not regained her strength.

All last week I could not write on account of a severe stiff neck—which was quite painful—then last Friday we got the terrible word of dear Uncle Moses death it is so dreadful to think of it all his Kindness and love to me since I was a little girl comes fresh to my mind—it would have been some comfort to me to have seen him once more—poor little Sallie she will miss her father—Aunt Margret has been so feeble this fall—that we have constantly felt anxious about her—but Uncle Moses so healthy and strong—I feel so badly if you were only with me what a comfort—oh darling I never felt your absence as much never longed to have you

FIRST LADY LUCY WARE WEBB HAYES DISPLAYS THE SERENITY
AND PATIENCE THAT SHE WOULD REQUIRE WHILE BALANCING THE
NEEDS OF HER SEVEN CHILDREN AND HER ROLE IN HER
HUSBAND'S MILITARY AND POLITICAL CAREERS.

with me so much. My little boys are dear good children—living affectionate and sympathizing happy—I have had several calls to day—and Georgie more fretful than usual. I have almost failed to get my letter off—then my Ward robe Key has got a spell and will not open so your envelopes are mine.

Good bye darling—so lonely without you—"the days so sad and dreary"—boys all send love—yours only always.

Tuesday evening—this letter for you is fated. I wonder if you will ever receive it—forgot to send it this morning—then calling at Harriet's got to John to direct. I ought to say Wardrobe with envelopes was tightly locked finally got Mr. Cramsy from the corner and getting it open now have those you left.

Georgie has been so fretful this evening that I have not been able to write before. Birch has just received the paper you sent here they come joyous happy and noisy—three bears.

Good bye. Loving

ULYSSES S. GRANT
TO
JULIA GRANT

*P*resident Grant and his wife were concerned with some of the routine dental issues that come with age. They could not know that a fatal bout with throat cancer awaited Ulysses in the near future.

June 15th 1880

Dear Julia

I am sorry you are sick. We can go home to-morrow as well as any other day. But do you not think we had better remain over one day longer? No dispatches received yet from New York.

Probably Buck will not receive the dispatch sent last night until this morning. If he did he could not answer until he could see Harry Honori this am. say eleven o'clock. I have had my tooth pulled. Saw Maj. Lydig who says Tilly got off friday. He placed him in charge of the Executor—fast train—who said they woud be due in Wheeling next morning.—Saturday at 8 am. I have to go to the Dentist between 2 & 3 this pm to have another tooth set in the place to take the place of the one pulled. Yours U. S. G.

JAMES GARFIELD
TO
LUCRETIA GARFIELD

*J*ust the day before his assassination, President Garfield sent this brief telegram to his wife, who was vacationing in Elberon, New Jersey, asking about her health. It was the last written message that the couple would exchange.

Executive Mansion. Wash DC.
July 1, 1881

Mrs. J. A. Garfield

How are you this morning. I hope there is no doubt that you will be well enough for the New England trip. Does Harber go to Ohio with the boys and when does he leave. Answer. J. A. Garfield

---

WILLIAM HOWARD TAFT
TO
HELEN TAFT

---

*H*elen Taft remained in Paris on her European tour, while her husband worked as Chief Justice of the Supreme Court despite suffering from chronic heart palpitations. She wrote a letter of "indignant protest" at the doctor's suggestion that her grossly over-weight husband (reportedly the heaviest president ever) lose weight.

Supreme Court of the United States,
Washington, D.C. April 30, 1924.

My darling Nellie.

This is a rainy day but tomorrow is May day—I don't expect a queen of the May.

I haven't much to say to-day. I am getting along fairly well, but the Doctor thinks that quiet is what I need, and it would be better perhaps if I didn't go to Court, but this is the last week and I must get through. He thinks that everything is progressing favorably. He thinks there is nothing organic the trouble with the heart—that is due to some nervousness that acts on itself. I feel all right and seem to be able to do my work, but of course I am impatient at not being able to be up and about. Under the supervision of the Doctor, I am going to follow a stricter diet than I have heretofore, and see if I can not reduce myself to about 240 pounds—certainly to 250. I think that will help me in the matter of the heart and in the matter of my general comfort. He is going to get me a set of scales so that I can weigh my food. He thinks that the diet that I have given him is rather a lean diet, and that unless I am tempted to eat more than that, it will bring about a gradual reduction. I was able to finish up my work this morning in digesting the cases that we had and getting through my correspondence. Then I had to go to the Capitol to be photographed, in order that my picture should be upon the walls of the Convention at Cleveland with those of other worthies.

I am trying to prevent the passage of a bill aimed at the usefulness of the Federal Courts, which seeks to deny to Federal Judges the power to comment on the evidence as the English judges do. This has always been done in the Federal Courts and has contributed much to their effectiveness. Now these demagogues and damage lawyers are attempting to put the Federal Courts on the basis of the State courts in this regard. The bill has passed the Senate and the Senators yielded supinely, except Reed of Pennsylvania. It has been reported out of the House Judiciary Committee, but I am hoping to hold it over until the next session, in which case I feel fairly confident that I can induce the President to veto it, and I believe his veto would prevent its passage. There is a serious question as to whether it is constitutional, but I would prefer much to have it beaten through a veto that to throw upon the Court the questions of its constitutionality. Congressman Snell, who is the Chairman of the Committee on Rules in the House, promised me that he could postpone the bill. I saw the Chairman of the Judiciary Committee, Mr. Graham, and he thinks he can. I think I shall try and see Nick Longworth, the leader of the House, tomorrow, and with those agreed, I hope the plan of delay can be carried out. It would be a good deal easier to induce the President to veto the bill after the election than before.

I had a letter from Annie Jennings to-day, asking me to give a little opinion to Miss Comegys, urging a kind of Civil Service system in the Mount Vernon Association. Annie intimates that there are quite a number of the sisters who would like to land on the Association kinswomen and kinsmen as employees, and Miss Comegys is anxious to exclude them. I haven't hesitated to aid her in urging a general policy of not allowing favor to control such appointments.

I am very anxious to go to the dinner that Mrs. Grant gives me next Saturday night. The Doctor is a little anxious about it, but says he thinks I can go, but he thinks I ought not to go to Therese's on Sunday. Of course Therese's is not a big dinner— only a Sunday luncheon, and that is not so important.

Annie tells me that Sadie wants to go home to Montreal because her mother is sick, though I believe she does not want to give up the place. Annie is trying to arrange to have Sadie's sister come here to take her place. I have turned the matter over to Annie to do what she thinks wise.

I haven't anything more to-day.

I do hope that you are getting great enjoyment out of the trip but don't over do. Love to Maria. Cooledge beat Johnson in Ohio by six or seven to one. Daugherty was elected a delegate by four to one. He was last in the list of delegates but he was elected. Cooledge carried Mass. overwhelmingly also. Cox beat...in Ohio. Lovingly yours Will

---

CALVIN COOLIDGE
TO
GRACE COOLIDGE

---

*G*race Coolidge was in Northampton, Massachusetts, caring for her very ill mother when Calvin wrote this letter of concern that included some cheery news about life in Washington.

April 7, 1928

My dear Grace:

Your letter of this morning gives a much more encouraging report about your mother than what I had been getting from the doctor. We are having another bright sunny day. The cherry blossoms are coming out. The south grounds are all prepared for Easter Monday and I hope it will be fair weather, so the children can enjoy themselves. Mr. And Mrs. Stearns both seem to be very well.

I do not think I am quite so tired as when you went away. I hope the change, even with all the anxiety, may be helpful to you.

With much love.

---

*I*n the summer of 1937, doctors warned Harry S. Truman that he might have heart problems, so he checked into the U.S. Army and Naval Hospital in Hot Springs, Arkansas, for a thorough exam. The doctors found nothing wrong, and he resumed his place in the U.S. Senate.

Hot Springs, Ark. Sept. 16, 1937

Dear Bess:

Well, this is a gala day. I walked down to the Hotel awhile ago and there were four letters from you, one from Marge and one from Mary. Fred Caufil walked in on me about five minutes after two and we had a fine visit. He'll see you when he gets back. I was glad to get the Lodge letter and J.K.V's too. Of course J.K. can't make his arrangements until he knows what mine are and of course he doesn't Know. Does the St. Louis Mayor want us Sunday or Monday? I thought it was Monday. Caufil wasn't sure. You make him read you the Mayors letter and then I'll wire that St. Louis Lodge.

They photographed my teeth today, and finished my eye examination. This eye man is as good as I've had. The glasses needed a change. The heart photo was analyzed and found all right. One valve is smaller than it should be, but it isn't the one that gives trouble, so they say. The blood test isn't finished, but I've had enough to eat four days hand running anyway. Fred can tell you how grand I'm fixed up. There are four doctors giving me special care, and I'm nearly rested. Will stay as long as I can, though. Wish you'd come down when the notion hits you.

Do you need any money? Love to you both, Harry

*I*n this flirtatious letter from the Mediterranean just before the Allied invasion of Sici-
ly, Ike tried to alleviate Mamie's concern over his health and his unwillingness to allow
her to visit him at his North African headquarters.

September 8, 1943

Dear Mamie:

Don't be shocked to get a typewritten note, but at the moment I
am just too worn down to go over to the office and start writing.
I wanted you to have the enclosed copy of a letter I am writing to
Mr. Norton.

Please don't think I am sick or in any danger of being so, but
this is September 8 and long before you get this note you will have
read in the papers enough that will show you why I happen to be
rather stretched out at the moment.

I am delighted that John had a week end with you and of course
it was all the more fun for you because it was unexpected. It is
also nice to know that you have a prospect of spending a week or
so at Hot Springs. I am sure you will thoroughly enjoy it.

The only reason that I have always suggested meeting me somewhere else in the event I could get away for a day or so is because
I cannot allow, as a matter of policy, wives of soldiers to come
into this theater. Consequently, I couldn't allow you to come
because it would be taking advantage of my own position. But at
one time I thought there was a very fine chance of my being sent
to England for four or five days and I figured it would be a wonderful thing to have you there while I was on the trip. They would
have had a hard time getting any work out of me because I would
have wanted to visit with you all the time.

This minute, in my desk drawer, is a half-finished letter to you.
I will get it finished as soon as I can and send it on. Incidentally,

your letter of September 1 reached me far to the east of Algiers on the 8th. The magazines (Westerns) and the cigars of which you spoke, have not arrived.

As ever your Ike

P.S. Thank you so much for the pictures. They are splendid of both you and John. I must say that you look almost as young as he does. When I come home everybody will assume that I am the father of you both.

PRESIDENT DWIGHT EISENHOWER AND FIRST LADY MAMIE EISENHOWER ENJOY THEIR LOOK AT MAMIE'S WEDDING DRESS WHEN THEY OFFICIALLY HELP TO OPEN THE INAUGURAL GOWN EXHIBIT AT THE SMITHSONIAN INSTITUTION IN 1955.

PRESIDENT FRANKLIN D. ROOSEVELT AND HIS WIFE
ELEANOR READ AND CONVERSE IN A PHOTOGRAPH THEY
USED ON THEIR 1935 CHRISTMAS CARDS.

CHAPTER 8

GOOD WORKS

~𝒞

"*The Distresses of the inhabitants
of Boston are beyond the power of language.*"
—Abigail Adams to John Adams,
May 7, 1775

"*All his family is destroyed.*"
—Andrew Jackson to Rachel Jackson,
November 4, 1813

G O O D works and a concern for helping others have always been
on the agenda for presidents and their wives. Some have responded to society's victims with charity, others with indifference or
self-interest. Public appearance and political impact had always
to be considered, even in charitable matters.

*H*elp for the distressed inhabitants of Boston after the outbreak of fighting between the Americans and the British in 1775 was a major concern of Abigail Adams and her husband, who was serving in the Continental Congress in Philadelphia.

Braintree, May 7 1775

I received by the Deacon two Letters from you this Day from Hartford. I feel a recruit of spirits upon the reception of them, and the comfortable news which they contain. We had not heard any thing from N. Carolina before, and could not help feeling anxious least we should find a defection there, arising from their ancient feuds and animosities, than from any setled ill will in the present contest. But the confirmation of the choise of their Delegates by their assembly leaves not a doubt of their firmness, nor doth the Eye say unto the hand I have no need of thee, the Lord will not cast of his people neither will he forsake his inheritance. Great Events are most certainly in the womb of futurity and if the present chastisement which we experience have a proper influence upon our conduct, the Event will most certainly be in our favour. The Distresses of the inhabitants of Boston are beyond the power of language to describe. There are but very few who are permitted to come out in a day. They delay giving passes, make them wait from hour to hour, and their counsels are not two hours together alike. One day they shall come out with their Effects, the next Day merchandise are not Effects. One day their household furniture is to come out, the next only weareing apparel, and the next Pharoahs heart is hardned, and he refuseth to hearken unto them and will not let the people go. May their deliverance be wrought out for them as it was for the Children of Israel. I do not mean by miracles but by the interposition of heaven in their favour.

They have taken a list of all those who they suppose were concernd in watching the tea, and every other person who they call obnoxious, and they and their Effects are to suffer distruction. Poor Eads escaped out of town last night with one Ayers in a small boat, and was fired upon, but got safe and came up to Braintree to day. His name it seems was upon the black list. I find it impossible to get any body in with any surty of their returning again. I have sent to Walthham but cannot hear any thing of Mr. Cushings Son. I wish you would write me whether Mr. Cushing left any directions what should be done in that affair. I hear that Mr. Bromfield has Letters for you, and young Dr. Jarvis has more, but cannot get them. Pray write me every opportunity every thing that transpires. Every body desires to be remembered to you—it would fill the paper to name them. I wrote you once before. Let me know whether you have received it. You don't say one word about your Health. I hope it was comfortable and will continue so. It will be a great comfort to know that it is so to your.

Portia

A N D R E W   J A C K S O N

T O

R A C H E L   J A C K S O N

---

*L*yncoya, a Creek Indian infant orphaned when Andrew Jackson's troop triumphed at the Battle of Talluschatchee during the War of 1812, was sent by Jackson to his home, the Hermitage, where he was reared as an adopted child by the Jacksons.

Headquarters 10 Islands Cosa river
Novbr. 4th. 1813

My Dear
In the hurry of the moment I have but a moment to write you. I detached Genl John Coffee with part of his Brigade of Cavalry and mounted men to destroy the Creek Town Talushatchey, he

PRESIDENT ANDREW JACKSON WAS A FORMIDABLE
OPPONENT, WHETHER IN WAR OR POLITICS, LEADING AMERICAN
ARMIES TO VICTORY IN FLORIDA AND NEW ORLEANS AND HIS
PARTY TO THE WHITE HOUSE IN 1829.

has executed this order in elegant stile leaving dead on the field one hundred and seventy six, and taking 80 prisoners, forty prisoners was left on the ground many of them wounded, others to take care of them—since writing the above Genl. Coffee reports 180, found dead, and there is no doubt but 200 was killed. I have here forty two added to the thirty two heretofore captured & sent on to Huntsville, in all 74. I have been and is still badly supplied with provisions, as soon as I can get a supply will proceed on to the heart of the creek nation. Mr. Alexander and Jack Donelson were both in the action are safe & behaved like what I could wish & expected, all friends safe, Capt. Hammond had 5 of his men wounded—all behaved bravely and as I could wish. I send on a little Indian boy for Andrew to Huntsville—with a request to Colo. Pope to take care of him untill he is sent on—all his family is destroyed—he is about the age of <u>Theodore</u>. In haste your affectionate Husband Andrew Jackson

---

JAMES MADISON
TO
DOLLEY MADISON

---

*A*fter retiring from the presidency, James Madison restricted his outside activities to service on the University of Virginia Board of Regents, as well as nominal support for local agricultural societies and the American Colonization Society. Madison was in Charlottesville, performing his good work hearing examinations at the university, when he wrote this letter to his wife, who had remained at Montpelier.

University. July 11. 1827

My dearest,

We made out to get to Mr. Goodwins by 5 OC. where we luckily fell in with Genl. Cocke. After consultation as to our lodging &c at the University, he was left to make the arrangements on his arrival, which would be that evening. On our reaching the University the

morning after, we found, much to our satisfaction that he had provided by treaty with Mr. Brokenborough, that we shd. all lodge in
the Pavilion evacuated by Mr. Key, and be there supplied with a
table & every other accomodation requisite. Our situation is thus
made as convenient as possible, all the Visitors being together and
able to proceed on their business, at every interval left by the Examinations. These commence at 5 OC. in the morning, are resumed
at half after 8 OC. & continue till Eleven; & after an interval of half
an hour are again continued till one OC. I have seen Mrs. Blatter-
man and Mrs. Conway, and said to them what you would wish. I
shall call on Mrs. D. & the other Ladies of your acquaintance as I
can. Mr. Trist says they are all well at Tufton, except Mr. J. Randolph;
who is not so. Late accts. from Mrs. R. are favorable. Every body is
full of expressed regrets that you did not come with me. Mr. Monroe was a little indisposed yesterday forenoon, but I hope is again
well. By not getting off early from Mr. Goodwin's I lost the opportunity of writing by the last post. The mail of this morning brought
me nothing, which is explained by what Mr Chapman mentioned
to you. We are not, without hopes that the examinations will be
closed on the 18th. instead of the 20th. Mean time be assured of
my greatest anxiety to hasten the moment of being where my heart
always is.

Mr. Cabell saw Mrs. Stephenson on his way, and was desired
to let her know whether you were here, intending, with her sister, to come to you. He has got her word that you were not. She
is low, but rides about.

L U C R E T I A   R U D O L P H

T O

J A M E S   G A R F I E L D

---

*I*n the years before their marriage, James Garfield and Lucretia Rudolph met frequently in Cleveland, Ohio, where Lucretia was attempting to help children through her
teaching at the Brownell Street School.

James Dearest:

Indeed you were a very naughty boy to make me promise to write you a letter, for I had fully determined that no letter you should get until I had received one from you; still I don't care much just now for I have wanted you here so much this evening to enjoy with me one of the most enrapturing sights I have ever witnessed. Smith's Panorama of the Tour of Europe. From Rouen France we have followed the artist through France Belgium, Germany, Prussia, Switzerland and Italy, stopped at many of the principal cities, lingering beside beautiful fountains, gazing at the most exquisite specimens of art—then away among the terrible sublimities of the Switzers pride, the snow clad Alps, first viewing them in the clear full sunlight, then at the twilight hour when every peak and crag was tinged with rosy hue—now standing upon the verge of Vesuvius' crater looking down into its yawning depths—then with the Neapolitan watching it when wrapt in lurid flames and pouring into the sea rivers of fire.

But don't think I am crazy, running on at such a rate as this. I have only been lost in most delightful raptures, and can scarcely restrain tongue or pen from pouring forth the most ludicrous extravagancies. It is all in vain however. I can give you only the faintest idea of the beauty and perfection of those paintings. I only wish you could see them. I do not believe I could have felt any more powerfully the overwhelming grandeur and magnificence of Alpine scenery had I looked upon the original. If you were only to be here tomorrow night, then you too could see and feel it all yourself. But when do you come again? There is so much here to enjoy that I long for some <u>old</u> friend to share it with me. I am at my new boarding place now and have a very pleasant roommate—one of the teachers, a graduate from Mount Holyoke—but I cannot love her yet as one of my old friends and whenever we go out upon the lake-shore or visit any place or thing interesting, somehow I cannot help wishing it were an old <u>heart friend</u> near. I cannot learn to love the changes which life seems to bring, and I often find my heart asking for the sweet hallucinations of my early dreams. I love my little school very much—never felt better satisfied with my efforts than now. I am continually becoming more and more pleased with the method of teaching and drilling in these Union Schools. It may be faulty in some respects, but I am sure is far ahead of anything I have known anything about before. I am getting every day slower and more thorough—I try to teach the children only a very few things, but try to make those few thoroughly understood and leave them impressed. A dissertation on school teaching now!! Well, good night; perhaps my brain will be cooler when the morning breezes blow.

Another beautiful morning. How refreshing the sunlight after so many dark, rainy days. Such a nice time I had getting home the morning you left me. Noon. The breakfast bell called me, and I have been busy ever since. I can never tell how much I love you all at Hiram. It seems as though I had no heart left for anyone else. And then to be away from you all and every hour miss you so much. Harry is going to call here soon, and a fine visit I am promising myself. I am so glad Mr. Harden sent him out here—I wish he would send some of you every day. Harry writes me such a good letter—speaks of Barbara's marriage, but does not regret it—says he is happier in his new love. I am glad if he can be. Dare I hope for an answer to such a thing as this! I believe I might if you could only know how happy it would make me. Tell Almeda I am waiting very patiently for a letter from her. Loving Crete

---

MARY LINCOLN
TO
ABRAHAM LINCOLN

---

*M*ary was in New York when she wrote this letter to her husband, asking him to provide funds for the aid of the black "contrabands," former slaves who had fled the South for the safety of Washington and other Northern cities.

My Dear Husband.

I wrote you on yesterday, yet omitted a very important item. Elizabeth Heckley, who is with me and is working for the Contraband Association at Wash. is authorised by the White part of the Concern by a written document to collect any thing for them here that she can. She has been very unsuccessful. She says the immense number of Contrabands in W–are Suffering intensely, many without bed covering & having to use any bit of carpeting to cover themselves. Many dying of want. Out of the $1000 fund deposited with you by Gen Corcoran I have given her the privelege of investing $200 here, in bed covering. She is the most deeply grateful being, I ever saw, & this Sum, I am sure you will not object to being used in this way. The cause of humanity requires it—and there will be $800 left of the fund. I am sure, this will meet your approbation. The soldiers are well supplied with comfort. Please send check for $200 out of that fund. She will bring you on the bill.

    Please write by return mail

With much love, yours ML

U L Y S S E S   S .   G R A N T
T O
J U L I A   G R A N T

---

*E*llen Grant, the Grants' daughter, had been raising money for the care of wounded troops by posing as the Little Old Lady Who Lived in the Shoe and selling dolls. Ulysses acknowledges her activities and discusses other relatives in this letter to his wife, sent just after one of the bloodiest battles of the Civil War. Julia later wrote the following comment on the verso of the letter: "Gov. Morton was one who in after years counted on the influence of Genl Grant and rced it much. Julia D. Grant."

Cold Harbor Va. June 6th 1864

Dear Julia,

The photographs of "the old woman who lived in the shoe" and little Jess are received. I also received yours and Jess' a few days before. They are all very fine. Gen. Rawlins asks me to get one of Missie's for him. She looks right cunning dressed as an old woman. This is very likely to prove a very tedious job I have on hand but I feel very confidant of ultimate success. The enemy keeps himself behind strong intrenchments all the time and seems determined to hold on to the last. You ask me if I have received Cousin Louisa's letter? I have not received a letter from her since leaving Culpepper. At that time I was very busy and neglected to answer and since forgot it until your letter reminded me of it. She asked me to recommend her brother who is a soldier at Indianapolis Ia. I intended to write to her that she did not probably understand what that position was and that I would not advise him to accept such a position. Further that likely a recommendation from me to Governor Morton for his promotion might injure his prospects.

Governor Morton I believe is one of the influential men who tried to have me removed from the command of the Dept. of the Ten. He complained to Jo Reynolds about some remarks I had made also and I replied that they were well founded and he, the Gov, must acknowledge it. I wish you would tell Cousin Louisa this and apologize for my not answering before. You need not tell her that you had picked her out for my second wife forgetting all about her having a husband already.

Kiss all the children for me. I wrote to Nelly the other day and told her to send the letter to you. I sent you $800. the other day. June pay I must send to pay my debts. I think that will about let me out. Kisses for yourself and love to all at your house. Fred is just getting out again. Ulys

---

RUTHERFORD B. HAYES
TO
LUCY WEBB HAYES

---

*R*utherford Hayes was in the White House when he wrote this letter about his children helping to decorate the graves on Memorial Day—or Decoration Day, as it was then called.

Executive Mansion, Washington 1 June 1878

My Darling:

I did hope you would be home today, but the published dispatches indicate that you will not leave Malone, for four days. We had a good Decoration day at Gettysburg in spite of a rainy afternoon. You would have enjoyed it. Two Misses Austin spent a few days with us, coming from the South to Hamton Institute. Miss Kent is still here. We miss you at all times, and dear Fanny the little treasure! Tell her she must come home soon. Winnie and Scott had a glorious time decorating the graves of our heroes at Arlington. They were at the head of the Orphans Column. I support your absence at the Adirondacks, and mine at Gettysburg, authorised the Committee in marshalling Scott as an orphan!

The weather here is cool and wet. The Magnolia is fragrant with large white flowers. The scenery is now at perfection so far as depends on the verdure of grass and trees. Congress will adjourn the 17th, it is probable. If you are to go with me to West Point you ought to be here. It is not certain that I can go to W.P. "S. Much" Aff. R

PRESIDENT FRANKLIN D. ROOSEVELT POINTS OUT
SOMETHING INTERESTING TO HIS WIFE ELEANOR AS THEY
CAMPAIGN IN POUGHKEEPSIE, NEW YORK, IN 1944, NEAR THE
END OF THEIR FINAL CAMPAIGN TOUR.

FRANKLIN D. ROOSEVELT
TO
ELEANOR ROOSEVELT

*T*he use of the Roosevelts' "big house at Hyde Park" for convalescents from wartime wounds was the topic of this exchange between Franklin and Eleanor.

The White House, Feb. 9, 1942

Memorandum for E. R.

I see no reason for listing rooms in the big house at Hyde Park for convalescents, in view of the fact that there are half a dozen big houses completely unoccupied between Beacon and Barrytown–room for several hundred convalescents, etc.

Incidentally, if we were to put the big house at Hyde Park to that use I could not go there at all, as the one essential in war time is complete lack of any distraction on the very occasional weekend I can get away from Washington. It is, of course, impossible for me to take any cruise this Spring and Summer and I doubt if I can use the Potomac at all on account of the obvious target she would make for any planes from a hostile aircraft carrier. F.D.R.

ELEANOR ROOSEVELT
TO
FRANKLIN D. ROOSEVELT

[February 9, 1942]

For the President:
O.K. My conscience is free! E.R.

Then commander in chief of Allied Forces in Europe, Ike congratulated his wife on the good volunteer war work she had been doing, while reassuring her that the rumors of his close relationship with his personal aide, Kay Somersby, were not true.

Tuesday, March 2, 1943

My Darling:

What a morning! Two fine long letters from you—both written on February 22 and this is only <u>Mar.</u> 2. You told about being with Mrs. Wallace, Mrs. W. Wilson, pulling out numbers for blood donors and signing an article for New Yorker. Also you spoke of a uniform. What it is I don't know—but I can tell you this; if you've gone into a uniform of any kind for any kind of war work my admiration for you is even greater than before. All through this publicity storm you've been tops—sensible, considerate and modest. But your example is showing the women of America how definitely they must get down to brass tacks in this thing is marvellous. God—how I wish I could help make all Americans feel the <u>deadly</u> seriousness of this task. You are all that any man could ask as a <u>partner and a sweetheart</u>.

So Life says my old London driver came down! So she did— but the big reason she wanted to serve in this theater is that she is terribly in love with a young American Colonel and is to be married to him come June—assuming both are alive. I doubt that Life told that. But I tell you only so that if anyone is banal and foolish enough to lift an eyebrow at an old duffer such as I am in connection with Wacs—Red Cross workers—nurses and drivers—you will know that I've no emotional involvements and will have none. Ordinarily I don't try to think of all the details surrounding my existence when I write to you—they are all unimportant compared to the real things I like to talk to you about. And, by the way, <u>my own</u> driver is a Sergeant Drye!

There was so much in your two letters that interested me that I feel inept in writing the kind of note I usually send you. I do hope you take the Florida trip. I'm sure you'd enjoy it. Also will you drop a note to Loreen Robertson and thank her for the nice letter she wrote to me. I just don't have time to write long hand letters. You are the only person in the world to whom I send them—and she'd probably be hurt if I sent a dictated message.

You speak of the hundreds of messages—congratulatory and so on—that come in to you. There is no point in trying to send on the letters, but could you give me the names of the writers. If the list is long Charley Gailey would probably send out a secretary for an hour to whom you could dictate them! I like to know the identity of those who are nice to you—and who don't think we (you and I) are trying to be haughty because heavy responsibilities have been heaped upon me. But don't do a lot of work on such a thing—after all, some day we can go over those letters together (if you're saving them) and that will be a lot of fun, because we'll say "<u>That's when we were big shots.</u>" Then we'll chuckle!

Darling, it's time to see some of the people collecting in Lee's office. But in case I haven't said it before in this letter, and you have any interest in the matter (<u>you'd better!!</u>) I love you—only.

Send my best to Johny & please remember me to such people—when you see them as—Harry Hopkins, George Allena, Palleys, Garys, Gartleys, Tom Handy, Mrs. Nevis, Mrs Littlejohn, Kid Hylos, etc. etc. etc. & Harlen & <u>Milton</u>. Special also to Ruth & Bev.

Always your Ike

P.S. I'm not astonished at the price for the robe—it is a beauty.

*C*oncern for the displaced people in Europe and the return of U.S. soldiers after the end of World War II is evident in this letter Ike later sent to Mamie.

Reims, May 12, 1945

Darling:

For a month I've been trying to figure out the earliest date on which I could get home, even briefly, to see you and my mother. While I know (or at least I think I do) that I can make it within a reasonable time—it is still as difficult as ever to make any definite plan.

One of the troubles all senior officers will encounter (I probably most of all) will be the necessity of going through certain <u>formal</u> receptions. Possibly, in my case, I may have to face two, three, or even more. As a matter of courtesy these must be carried out—troops here would feel their long fighting record unappreciated if their senior commanders were not received with some acclaim on their first trip home. (<u>All this is very secret.</u>)

The need for arranging these things takes some time. Moreover, the receptions themselves will cut into the private time I will be wanting with you.

But one thing I hope for is to work out some "policy" by which families can come over here; the difficulty will be so to formulate it that the lowest private has the same right as the highest general. This, I <u>must insist</u> upon!

One of the greatest drawbacks will be lack of suitable quarters in Germany. The country is devastated. Whole cities are obliterated; and the German population, to say nothing of millions of former slave laborers, is largely homeless. There is certain to be unrest, privation, and undoubtedly some starvation next winter. It is a bleak picture. Why the Germans ever let the thing go as far as they did is completely beyond me!

There are now so many men thronging the outer office that 2 secretaries are having a hard time entertaining them. Gosh! These are busy times! In thirty minutes I must run out to see some returned prisoners of war. We're evacuating them as rapidly as possible—but there are so many!

Well Sweet—here's to an early meeting, but just when, I can't say. John is coming to see me today & I'll have him write to you. I love you, Always your Ike

P.S. I have to go to London Tues. p.m. Some good friends of John's and mine have asked us to a theater & supper party. So for the first time in this war I hope to go out—unless John doesn't want to do so. It would be fun, I think. Haven't seen a show & eaten in a restaurant in 3 years.

PRESIDENT WILLIAM HOWARD TAFT
SPEAKS AS HIS WIFE HELEN WATCHES FROM
A TOURING CAR IN 1910.

CHAPTER 9

FOREIGN TRAVEL

~⁀

"You have not missed much by not coming here."
—Ulysses Grant to Julia Grant,
September 11, 1878

"Infer you have had a very fine time in Japan."
—Helen Taft to William H. Taft,
August 2, 1905

"The Mexicans put on a real show for me."
—Harry Truman to Bess Truman,
March 4, 1947

ALTHOUGH some of our earliest presidents, Thomas Jefferson, John Adams, James Monroe, and John Quincy Adams, had extensive foreign service experience, they did not travel abroad as president, nor did their first ladies. Now, presidents and their wives frequently travel overseas—often together, thus unfortunately eliminating the need for correspondence. Because presidential families traveling abroad have always been seen as representatives of the U.S. government, presidential couples have often discussed foreign affairs and travel in their correspondence.

JOHN ADAMS

TO

ABIGAIL ADAMS

---

*J*ohn Adams had returned to Paris from The Hague in order to negotiate a peace treaty with Great Britain. Despite his positive response to one of Abigail's many requests to join him in Europe and "Permit me my Dearest Friend to renew that Companionship," she did not go abroad until 1784.

Paris November 8. 1782

My dearest Friend

The King of Great Britain, by a Commission under the great Seal of his Kingdom, has constituted Richard Oswald Esqr. his Commissioner to treat with the Ministers Plenipotentiary of the United States of America, and has given him full Powers which have been mutually exchanged. Thus G.B. has Shifted Suddenly about, and from persecuting acknowledged us a Sovereign State and independant Nation. It is surprizing that she should be the third Power to make this Acknowledgment. She has been negotiated into it, for Jay and I peremptorily refused to Speak or hear, before We were put upon an equal Foot. Franklin as usual would have taken the Advice of the C de V and treated, without, but nobody would join him.

As to your coming to Europe with Miss Nabby, I know not what to say. I am obliged to differ in Opinion so often from Dr. Franklin and the C. De Vergennes, in Points that essentially affect the Honour Dignity and most precious Interests of my Country, and these Personages are so little disposed to bear Contradiction, and Congress have gone so near enjoining upon me passive Obedience to them, that I do not expect to hold any Place in Europe longer than next Spring. Mr. Jay is in the Same Predicament, and So will every honest Man be, that Congress can Send.

Write however to Mr. Jackson in Congress and desire him candidly to tell you, whether he thinks Congress will continue me in Europe, upon Terms which I can Submitt to with honour, another Year. If he tells you as a Friend that I must Stay another year, come to me, in the Spring with your Daughter. Leave the Boys in good Hands and a good school. A trip to Europe, for one Year may do no harm to you or your Daughter. The Artifices of the Devil will be used to get me out of the Commission for Peace. If they succeed I abandon Europe for ever, for the Blue Hills without one Instants Loss of Time or even waiting for Leave to return. For whoever is Horse Jockeyed, I will not be. Congress means well, but is egregiously imposed upon and deceived.

Mrs. Jay and Mrs. Izard will be excellent Companions for you and the Miss Izards for Miss Nabby.

ABIGAIL ADAMS
TO
JOHN ADAMS

Abigail ventured to Europe in the spring of 1784, after her husband had been directed to remain there by the Continental Congress. In this lengthy letter, she detailed some of the preparations for her trip, including an intriguing paragraph about "Pheby," a slave freed by her father, the Rev. William Smith.

Febry. 11th. 1784

Two days only are wanting to campleat six years since my dearest Friend first crost the Atlantick. But three months of the Six Years have been Spent in America. The airy delusive phantom Hope, how has she eluded my prospects. And my expectations of your return from month to month, have vanished "like the baseless Fabrick of a vision."

You invite me to you, you call me to follow you, the most earnest wish of my soul is to be with you—but you can scarcely form an Idea of the conflict of my mind. It appears to me such an enterprize, the ocean so formidable, the quitting my habitation and my Country, leaving my Children, my Friends, with the Idea that perhaps I may never see them again, without my Husband to console and comfort me under these apprehensions—indeed my dear Friend there are hours when I feel unequal to the trial. But on the other hand I console myself with the Idea of being joyfully and tenderly received by the best of Husbands and Friends, and of meeting a dear and long absent Son. But the difference is; my fears, and anxieties are present; my hopes, and expectations, distant.

But avaunt y Idle Specters, the desires and requests of my Friend are a Law to me. I will sacrifice my present feelings and hope for a blessing in persuit of my duty.

I have already arranged all my family affairs in such a way that I hope nothing will suffer by my absence. I have determined to put into this House my Pheby, to whom my Father gave freedom, by his Will, and the income of a hundred a year during her Life. The Children furnished her to house keeping, and she has ever since lived by herself, untill a fortnight ago, she took unto her self a Husband in the person of Mr. Abdee whom you know. As there was no setled minister in Weymouth I gave them the liberty of celebrating their nuptials here, which they did much to their satisfaction.

I proposed to her taking care of this House and furniture in my absence. The trust is very flattering to her, and both her Husband and She Seem pleased with it. I have no doubt of their care and faithfulness, and prefer them to any other family. The Farm I continue to let to our old tennant, as no one thinks I shall supply myself better.

I am lucky too in being able to supply myself with an honest faithfull Man Servant. I do not know but you may recollect him, John Brisler, who was brought up in the family of Genll. Palmer, has since lived with Col. Quincy and is recommended by both families, as a virtuous Steady frugal fellow, with a mind much above the vulgar, very handy and attentive. For a maid servant I hope to have a Sister of his, who formerly lived with Mrs. Trott, who gives her a good character. It gave me some pain to refuse the offerd service of an old servant who had lived 7 years with me, and who was married here, as I wrote you some time ago. Both she and her Husband solicited to go, but I could not think it convenient as Babies might be very inconvenient at Sea, tho they offered to leave it Nurse if I could consent to their going, but tho I felt gratified at their regard for me I could not think it would answer. On many accounts a Brother and sister are to be prefered. This far have I proceeded but I know not yet what Ship, or what month or what port I shall embark for, I rather think for England.

I wrote you largely by Capt. Love, who saild for England 3 weeks ago. By hime I mentiond a set of Bills which I expected to draw in favour of Uncle Smith for 200 dollors. He did not send me the Bills untill yesterday. Instead of 60 pounds Lawfull, he requested me to sign a Bill for 60 Sterling, as that was just the sum he wanted, and that it would oblige him. I have accordingly drawn for that; as I supposed it would not make any great odds with you; whether I drew now; or a month hence, as I suppose I shall have occasion before I embark. You will be so kind as to honour the Bill.

I have not heard from you since Mr. Robbins arrived. I long to hear how your Health is. Heaven preserve and perfect it. Col. Quincy lies very dangerously ill of the same disorder which proved fatal to my dear and honoured parent. The dr. is apprehensive that it will put a period to his life in a few days.

However, kind sons may be disposed to be, they cannot be daughters to a Mother. I hope I shall not leave any thing undone which I ought to do. I would endeavour in the discharge of my duty towards her, to merit from her the same testimony which my own parent gave me, that I was a good kind considerate child as ever a parent had. However undeserving I may have been of this testimony, it is a dear and valuable Legacy to me and will I hope pruve a stimulous to me, to endeavour after those virtues which the affection and partiality of a parent ascribed to me.

Our sons are well. I hope your young companion is so too. If

I should not now be able to write to him, please to tell him I am not unmindfull of him.

I have been to day to spend a few Hours with our good Uncle Quincy, who keeps much confined a winters and says he misses my two Boys almost as much as I do; for they were very fond of visiting him, and used to go as often as once a week when they lived at home.

There is nothing stiring in the political world. The Cincinati makes a Bustle, and will I think be crushed in its Birth. Adieu my dearest Friend. Yours most affectionately A. A.

LOUISA CATHERINE ADAMS
TO
JOHN QUINCY ADAMS

---

*A*lthough Adams had been serving as U.S. minister to Russia, he was recalled to Ghent to head the delegation to negotiate peace with Great Britain. Catherine was left behind in St. Petersburg to help maintain the U.S. legation and ultimately to bring her family to France.

St. Petersburg May 11th. 1814

Your kind letter arrived just in time to cheer us. Charles and I were both quite sick, but are now thank God much better, though Dr. Galloway has ordered me to keep him at home for some days, the weather being uncommonly cold and the Bridge not likely to be put up for some days.

We have nothing new there is some talk of the Emperor's return, some say immediately, others not until August. The two Mr. Lewis's dined with me last Sunday with Dr. Beresford who told me that Lord Byron in consequence of some lines which he wrote on the quarrel which took place between the P. B. and Lord Lounderdale (which was said to have produced a flood of tears from the P.C.) is to be called before the house of Peers. if I can procure the lines I will send them to you.

We have been amusing ourselves with the rejected addresses which are very laughable, and certainly very well done. I believe you never saw them, they would afford you half an hours amusement, and I wish you had them in your Carriage. they are just calculated to while away the time which sometimes hangs heavy on the road, and most profitable than musing on enjoyments out of our reach. I have not seen the Countess, but will deliver your message without fail.

Dr. Galloway has just left me, and informs that the Senate have had a meeting to consult upon the great question, of making a new title for the Emperor. this important business is terminated and three Gentlemen whose names are Alexander, are to leave this place immediately, as bearers of it to his Imperial Majesty Prince Kournkin, Count Saltzburg and another whose name I do not recollect. it is in future to be Alexander the Blested.

Among the circumstances which afford matter for conversation, the seizure of Sir James Biddle's Trunk, excites the most visibility. It was seized, on account of a small Copper Plate for printing Cards with his name. the Custom House have declared it contraband and his little Lordship has been obliged to interfere, after Mr. Cugley's having been forced to appear before the Court on account of Sir James. and I understand much warmth has been produced, but all is happily settled.

I was really grieved at the loss of your poor Servant but very happy to think the accident was no worse. I congratulate you upon your good fortune in arriving so exactly in time to participate in all the rejoicing at Revel. I am fully sensible of the pleasure it must have afforded you.

It is quite unnecessary to send me the paper which you mention, as I trust our separation is to be a short one, and that such an one will ever be useless to me.

We are anxiously waiting to hear from you at Guttenburg, and to receive the letters which we have the happiness to Know Mr. Clay keeps for us. you may judge of our impatience.

Mr. & Mrs. Smith desire to be remember'd , Charles says he

shall write you again soon, the last was all his own. My paper is out and my letter very tedious, so I will only bid you adieu with every good wish. L. C. A.

U L Y S S E S   S.   G R A N T
T O
J U L I A   D E N T

---

*N*ear the end of the Mexican War, Ulysses wrote this observant letter about the people and country to his then-fiancée.

Tacubaya Mexico January 9th 1848

My Dear Julia

Since I wrote you last one Brigade has moved to this place which is about four miles from the City of Mexico and from being so much higher than the City is much more healthy. One Brigade has gone to Toluca and it is rumored that before a great while we will move to some distant part, either Queretero, Zacetecus, San Louis Potosi or Guernivace unless there is a strong probability of peace. It is now however strongly believed that peace will be established before many months. I hope it may be so for it is scarsely suportible for me to be separated from you so long my dearest Julia. A few weeks ago I went to the Commanding Officer of my Regiment and represented to him that when the 4th Infy left Jefferson Barracks, three years ago last May, I engaged, and that I thought it high time that I should have a leave of absence to go back. He told me that he would approve it, but I found that it would be impossible to get the Comdg. Gen. To give the leave so I never made the application. I have strong hopes though of going back in a few months. If peace is not made it is at all events about my turn to go on recruiting Service. As to getting a sick leave that is out of the question for I am never sick a day.

Mexico is a very pleasant place to live because it is never hot nor never cold, but I believe every one is hartily tired of the war. There is no amusements except the Theatre and as the Actors & Actresses are Spanish but a few of the officers can understand them. The better class of Mexicans dare not visit the Theatre or associate with the Americans lest they should be assassinated by their own people or banished by their Government as soon as we leave. A few weeks ago a Benefit was given to a favorite Actress and the Governor of Queretero hearing of it sent secret Spies to take the names of Such Mexicans as might be caught in indulging in amusements with the Americans for the purpose of banishing them as soon as the Magnanimous Mexican Republic should drive away the Barbarians of the North. I pity poor Mexico. With a soil and Climate scarcely equalled in the world she has more poor and Starving subjects who are willing and able to work than any country in the world. The rich keep down the poor with a hardness of heart that is incredible. Walk through the Streets of Mexico for one day and you will see hundreds of beggars, but you never see them ask alms of their own people, it is always from the Americans that they expect to receive. I wish you could be here for one short day then I should be doubly gratified. Gratified at seeing you my dearest Julia, and gratified that you might see too the Manners and customs of these people. You would see what you never dreamed of nor you form a correct Idea from reading. All gamble Priests & Civilians, Male & female and particularly so on Sundays. But I will tell you all that I know about Mexico and the Mexicans when I see you which I do hope will not be a great while off now. Fred is in the same Brigade with me. I see him every day. He like myself is in excellent health and has no prospect of getting out of the Country on the plea of Sickness. I have one chance of getting out of Mexico soon besides going on recruiting Service. Gen. Scott will grant leave of absence to officers when there are over two to a Company. In my Regt. There is three or four vacancies which will be filled soon and will give an oportunity for one or two now here to go out. Give my love to all at White Haven and do not fail to write often dearest Julia. I write but seldom myself but it is because a Mail but Seldom goes from here to the Sea Coast. Coming this way it is different for the Volunteers are Constantly Arriving.

When you write next tell me if Mrs. Porter and Mrs. Higgins are married or likely to be.

Adieu My Dearest Julia Ulysses

WILLIAM   HOWARD   TAFT

T O

HELEN   TAFT

---

*W*illiam H. Taft, then Secretary of War, was on an official visit to Japan and the Philippines, and his wife was on a family vacation in Oxford, England, when they exchanged these charming but occasionally acerbic letters. Helen had her hands full with the English, and William had his full with Alice Roosevelt.

Steamship "Manchuria" July 31 [1905]

My darling Nellie,

My last letter was written just before the luncheon of the Emperor. We all attended promptly, although as usual on such occasions Monico was wanting in that he had sent my trousers to be pressed instead of pressing them himself and nearly delayed me beyond the time when it was necessary for me to start. Attending an Emperor's luncheon without trousers would create a sensation but could hardly be called pleasant. We were all assembled in the room as you will remember it and I am bound to say that our party had prepared themselves well so that they all looked very well dressed and quite used to their surroundings. We went in by squads to hold audience with the Emperor and the Crown Princess received us instead of the Empress who was ill in the country. The luncheon was just like the one you attended except that it was larger. The arrangement of seats I enclose. After the luncheon, Alice Roosevelt, Griscom and Mrs. Griscom and I went up and were received by the Emperor and the Princess, and the Emperor seemed to be in very great good humor, shook hands with me most cordially and on the whole was greatly pleased with his successful function which really passed off as smoothly as if there were but three or four present. Everybody was delighted and we all went away pleased.

That evening we attended a function tendered us by the Prime Minister, a dinner at the Imperial Hotel. He made quite a long speech and I responded. I received quite a number of compliments on the speech because of its diplomatic character and the fact that it did not slop over or involve us with Russia. I send you a copy of the Japan Times which contains the speech together with a number of comments of the Japanese press which will interest you.

The Prime Minister said that he was very anxious to have an interview with me and so I fixed the next morning at ten o'clock. He came around and we talked so much that we consumed all the time between that and twelve and this made us late to the luncheon given us by Prince Fushimi, the Japanese prince who came to the United States last year. As a result of the conversation, I sent a long cable to Mr. Root at Washington. The Prime Minister requested me to do so and I did not see any way out, although it was pretty expensive to do so for it cost twenty one hundred yen to send the dispatch. It bore on three points: on the Japanese relation to the Philippines, on a proposed informal alliance between the United States and Japan for the maintenance of peace in the East, and third, the question of suzerainty over the Empire of Korea by Japan. I don't know but that I was "butting in" in this matter, but as they were so anxious, I concluded that I ought to act and telegraph which I did.

The lunch at Prince Fushimi's was very nice. I took out his daughter-in-law, the Princess something or other, who was the daughter of the late Shogun. Her husband was the son of Prince Fuchimi, who was present. In the evening we paid a great many calls accompanied by Mr. Nagasaki. His attentions and care of us have been such that I never can repay him. He was put in charge of me and Mrs. Nagasaki in charge of Alice, together with Count and Countess Terashima. The present Count Terashima was educated at the University of Pennsylvania and speaks English very well. His wife does not speak English. She was the daughter of a rich resident of Kioto, one of the bank people and had been married about four months and had put on European dress for the first time. We had formal meals every day at the Palace, when not otherwise engaged, with menus of which I send you a sample. In the evening of the third day, we went to the Maple Club where we had a Japanese dinner and a geisha dance. The next day the Minister of War gave us a Garden Party at the arsenal. I ought to say that we had to make speeches at the Maple Club in response to a speech by the President of the Commercial Associations that gave us that entertainment. I spoke and Senator Warren and Representative Grosvenor. The Garden Party of the Minister of War was a great success, although we all suffered intensely from the heat because we were obliged to wear Prince Alberts and top hats. It was gotten up with a great deal of elaboration and all the great men of Japan were there, including Ito. The Minister made a speech and so did I and Marquis Ito sang a poem to express his feelings. Griscom also made a speech. After that we had Japanese wrestling. They had one man that they said weighed one hundred pounds more than I, but I do not think that they were correct. However, the wrestling was exceedingly interesting and I enjoyed it as I had never seen it before.

We went afterwards to call at the Minister's and on the First, Second and Third Secretary. Laughlin, the Second Secretary, Lucy's brother-in-law has a Japanese house constructed as they are and lives very elegantly and comfortable in this way. That night we left at half past nine for Kioto. As we drove up to the station the large square in front of the station was filled with shouting crowds who had assembled to give us a farewell calling out "Banzai, banzai." I have never seen such a popular tumult and gathering. We drove into the station where they had a room for us and from which we could look out on the crowd. Every member of the party was cheered to the echo, especially Alice. Then the people or those of them who could get in followed us to the train and there were cheers and cheers and cheers. Marquis Ito was among those who came and it was really a most thrilling popular reception. All the way down the railway track from Tokio to Yokahama were crowds gathered to cheer the train and at Yokahama we found a great crowd assembled with our friends among the municipal officials to say goodbye again. During the night whenever we stopped at a provincial capital they brought in presents for Alice Roosevelt or for me and that continued until eleven o'clock the next morning when we reached Kioto.

At every station during the morning there were crowds that cheered and cheered and when we reached Kioto we had another popular ovation and drove through crowded streets to the hotel. The train was called "The Welcome Express" and its time for stopping was advertised throughout the country which enable the people to be there when we went by. The most complete preparations were made for us by the Government. The train was put at our disposal, and at the Kioto Hotel, Alice, my staff, and Miss Boardman and Miss McMillan were the guests of the Government.

We went out to the palaces at Kioto and saw them thoroughly under the guidance of Mr. Nagasaki, and we went to an exhibition of the jiu jitsu and the fencing under the auspices of a great Athletic Club, to which Alice and I were elected as honorary members. In the evening we dined and invited to dine with us the various municipal officials of Kioto, the Governor and his wife, the Mayor, the Chief of Police and Custodian of the Royal Palaces. After that we went to a geisha dance which in Kioto is said to be better than that in Tokio and saw the cherry blossom dance. I was about exhausted and could hardly keep awake.

The next morning we went to the Temple where for our convenience all the merchants in Kioto had assembled their rarest wares and we were able to go through them all by one visit to the Temple. We went to some silk factories in addition. In the afternoon we left for Kobé and had a similar experience about leaving Kioto where crowds cheered and cheered. We were met at Kobé by the same kind of a cheering crowd. We stopped at the consulate a few minutes to receive the municipal officials and the Society of Patriotic Women. The Nagasakis and Terashimas came with us and dined aboard the ship. Tired but pleased that they had got us safely aboard the steamer without any mishap. I was exceedingly worn out after our experience and while I slept some today and have not attempted to do a great deal in the way of exercise. The Inland Sea of course to me is an old story, but I enjoyed it.

At Shimonoseki and Moji we were met by some fifteen or sixteen decorated launches that followed us down nearly to the mouth of the straits. Tomorrow morning we expect to reach Nagasaki where we shall be the recipient of a garden party I believe, and we shall then go rejoicing on our way to Manila.

It has not always been easy to secure from Alice the graciousness that our treatment here deserves, because she seems to be so much taken up with Nick. She becomes absorbed in him and pays but little attention to anybody else. She is however amenable to persuasion and has quite winning ways when she devotes her attention, so that I think the Japanese generally thought she was very nice and very gracious. Although I believe that they are nominally engaged, I shall never believe that they are permanently engaged until I hear that they are married. Mabel Boardman and Amy McMillan are most useful in the management of Alice, but I confess I don't feel at all certain of myself in the Philippines for the Lord knows what she may do.

There was some failure to notify the Senators and Congressmen of the intention to stop at the Consulate at Kobé, which led to some sharp words about the treatment they had received at Kioto, a most unreasonable complaint considering the enormous pains that the Japanese took in order to accommodate us all. I suppose there was some little jealousy growing out of the fact that more attention was given to Alice and to me than to anybody else in the party, but I think they are getting over that feeling today. Noble came in upon us at Kobé and has given us some idea of affairs at Manila. They are preparing a series of festivities that are enough to kills us. If I have anything else to add, I will add in my own hand.

6 Bradmore Road
August 2nd [1905]

My dearest Will

I am seeing all about you in the papers and infer you have had a very fine time in Japan. I am so anxious to hear from you about your Experience with the party. I had a note from Eleanor Davenport this morning, enclosing clippings from San Francisco papers. It had been ten days at the bank, as it seems I left my address at a Branch Bank, not thinking but that it was all the same. I am sorry you did not take the house address, they seem so unreliable at the Bank. Now that you have left Japan, I shall not see so much in the papers. I don't remember whether I wrote you about the End of our trip. We went to Exeter saw all there was in a short time and came back Sunday sooner than we had Expected. The children got on perfectly well and seem contented enough, though there is very little variety for them. Tuesday the Uslers took us with them to a cricket match at Mr. Abbey's, the artist. He lives in Fairford about an hour on the railroad from here. And we had a delightful day. Two doctors were staying with them and a Mr. Schofield, professor at Harvard joined us. We got a fairly good lunch at the Bull Inn, and then went to see the British church which rejoices in the finest old stained glass windows in England, and a quaint old berger who describes them with the help of a fishing pole. The Abbeys have a lovely place there and once a year have a house party of artist cricketers...of them, who spend a week and play all the teams in the vicinity. Mrs. Abbey was charming and remembered your family when in Mt. Auburn. We saw some interesting work in the studio designed for the Harrisburg State House. There were a good many people there, but as usual we only met two or three. The wife & daughter of Sir Michael Hicks-Beach. When we came back we found an invitation to play Bridge, an unusual excitement with Fredericks tutor and another young man. The mother is a near neighbor and a very decent woman. She is a Canadian which accounts for it. You can tell immediately any one from the other Continent they are so much more presentable. I do not like the English at all, and the women are hopeless. Perhaps the upper ten may be different. I have a very polite note yesterday from Admiral Sir Cyprian Bridge, regretting that he was just leaving England. It was very nice of him to think of writing. The Uslers go away in a few days. The Hoadlys have arrived and are established in lodgings. They were coming to play Bridge last night but their boy was threatened with Croup. It is raining this morning the first time since I have been in England. Every thing is dried up. With best love and Kisses from us all.

Yours ever Helen

[P.S.] Bob writes often & is radiant.

F R A N K L I N   D .   R O O S E V E L T
TO
E L E A N O R   R O O S E V E L T

---

*P*resident Franklin Roosevelt was on an inspection trip to the Panama Canal Zone when he wrote this typically "friends" letter to his wife.

U.S.S. Houston Balboa, C. Z. [August 1938]

Dearest Babs:

Safely here and the last plane mail goes tomorrow early. I have given a tea for President Arosemena and his cabinet and the Canal officials and army and navy officers. Ex-Pres. and Mrs. Arias came and both sent you their warm regards.

Tomorrow I inspect the West Side of Canal Zone taking Arosemena with me and lunch with Governor Ridley. Then by train across the Isthmus, inspect at Cristobal and rejoin the ship at

Gatun Locks, sailing about 6 p.m. A long day but it is not very hot now and I hope the breeze keeps up tomorrow.

Saturday we explore old Providence Isl. off the Nicaragua coast—the haunt of Sir Harry Morgan and the other buccaneers. Then straight to Pensacola arriving Tues. p. m.

I wired you today about the plans for Canada the 18th. I do so hope you can come.

All goes well. I caught a 230 lb. shark yesterday—1 hr. and 35 minutes—so I win the pool for the Biggest Fish! Devotedly F.

HARRY S. TRUMAN

TO

BESS TRUMAN

---

*I*n the aftermath of World War II, President Truman undertook a "Good Neighbor" trip to South America. He wrote this letter to his wife from Mexico City, during the first visit of an American president to Mexico.

March 4, 1947

Dear Bess:

We arrived on the dot at 10 a.m. Left K.C. at 3:04 and had to slow down so we would not arrive too soon. I rode with the pilot as we went over the 10000 foot rim of the Valley of Mexico City. Popocatgetl came into view, about a hundred miles from the valley, but we couldn't see Orizaba because of the haze. Orizaba is just west of Vera Cruz and rises right out of the sea level plane to 18700 feet. Popo is a thousand feet lower.

The airport was lined with people and the Mexicans put on a real show for me. The Mayor of the city and Gov. of the Federal District (the same man) made me guest of honor and presented me with a solid gold medal weighing a half pound with the arms of the city on one side, and a replica of an Aztec calendar stone on the other. I wore it all day to the delight of the Mexican President.

BESS TRUMAN PROVIDED SUPPORT AND "POLISHED
THE MANNERS" OF HER HUSBAND HARRY.

He has a most beautiful home where I called on him, and three lovely children, two boys and a girl. I met the First Lady of Mexico and she is a charming person.

The President told me at the banquet that she was highly pleased with the presents you sent. They are sending you a silver tea service.

Last night's affair was a colorful one. The streets were packed from the embassy to the palace and at least 10,000 were in the square in front of it. The President & I had to greet them from the balcony in Franz Josef style. Never had such a welcome.

Hope everything is going well. Tell Margie to behave. Lots of love. Harry

PRESIDENT AND MRS. GEORGE WASHINGTON
SET PRECEDENTS OF POLITICAL AND SOCIAL BEHAVIOR
FOR MANY FIRST COUPLES TO COME.

HELLO   AND   GOOD-BYE

*"Every thing around and
within reminds me that you are absent."*
—James Madison to Dorothea (Dolley) Madison,
August 7, 1809

"Then come along, and that as <u>soon</u> as possible."
—Abraham Lincoln to Mary Lincoln,
June 12, 1848

"Till that sweet time—principally <u>love-making!</u>"
—Woodrow Wilson to Ellen Wilson,
June 4 1886

"I wanted to go home with you so badly last night."
—Harry S. Truman to Elizabeth (Bess) Truman,
July 27, 1923

A P E R S O N does not become president by staying home and plowing the lower forty. These men traveled early and often, leaving their spouses to maintain the family and often to run the family business. These letters show the strains of separation and the joys of reunion.

MARTHA WASHINGTON
TO
GEORGE WASHINGTON

*T*his affectionate letter is the only known one written by Martha Washington to her husband. He'd been attending the House of Burgesses in Williamsburg and made a commercial side trip to the Dismal Swamp.

March 30, 1767

My Dearest

It was with very great pleasure I see in your letter that you got safely down. We are all very well at this time but it still is rainey and wett. I am sorry you will not be at home soon as I expected you. I had reather my sister would not come up so soon as May would be much plasenter time than April. We wrote you last post as I have nothing new to tell you I must conclude myself. Your most Affectionate Martha Washington

MARTHA WASHINGTON

John and Abigail had been married only three years, but she had already experienced the pain of separation from her husband. If she could have seen the future she might not have been so sanguine about his absence while attending the Massachusetts Superior Court in Worcester.

Sunday Eveng. Weymouth Sepbr. 14 1767

My Dearest Friend

The Doctor talks of Setting out tomorrow for New Braintree. I did not know but that he might chance to see you, in his way there. I know from the tender affection you bear me, and our little one's that you will rejoice to hear that we are well, our Son is much better than when you left home, and our Daughter rock's him to Sleep, with the Song of "Come pappa come home to Brother Johnny." Sunday seems a more lonesome Day to me than any other when you are absent, For tho I may be compared to those climates which are deprived of the Sun half the Year, yet upon a Sunday you commonly afforded us your benign influence. I am now at Weymouth. My Father brought me here last night. To morrow I return home, where I hope soon to receive the Dearest of Friends and the tenderest of Husbands, with that unabated affection which has for Years past, and will whilst the vital Spark last, burn in the Bosom of your affectionate A Adams

PS poor Mr. Gridly died a thursday very suddenly, we hear and was yesterday buried.

ANDREW JACKSON
TO
RACHEL JACKSON

*A*ndrew Jackson wrote this "sincere" letter to his wife Rachel, promising to retire from public life, after serving as a delegate to the Tennessee Constitutional Convention while engaged in his duties as a district attorney. Despite his protests and assurances, within the year Jackson was serving as a U.S. representative in Washington.

Knoxville, May 9 1796.

My dearest Heart

It is with the greatest pleasure I sit down to write you. Tho I am absent My heart rests with you. With what pleasing hopes I view the future period when I shall be restored to your arms there to spend My days in Domestic Sweetness with you the Dear Companion of my life, never to be separated from you again during this Transitory and fluctuating life.

I mean to retire from the Buss of publick life, and Spend My Time with you alone in Sweet Retirement, which is My only ambition and ultimate wish.

I have this moment finished My business here which I have got in good Train and hope to wind it up this Touer, and will leave this tomorrow Morning for Jonesborough where I hope to finish it, and tho it is now half after ten o'clock, could not think of going to bed without writing you. May you be blessed with health. May the Goddess of Slumber every evening light on your eyebrows and gently lull you to sleep, and conduct you through the night with pleasing thoughts and pleasant dreams. Could I only know you were contented and enjoyed Peace of Mind, what satisfaction it would afford me whilest travelling the loanly and tiresome road. It would relieve My anxious breast and shorten the way–May the great "I am" bless and protect you until that happy and wished for moment arrives when I am restored to your sweet embrace which is the Nightly prayer of your affectionate husband, Andrew Jackson

P.S. My compliments to my good old Mother Mrs. Donelson, that best of friends. Tell her with what pain I reflect upon leaving home without shaking her by the hand and asking her blessing.

JAMES MADISON

TO

DOLLEY MADISON

---

*J*ames Madison wrote this letter from the President's House during his first term as president.

Washington August 7th. 1809

My Dearest,

We reached the end of our journey yesterday at one o'clock; without interruption of any sort on the road. Mr. Coles had been here sometime, arrived, and Mr. Gilston after a short passage from France, entered Washington about the moment I did. You may guess therefore the volumes of papers before us. I am but just dipping into them; and have seen no one as yet except Mr. Smith for a few minutes last evening. What number of days I may be detained here it is impossible to say. The period you may be sure will be shortened as much as possible. Every thing around and within reminds me that you are absent, and makes me anxious to quit the solitude. In my next I hope I shall be able to say when I shall have this gratification; perhaps also to say something of the intelligence just brought us. I send the paper of this morning which has something on the subject. I hope the communications of Gilston will be found more favorable than is stated. Those from England can scarcely be favorable, when such men hold the reins as we have latterly had to do with. Mr. And Mrs. Ekrsine are here. His successor had not sailed on the 20th of June. God bless you and be assured of my constant affection. J. Madison

*S*arah Polk was making one of her infrequent trips away from the White House when her husband wrote this letter describing life in her absence.

Washington City July 12th. 1847.

My Dear Wife:

I wrote you on yesterday and after closing my day's labour, write again to night, not that I have any thing of interest to communicate, but to comply with my promise & to let you know how much I miss you in the White House. When I went down to breakfast this morning none of the family appeard. They are all fine-sleepers except <u>Wm. Polk's</u> wife who is an early riser. I asked <u>Henry</u>, if he had notified them. He answered, <u>Yes Sir, but things was a heap straighter when Miss Sarah was here</u>, and so I thought. I gave a

JAMES K. POLK WAS A PROSPEROUS PLANTER AND BUSINESSMAN
IN TENNESSEE BEFORE SERVING AS GOVERNOR AND PRESIDENT. HE LED THE
NATION TO VICTORY IN THE MEXICAN WAR OF 1846-1848.

small dinner party to <u>William's</u> wife to day. It consisted of <u>Mr.</u> <u>Buchanan, Mr & Mrs. Mason, Mr & Mrs. Marcy, Mr. and Mrs.</u> <u>Graham, Senator Downs</u> of Louisiana & two young ladies who came with him, <u>Judge Wadswroth</u> of N. York, and one or two other gentlemen. The Dinner was well got up. <u>Bauman</u> you know would attend to that.

The weather is extremly warm, & I fear you will have a disagreeable journey on your return.

Your affectionate Husband, James K. Polk

A B R A H A M   L I N C O L N

T O

M A R Y   L I N C O L N

---

*A*braham Lincoln was serving as a U.S. representative from Illinois when he wrote this excited letter to Mary, who had unwillingly been left behind.

Washington, June 12. 1848

My dear wife:

On my return from Philadelphia, yesterday where, in my anxiety I had been led to attend the whig convention I found your last letter. I was so tired and sleepy, having ridden all night, that I could not answer it till to-day; and now I have to do so in the H.R. The leading matter in your letter, is your wish to return to this side of the Mountains. Will you be a <u>good girl</u> in all things, if I consent? Then come along, and that as <u>soon</u> as possible. Having got the idea in my head, I shall be impatient till I see you. You will not have money enough to bring you; but I presume your uncle will supply you, and I will refund him here. By the way you do not mention whether you have received the fifty dollars I sent you. I do not much fear but that you got it; because the want of it would have induced you say something in relation to it. If your uncle is already at Lexington, you might induce him to start on earlier than the first of July; he could stay in Kentucky longer on his return, and so make up for lost time. Since I began this letter, the H.R. has passed a resolution for adjourning on the 17th July, which probably will pass the Senate. I hope this letter will not be disagreeable to you; which, together with the circumstances under which I write, I hope will excuse me for not writing a longer one. Come on just as soon as you can. I want to see you, and our dear-<u>dear</u> boys very much. Every body here wants to see our dear Bobby.

Affectionately A. Lincoln

ULYSSES S. GRANT
TO
JULIA GRANT

---

*U*lysses and Julia were suffering through an extended separation because of his army assignments on the West Coast, leading this Mexican War veteran to resign his commission later in 1854.

Fort Humboldt. Humboldt Bay, Cal.
February 2, 1853[4]

My Dear Wife

You do not know how forsaken I feel here! The place is good enough but I have interests at others which I cannot help thinking about day and night; then too it is a long time since I made application for orders to go on to Washington to settle my account but not a word in reply do I get. Then I feel again as if I had been separated from you and Fred. long enough and as to Ulys. I have never seen him. He must by this time be talking about as Fred. did when I saw him last. How very much I want to see all of you. I have made up my mind what Ulys. looks like and I am anxious too see if my presentiment is Correct. Does he advance rapidly? Tell me a great deel about him and Fred. and Freds pranks with his Grandpa. How does he git along with his Uncle Lewis?

I do nothing here but set in my room and read and occasionally take a short ride on one of the public horses. There is game here such as ducks, geese &c. which some of the officers amuse themselves by shooting but I have not entered into the sport. Within eight or ten miles Deer and occasionally Elk and black Bear are found. Further back the Grisley Bear are quite numerous. I do not know if I have told you what officers are at this post? Col. Buchanan, Hunt, Collins, Dr. Potts and Lt. Latimer to join. Expected soon. Col. B expects promotion by every Mail which, if he gets, will bring Montgomery and leave me in Command of the post. Mrs. Collins is the only lady at the post. Dr. Potts however will have his wife here in a short time. The quarters are comfortable frame buildings backed by a dense forest of immense trees. In front is the Bay. We are on a bluff which gives us one of the most Commanding views that Can be had from almost any point on the whole Bay. Besides having a view of the Bay itself we can look out to sea as far as the eye can extend. There are four villeges on the Bay. One at the outlet, Humbolt Point is the name, where there are probably not more than 50 inhabitants. What they depend upon for support I don't know. They are probably persons who supposed that it would be the point for a City and they would realize a California fortune by the rise of the lots. Three miles up the Bay is Bucksport and this Garrison. Here geting out lumber is the occupation, and as it finds a ready market in San Francisco this is a flourishing little place of about 200. Three miles further up in Eurieka with a population of about 500 with the same resourses. The mills in these two villages have, for the last year, loaded an average of 19 vessels per month with lumber and as they are building several additional Mills they will load a greater number this year. Twelve miles further up and at the head of the Bay, is Union, the largest and best built town of the whole. From there they pack provisions to the Gold Mines, and return with the dust. Taking all of these villeges together there are about enough ladies to get up a small sized Ball. There has been several of them this winter.

I got one letter from you since I have been here but it was some three months old. I fear very much that I shall loose some before they get in the regular way of Coming. There is no regular Mail between here and San Francisco so the only way we have of get-ing letters off is to give them to some Captain of a vessel to Mail them after he gets down. In the same way Mails are received. This makes it very uncertain as to the time as letter may be on the way. Sometimes, owing to advers winds, vessels are 40 and even 60 days making the passage, while at others they make it in less than two days. So you need not be surprised if sometimes you would be a great while without a letter and then likely enough get three or four at once. I hope the next Mail we get to have several from you. Be particular to pay postage on yours for otherwise they may refuse to deliver them at the San Francisco Post Officer. I Cant pay the postage here having no Stamps and not being able to get them. I have sent below however for some.

I must finish by sending a great deal of love to all of you, Your Pa Ma brother and sisters, niece and nepews. I have not yet fulfilled my promise to Emmy yet to write her a long letter from Humboldt. Kiss our little ones for me. A thousand kisses for yourself dear Julia.
Your Affectionate husband Ulys

LUCY   WEBB   HAYES
TO
RUTHERFORD   B.   HAYES

---

*G*eneral John Fremont had declared martial law in Missouri and issued an order free-ing the slaves when Lucy wrote this letter that included keen political insights. Rutherford was serving as an officer in the Union Army at the time.

Cincinnati. Sept 23rd 1861

Dearest Ruddy.

It has been a long time since I wrote you but every day and hour I think of you and long so much to see you. I received your letter dated the 11th on the 20th—but I knew before that you were in the battle from the paper—I sent your letter on as you desired.

Uncle Birchard has been making a long visit at Columbus. Laura wrote he was quite well and enjoying himself. I was in hopes he would come and see us before he returned to Fremont. It is three weeks Wednesday since I came home—of which ten days I have been quite unwell. My head feeling so badly as to totally unfit me for writing you know your wife is of a Bilious turn but now I am as well as ever. Little Ruddy the darling also has been right sick, but we think now he is better, and soon will be well. He insisted to day on going to see his Pa Pa—wonders when you will come home. It is pleasant to be at home, but each day we miss you more and more—this winter but I will not anticipate you are doing right, I feel and know it—and would not have you otherwise. At times we have such conflicting rumors of troubles in the Cabinet—then the present trouble with Gen. Fremont, till I feel almost crazed and think there are no true men among our leaders. President Lincoln I fear lacks decision—he is too easy—but as silence is the best plan I try to keep so, and avoid hearing all discussions if possible. What do you think of Gen. Fremont—the dispatch this Afternoon is that Lexington, Mo. has been taken by Price—Then if Fremonts Proclamation was right—why must it be modified for Ky. I have no patience nor sympathy nor confidence in the Ky stripe of Union Men—but you will think I am spending my time very unprofitably—but no I am taking care of my three dear boys—thinking of a dear husband and brother all the time.

Mr. Stevenson has been to see me twice. The last time, he wanted a deed of Mrs. Willers. Mrs. W's school opened with 30 Scholars a very good beginning and a prospect of more.

Mrs. Mary Kibleth has a son about one week old—our old friends Auntti and Uncle George are as Kind and attentive—his rents still trouble him—but I read you and brother Joes letters, and he says why how cheerfully they write—and he always appears to feel better.

Our friends in Chillicothe are well. Grandfather Boggs, and his wife, are at Uncle Moses's—the old gentleman is very sick, indeed I do not think he will ever get back to Zanesville.

This morning paper says that, Capt. M'Groaty was a little better, some hopes entertained of his recovery. Where are you to night in what scene of danger or peril. God grant to guard and keep you. Birchie is sitting by me—he wants you to know, that he is trying to work—he sweeps the back pavement—takes down the ashes, and brings up coal for Fannie, says good lessons—and as soon as Ruddy gets well, expects, to start to school. And now dearest good bye once more, or how dear doubly dear—you are to us—We do not forget, or cease thinking at any time, every thing brings you to my mind. Blessings and Kisses from us all.

Your Affec Wife, Lu

[P.S.] Jim has been having chills. I do not know what he intends doing, he is studying hard. Tell brother Joe that for my sake— Mother is willing and glad he is with you—we do not get low spirited—but always look forward to the happy reunion.

BENJAMIN HARRISON
TO
CAROLINE HARRISON

---

*B*enjamin Harrison wrote this thoughtful, reflective, but melancholy letter to Caroline as the Union Army stood before Atlanta, Georgia, in 1864.

HeadQuarters 1stBrig 3Div 20VC.
Before Atlanta Ga
Aug 20th 1864

My dear wife

I wrote you yesterday in great anxiety & in rather low spirits, as I had not heard from you since the 8th where you were quite sick. My mind has been relieved today by the receipt of your two letters of the 10th & 14th inst and my spirits have gone up at a bound. I feel as if I ought to write today not only to acknowledge the receipt of those letters, but because it is my <u>birthday</u> & suggests many memories of the past, among the happiest of which your

BENJAMIN HARRISON, HIS WIFE CAROLINE, AND SOME FRIENDS
STAND ON THE REAR PLATFORM OF THEIR TRAIN ON THE WAY
TO HARRISON'S 1889 PRESIDENTIAL INAUGURATION.

sweet form is closely interwoven. Perhaps you will not remember the day, as it is not the anniversary of an event so important to you as to me, but still perhaps you will think of me today a little oftener & more tenderly than usual. I am <u>thirty one</u> years old today, & nearly Eleven years of this period we have been man & wife. For how many more years God has decreed my life to be lengthened out, He only knows & whether they shall all be as full of blessing as those that are gone. But whether they be many or few I hope they will bear better witness of a faithful discharge of duty both those I love on earth & my Father in Heaven. Who is there that could not mend his life if he could live his years over again, & how many think more of the errors of the past, than of the promise and opportunities of the future. I hope to be a better husband & father, a better Citizen and a better Christian in the future than I have been in the past.

You may think it strange that I promise nothing to my present profession as a soldier. The reason is that I hope my mission as a soldier will end before another birthday. Certainly my present term of enlistment will expire before next August 20th, and unless Gen. Hooker should accomplish his threat of making me

HELLO AND GOOD-BYE 319

a Brigadier General, I will be a citizen again. For after three years of the best service I could render, if they don't promote me, I shall think the public does not need my help in that department and shall try to help myself in some other pursuit. The very complimentary notice which Gen. Hooker made of me in conversation with Halstead was, of course, very gratifying to me; but in all candor I do think "Uncle Joe" was somewhat extravagant & hope he will not push me <u>too</u> rapidly, as that has been the ruin of more than one good officer in the war. On your account and my children, I should like to wear the "lone star" when I can feel that I have <u>won</u> it, but my own ambition does not soar very high; and as such favors have been generally obtained through political influence and hard begging, I fear we need not look with much confidence to my obtaining it. The high compliment which Gen. Hooker has bestowed upon me, and the confidence which I have won among the brave officers and men of my command is worth more to me than a Brigadier's star, though the public will of course look to the latter as the evidence of the former. Genl H's official report will I am sure speak very formally of my conduct in the fight of the 20th & whether promotion follows or not his testimony will go before the public & there is no General officer in the Army from whom I should prize such testimony more. By the way how suddenly you have changed your opinion of the General since he has shown me some Kindness. When we first came under his command I remember that you did not much like it & spoke of him as ambitious & careless about sacrificing men. Now this only shows that your affection for my unworthy self, makes you like those who show me kindness & favor & I fear hate those who do not.

But I confess to some such inconsistency myself, though I shall of course claim that my change of opinion was brought about by observation of him in the field & not by any favors shown me. But I have talked enough of myself and my humble military career. Lest your affection might lead you to exaggerate my merits as a soldier, let me assure you that I am not a Julius Caesar nor a Napoleon, but a plain Hoosier Colonel with no more relish for a fight than for a good breakfast & <u>hardly</u> so much.

Your letter of the 14th was a real treasure & shows that you can write <u>long</u> letters when you try very hard & this fact being more <u>demonstrated</u> I shall be satisfied with <u>nothing less</u> than <u>eight</u> pages of the note paper you use. You make a great error when you say that you are not egotistic enough to fill a letter with matters about yourself. If you do not doubt my affection for you, you must Know that such things are just what I most want to hear about. How can true marital affection so well display itself as in a full & thorough communion in all matters of the heart, mind & life. Let me know all your feelings, hopes wishes, trials & joys that I may share them all with you.

As to the boots, I am much obliged to you for anticipating my want. You may have me a pair made, good heavy soles, upper rather light & wide tops reaching a little below the Knee. The best way to send them will be by mail unless you can find some one coming direct to the Regt. I don't think Henry has ever got his, at least John Wallace has not been here. Soldiers in returning are frequently stopped for weeks at the posts along the route at the different forts. Such packgs are constantly coming my mail & the postage will not be very much.

As to my complaint about Henry's treatment of me, you had better say nothing to any of the family. I have no bad feeling towards him & will still do him any kindness that I can, but he has taken his path and any very intimate relations between us are not possible until he makes amends for the past. Genl Ward will make a good patron for him & he will possibly not need any good offices from me, though he has profited by a good many in the past.

I have concluded to have Mark Ohm upon my staff as Inspector. He is a very agreeable gentleman, a good officer & deserves some relief from duty in the line.

The extract you sent me from the Cinti. Com was I have learned, from the pen of Maj. Higgins 73 Ohio in our 3 Brigade. I have only a slight acquaintance with him but I suppose Col. Coburns friends will view this as another evidence of my seeking notoriety with papers & etc. My under cloths particularly shirts & socks are getting quite dilapidatted. Both my big toes have made their way through both socks & boots & are constantly peering up at me, as if in reproach for leaving them uncovered. I think I shall have to select the most torn pair of socks & unravel them to get yarn to mend the others. Our black-woman I suppose has skill sufficient to accomplish the repairs. Some of my shirts have shrunk so that I can scarcely bend my arms in the sleeves & have had to cut through the band behind to get them buttoned around the neck, which has so shortened the tail behind that by the <u>severest stretching</u> that it can be made to reach my pants. However these things do very well in the army, at least when on Campaign and I shall look to my bureau drawer for a better outfit when I come home.

We have today succeeded in making a sort of armistice on the picket line which has stopped the constant firing which has annoyed us so much inside the lines. The agreement is simply that we wont fire if they wont. One Reb came half way today & traded a plug of tobacco for one of our newspapers. They said they had no newspapers to give in exchange. The danger is now that they will become too careless and carry their intimacy too far. We can hear nothing definite from the right, but are daily hoping that the movements there will compel them to evacuate & close the Campaign. It is said we have the Macon RR but I don't know how true it is, as we have a thousand false rumours daily.

Col Merrill had his application for leave returned today, with an order sending him to Hospital at Chattanoga for treatment, but I have an idea that he will get home yet before he Comes back to the Regt. He is doing duty all the time & don't look very sick, but he may be worse than he appears. I am inclined to think that the condition of his business & a desire to get home, rather than his Condition of health was the motive in seeking the leave. I should not like to leave my command on "Sick leave" unless I were utterly incapacitated for duty here. But every one for himself. Col M has certainly done his duty well during the Campaign.

I have labored faithfully for an hour to make out what it was the Dr said was the matter with your knee but the term seems to have given you some difficulty in the spelling & you have blurred it so I cannot make it out. I hope however it is nothing dangerous or chronic in its character & that you will not be troubled with it again. You must be <u>very</u> careful about exerting yourself too much or you will be sick again. Remember I want you & the children to be in perfect health when I come home, so that we can enjoy my short visit to the uttermost.

Well, I have again given you a very long letter & could write more but must go round the lines before supper to see how things look & for a little exercise.

Write to me often & tell me everything I am in excellent health & since I have heard of your recovery, in fine & hopeful spirits May God abundantly bless you & the dear Children & bring me to your arms again when my duty here is done.

Love to all friends. Your Affectionate Husband Benj Harrison

THEODORE ROOSEVELT

TO

ALICE LEE

---

*A*lice Lee had known Theodore Roosevelt, a student at Harvard College, only two months when she received this letter, but he had already decided to marry her.

Cambridge, December 6, 1878

Dear Alice,

I have been anxiously expecting a letter from you and Rose for the last two or three days; but none has become. You <u>must</u> not forget our tintype spree; I have been dextrously avoiding forming any engagements for Saturday. I send this by Minot Weld—who knows nothing of the contents, whatever he may say. Tell Rose that I never passed a pleasanter Thanksgiving than at her house.

Judging from the accounts I have received the new dress for the party at New Bedford must have been a complete success. <u>Your Fellow-conspirator</u>

THEODORE ROOSEVELT
TO
ALICE LEE ROOSEVELT

*W*hile serving as a New York assemblyman, Theodore wrote this longing letter to his wife. It would be just eight days before her death from complications giving birth to their daughter, also named Alice.

February 6, 1884. Albany

Darling Wifie,

How I did hate to leave my bright, sunny little love yesterday afternoon! I love you and long for you all the time, and oh so tenderly; doubly tenderly now, my sweetest little wife. I just long for Friday evening when I shall be with you again. Today I sparred as usual; my teacher is a small man and in the set-to today I bloodied his nose by an upper cut, and knocked him out of time.

In the House we had a most exciting debate on my Reform Charter bill, and I won a victory, having it ordered to a third reading. Tomorrow evening I am to dine at the Rathbones, at half past seven; it was very kind to ask me, but I do not anticipate much fun.

Goodbye, sweetheart. Your Ever Loving Thee

WOODROW WILSON
TO
ELLEN WILSON

*E*llen was in Gainesville, Georgia, recovering from the birth of their first child, Margaret Woodrow Wilson, and Woodrow was teaching at Bryn Mawr College in Pennsylvania, when he wrote this letter. He was on the verge of going to Georgia to bring his family home to Bryn Mawr.

Bryn Mawr, 4 June, '86

My own darling,

I have just returned from my last class exercise. Think of that! How much nearer it seems to bring me to you! I shall probably have to go on, an hour a day, with Miss Bancroft next week, but that does not mean any work outside of that one hour, and will. I think, by giving me something to do, save me the impatient feeling which would inevitably come with unoccupied days <u>on which I could not go to you</u>. True, I'll have packing to do, and I shall probably spread it over several days; but if I knew that I could go to you as soon as I finished my packing, it wouldn't take me many hours to finish! I could be off <u>to-night</u>! One week from tonight <u>I will</u> be off—Oh, isn't that just too good to be true!

I received a very sweet letter from Jessie this morning—and a pretty, embroidered, lined, and scented blanket for baby, which I am to bring to you. She did not know your address. Here's a passage from the letter: "And cousin Woodrow you must see that Ellie Lou does not exert herself too much, or she will sow the seeds of invalidism that will make you both miserable in years to come. When I was in Rome I heard that she had gotten up already, and it made me feel dreadfully sorry to hear it. I write you this for I am afraid she, like every young mother, through ignorance, may injure herself for life." Rather a remarkable statement, that 'every young mother injures herself for life'. I smile, and think of Beth; but, as my letters will prove, I can't help saying 'amen' to the advice conveyed. She says that 'we have started out to raise a family about as quickly as they did'! But you shall read the whole letter when I come. 'When I come'! How many things of all sorts I have been putting off till that sweet time—principally <u>love-making</u>! You may not think, Miss, from the character and contents of some of my letters, that such a postponement has been very evident in this correspondence; but it has been very evident to me almost impotent unless I can <u>say</u> them with my lips and interpret them with my eyes—not to mention that sweet lovemaking in which there are no words spoken at all. But <u>I'm coming</u>—and then we'll <u>see</u> if it isn't better! Kiss my precious baby ever so many times for her father. A kiss for little sister, love for Eddie, aunt Lou, and all. You are my sweetheart, precious, my queen, my life—and I am <u>all</u> your own Woodrow

[P.S.] I enjoyed the affair at the Garretts' very much indeed last night. I shall myself be the sixth letter after this!

GROVER CLEVELAND
T O
FRANCES FOLSOM CLEVELAND

---

*I*n between his two presidential terms, Grover Cleveland practiced law in New York while his wife sometimes stayed with friends or at their summer home in Massachusetts.

May 26 1891

Darling

Only a word to night to say that I am pegging away as fast as I can to get done with my work so that I can go for good next Friday. I got an...but I shall be with you Saturday whether I get done or not. I went to the Democratic Club to dinner and when I returnd to the hotel I found Dr. Bryants card. I am very sorry I did not see him. They told me that Col. Lamont had been here too. I have been here two days trying to get through but I ... I shall be so glad to get away and be with you. I breakfast every morning at 8 o.c. but this morning I slipped back to the old ways of 8:15.

I love you very much but you know that by this time. I send you ten dollars as you bid me to in your letter.

With all the love in the world and Kindest remembrances to all the Jefferson household I am Your loving husband G. C.

PRESIDENT GROVER CLEVELAND AND FRANCES FOLSOM,
THE TWENTY-ONE-YEAR-OLD DAUGHTER OF HIS DECEASED FRIEND
AND LAW PARTNER, WERE MARRIED IN THE FIRST AND ONLY WHITE
HOUSE WEDDING OF A PRESIDENT ON JUNE 2, 1886.

IDA McKINLEY
TO
WILLIAM McKINLEY

---

*W*illiam McKinley was the governor of Ohio and preparing to seek the Republican presidential nomination when Ida sent him these two telegrams.

Columbus Ohio Oct 8 1895

Governor McKinley

Feeling much better homesick for your arrival. Are you well.

Mrs. McKinley

Columbus O.

[October 18] 11 p.m. 1895

Governor McKinley

Received your Telegram. Delighted your well. Am comfortable but homesick.

Mrs. McKinley

WILLIAM McKINLEY
TO
IDA McKINLEY

---

*J*ust months before his assassination, President William McKinley sent this routine telegram to his wife. It is the only known extant message from him to her.

En Route Indianapolis to Canton,

March 17, 1901

Mrs. William McKinley

We are just leaving Indianapolis. Feel very well. Will be home seven o'clock to-morrow morning. William McKinley

Charge the President's private account, Executive Mansion, Washington, D.C.

WARREN G. HARDING
TO
FLORENCE M. HARDING

---

*W*arren's letter to his wife, written while on a trip to Florida, included news of a long-running card game, one of his overriding interests.

Friday 7–3:30 p.m

My Dear Florence:

We are due in Jaxonville in an hour. Trip has not seemed exceedingly long; because we have played heaps of auction en route—not to my profit. All six have played cutting in and out, and Mrs. Weeks has cleaned up nearly everybody. She can buy a new gown. Cummins had such bad luck yesterday afternoon that he grew petulant and swore off for the trip. We were then playing for 1 cent a point. He resumed this morning and is now playing for 21/2 cents a point. He hates to lose. So do I, but I never reveal it, if I can help it.

This is not a very attractive route for travel. Not so interesting as the Q & C. So much low-land and it is all flooded. Never saw so much water.

Peaches are in blossom and look very attractive. New foliage is out on many of the trees, but the country so far has not had an attractive appearance.

Train is not crowded. Has lots of empty space. Travel is a ll in the other direction. Everybody says Florida is full up.

FIRST LADY FLORENCE HARDING PINS A FLOWER ON THE LAPEL OF PRESIDENT WARREN HARDING IN THE WHITE HOUSE GARDENS DURING HIS PRESIDENCY.

HELLO AND GOOD-BYE   329

Sorry you are not along. So is everybody in the party. I think you could have made the journey "comfy" enough.

Mrs. Weeks expressed her disappointment several times. Hal has spoken of his disappointment often. He says you are a good sport. You would enjoy the bridge, but you would probably be broke. I am out $40, and I am supposed to be luckier than you.

There is nothing else to tell today. I scratch this while sitting out. Hope you and Stella are going on finely. I send you my love, and my regrets again that you are not along. W. G.

HARRY S. TRUMAN
T O
BESS TRUMAN

---

*B*ess Truman had just left her husband at military training camp at Ft. Leaven-worth when he wrote this letter. Her tooth problem turned out to be her pregnancy with daughter Mary Margaret.

Ft. Leavenworth, Kans. July 27, 1923

Dear Bess:

I wanted to go home with you so badly last night, I could hardly stand it. You just looked as if you needed a shoulder to put your head on, and I, of course, acted like a man brute usually does. I am dead sure you didn't feel a bit good, and that bumping did not make you any better. Well, it won't be but a couple of days more. I'll bet you'll feel fine though when all those teeth are fixed as they should be.

Well, yesterday you know was turnip day, and the instructions are to sow them wet or dry. If they'd been sown, they'd have been up tomorrow.

We had a trash over about 12:30 last night and I got up and loosened the ropes of our tent with assistance of Groves and Bliss to Keep it from pulling the pegs out and falling down. There was more racket and chasing around in Avenue A about that time than there is on the real one. (Our street is A.) We had a game of leapfrog this morning across the lot and back, and it was a circus. All the short-legged men got bumped or thrown, and it was almost a riot. Then double time and the usual light breakfast of prunes, oatmeal, fried eggs, milk, and oranges. We go on a communication problem today.

I hope you are feeling well. Lots of love. Yours, Harry

C A L V I N   C O O L I D G E
T O
G R A C E   C O O L I D G E

---

*G*race had been in Northampton, Massachusetts, caring for her ill mother, Lemira Goodhue, when President Coolidge wrote her this letter catching her up with what she was missing.

December 22, 1928

My dear Grace:
I do not seem to have any letter from you, so have no doubt you are getting along all right and expecting to return tomorrow or the next day.

I had Mr. Firestone and Mrs. Firestone and all the little Firestones, including the daughter of one son, in to luncheon today. Mrs. Firestone wanted me to be sure to tell you how sorry she was you were not there. They fed the dogs so much that finally Calamity Jane climbed on the table and ate up the ice cream of the Firestone boy that you love, and then grabbed a whole chocolate-covered cup cake. I suppose she does not like ice cream without cake.

I have sent the opossum to the Zoo, and I have received another turkey from Texas. Not much of anything is coming in for you. I presume that people have seen in the paper that you weren't at home. I hope that it is not too cold for you at Northampton. With love

FRANKLIN D. ROOSEVELT
TO
ELEANOR ROOSEVELT

*P*resident Roosevelt and his peripatetic wife were both traveling when Franklin wrote this letter describing his latest fishing adventure combined with a tour of Haiti, just before the withdrawal of U.S. Marines.

U.S.S. Houston
From Cap Haitien to Mayaguez
July 5 1934

Dearest Babs

The Lord only knows when this will catch up with my Will o' the Wisp wife, but at least I am proceeding according to schedule, and it is a grand trip thus far. Yesterday we had a good day's fishing, stopping for 9 hours in the S.E. Bahamas, and F and J and I all got fish—also the people in the other boat—Rudolph and Dick Jervis and Gus. The "3 Musketeers" watched the fishing for a while. They have been I fear rather shaken up on their destroyer but Eddie Raddan's leg seems really better.

Today's ceremony at Cap Haitien was most colorful and interesting. A gayly decorated barge, specially built up to let us go on it from a gang plank conveyed us to a specially built landing where stood President Vincent and his whole cabinet, with the Garde d'Haiti drawn up behind and a huge crowd of cheering populace lining the quays and the roofs. Vincent and I drove through many streets and a good many of the buildings date back to Spanish and French days—then to the Club where there was a reception, a speech and toast by Vincent and a speech and toast by me—part in French, but when I got to the serious part I shifted to English!

When we first anchored F. and J. went right ashore and drove to the Palace of Christopher Sans Souci and saw the "Citadel" from the foot of the mountains. They rejoined me at the Club and we all returned to the Houston and received Vincent and his cabinet for a 15 minute return call. Many guns and much ceremony all day but I hope it will do good to Haiti and that they won't start revolting as soon as we withdraw the last marines on August 15th. Perhaps the Haitians will recognize the vast amount of good things we have done for them in these 18 years. The <u>people</u> do, but the ruling mulatto class doesn't, I fear.

Tomorrow we land at Mayaguez at 7:30 a.m.—a long hot day I fear. I will try to send you a line from St. Thomas on Saturday, and then my next will be from Panama—you won't get that much before I see you on the dock in Portland.

The boys are really interested and perfectly fine about everything. We have movies in the well deck every night surrounded by the officers and crew—tonight a sharp thunder storm stopped it in the middle. In my mess we have Capt. Brown and Dr. McIntire—5 of us—and the mess boys from "Sequoia" take very good care of us.

Ever so much love and do take very good care of yourself.

Your devoted. F.

L A D Y   B I R D   T A Y L O R

T O

L Y N D O N   B .   J O H N S O N

---

*L*yndon was in Washington, D.C., working as a congressional aide and going to law school, and Lady Bird was in Texas, pondering her life choices after graduating from the University of Texas, when they exchanged these letters.

Monday Nite [September 24, 1934]

Dearest

Whatever are you doing in room #1? I didn't know they had such a number in hotels!

You know, love, its been quite several days since I've had a letter from you! But I shan't fuss 'cause I think its plain silly (besides presumptious) to fuss at someone you love—and besides I feel sure there'll be one for me tomorro morning when I go down.

Yesterday I set out through the woods for Mrs. Fox's in the quite early morning—and came upon more beautiful little glades and hollows in the woods. And finally emerged at a cornfield that was practically covered with the <u>bluest</u> blue Morning Glories! Mrs. Fox is a rich old lady-grand-daughter of a fine old Southern family and one of these professional "old Southerners." She heartily dislikes most everybody around here but happens to be quite fond of me. And she's one of the few people around here I enjoy being with.

She has a gold colly dog who weighs a ton and who pounces upon me every time I go over there. He nearly eats me up and I <u>love</u> him.

Lyndon, when I get up to Washington my brain will have reverted to the idiot stage! (That's the 3 to 7 year old, isn't it?) 'Cause I never use it for anything more exacting than the design I want for my garden seat and the best material to upholster the chairs in et cetera ad finitum. So I'm going to buy me two or three up-to-the-minute books on economics or government or what's-the-world-coming-to. And one good one on Russia, which I'm very interested in and know nothing about. Do you ever read this kind—I mean have you any suggestions?

O, dear. I <u>do</u> miss you so But its not a completely unpleasant feeling 'cause I can look forward to when I see you again! Write me some more about this Thanksgiving idea. Are you seriously considering it?

This afternoon I took the films to be developed. If they're any good I shall send you several. And when I go to Dallas Nov. 12 for the API I shall have you a big, <u>nice</u> one made—if you want me to! I wouldn't here for the <u>world</u>. The Marshall photographer makes people look like ogres. Here are two little ones made in my beloved Austin in the enchanting Month of April. Goodnight, My dearest, Please write me. I love you, Bird.

LYNDON B. JOHNSON
TO
LADY BIRD TAYLOR

House of Representatives Washington, D.C.
Tuesday [September 25, 1934]

My dear

All day Sunday I waited for Monday and a letter from you. Disappointed Monday I longed for Tuesday—longed for a word from you. The last mail has just been delivered—now I will look forward to getting a word from my love tomorrow.

Don't even have a picture to gaze at when I'm dreaming and planning—dreaming of you—planning for you.

Only one letter from Mother since my arrival. Her reference to you—altho' an unusual expression for her—yet a most gratifying one to her first born. Destroy Mother's letter and write if you want to. All my love. Lyndon

PAT NIXON
TO
RICHARD NIXON

*W*hile a naval officer during World War II, Richard Nixon exchanged these letters, exuding love and loneliness, with his wife.

[1942]

Dear Plum,

Always write the day on your letters so I can picture it—also because the service seems to get all mixed up. I mail you a letter every day so I don't know how you get three at a time.

It's two o'clock but I just had to write you to say <u>how very much I love you!</u> It was clear all over again when talking to you on the phone. Also want to say that I hope I said nothing to worry you! When you are working so hard, etc. it would be awful to add to the load. In talking with you tonight it was the first time I really felt it was you.

RICHARD NIXON
TO
PAT NIXON

[August 17, 1943]

It is just one year ago that I left you at the Union Station and went off to Quonset. I shall never forget the day—Jake taking us to the station—saying goodbye to you—that lonely ride up to Providence—every mile reminding me of the time you and I had taken it together. Then the first night in the barracks—meeting Nimms, trying to sleep. That first week was the longest I've ever known—what with shots—marching—studying etc. I thought of you so much.

DWIGHT D. EISENHOWER
TO
MAMIE EISENHOWER

---

*G*eneral Eisenhower defends his lack of "direct" communication to his wife during their long wartime separation that sometimes strained their personal relations.

I'm a bit puzzled over your outburst about me sending messages via aides and secretaries

Naturally I cannot go to telegraph offices myself whenever the spirit might move me. Sometimes, over miles of bad telephone cable I dictate a short message to you with instructions it is to be placed on the teletype at once. Naturally also it is an aide or a secretary that has to do the mechanical part of the transaction. To save me I can see nothing wrong in this—if there is then I'll just have to send messages when I get back to main headquarters, which is infrequently.

Today my brother Roy would have been 52 years old, had he lived. I'd like to send a message to Edna—but that's impossible.

Johnny has not written to me, as yet. Looks like he would have sent a "bread and butter" note—but I do know he is terribly busy, and so preoccupied that letter writing can be an awful chore.

In my present location I have a nice camp—much better than the one I recently left. But we're not really settled and won't be until we get our next main headquarters established. It is a long irksome business to move a staff the size of mine, together with all its collaborating bodies, and its signal communications. These last are enormous.

The phone has just rung, saying my plane is at the field. So I'll start back to main. For the next day or so I'll be making some inspections—then back here again.

RONALD REAGAN
TO
NANCY REAGAN

---

*R*onald and Nancy Reagan had been married only three years and he was traveling for General Electric when he wrote from Atlanta, Georgia.

Sunday [March 20, 1955]
Atlanta Biltmore, Atlanta, Georgia

My Darling

Here it is—our day and if we were home we'd have a fire and "funnies" and we'd hate anyone who called or dropped in.

As it is I'm sitting here on the 6th floor beside a phony fire place looking out at a grey wet sky and listening to a radio play music not intended for one person alone.

Never the less I wouldn't trade the way I feel for the lonliness of those days when one place was like another and it didn't matter how long I stayed away. With all the "missing you" there is still such a wonderful warmth in the lonliness like looking forward to a bright warm room. No matter how dark & cold it is at the moment—you know the room is there and waiting.

Of course when I say "you" anymore I'm talking a package deal—you and the two & a half year old you. Time goes so slowly and I'm such a coward when you are out of sight—so afraid something will go wrong if I'm not there to take care of you so be very careful.

It's time to move on to the next town now and every move is a step toward home and you. I love you so very much I don't even mind that life made me wait so long to find you. The waiting only made the finding sweeter.

When you get this we will be almost halfway through the lonely stretch.

I love you, Ronnie

SOURCES

Primary Sources

Adams Family Papers, Massachusetts Historical Society.
Charles Francis Adams, ed., *Letters of Mrs. Adams, Wife of John Adams.* Boston:
Charles C. Little and James Brown, 1840.
L. H. Butterfield et al., *Adams Family Correspondence.* 8 vols. Cambridge:
The Belknap Press of Harvard University, 1961–93.

Chester A. Arthur Papers, Library of Congress.

George H. W. Bush Family Papers, Houston, Texas. George Bush,
All the Best, My Life in Letters and Other Writings. New York: Scribner, 1999.

Rosalynn Carter, *First Lady from Plains.* Boston:
Houghton Mifflin Company, 1984.

Grover Cleveland Papers, Library of Congress.

Hillary Rodham Clinton, *Living History.* New York: Simon & Schuster, 2003.

Calvin Coolidge Papers, Library of Congress.
Calvin Coolidge Papers, Forbes Library, Northampton, Massachusetts.

Eisenhower Papers, Dwight D. Eisenhower Library, Abilene, Kansas.
Louis Galambos, Daun VanEe et al., eds.,
The Papers of Dwight David Eisenhower. 21 vols. Baltimore:
The Johns Hopkins University Press, 1970–2001.
John S. D. Eisenhower, ed., *Dwight D. Eisenhower: Letters to Mamie.* New York:
Doubleday & Company, 1978.

Gerald R. Ford, *A Time to Heal: The Autobiography of Gerald R. Ford.* New York: Harper & Row, Publishers, 1979.

James Garfield Papers, Library of Congress.
John Shaw, ed., *Crete and James: Personal Letters of Lucretia and James Garfield.* East Lansing: Michigan State University Press, 1994.

Ulysses S. Grant Papers, Library of Congress.
John Y. Simon, ed., *The Papers of Ulysses S. Grant.* 26 vols. Carbondale: Southern Illinois University Press, 1967–.

Warren G. Harding Papers, Ohio Historical Society.

Rutherford B. Hayes Papers, Hayes Presidential Library, Fremont, Ohio.

Lou Henry Hoover Papers, Herbert Hoover Presidential Library, West Branch, Iowa.

Andrew Jackson Papers, Library of Congress.
Sam B. Smith et al., eds., *The Papers of Andrew Jackson.* 6 vols. Knoxville: The University of Tennessee Press, 1980–.

Thomas and Martha Jefferson in Hooe Papers, James Monroe Museum and Law Library.

Bill Adler, ed., *The Eloquent Jacqueline Kennedy Onassis.* New York: HarperCollins Publishers, 2004.

Abraham Lincoln Papers, Library of Congress.
Abraham Lincoln Papers, Illinois Historical Society.
Roy P. Basler, ed., *The Collected Works of Abraham Lincoln.* 9 vols. New Brunswick, New Jersey: Rutgers University Press, 1953–55.

James Madison Papers, Library of Congress. James Madison Papers, American Philosophical Society, Philadelphia, Pennsylvania.
Mary Estelle Cutts Papers, Schlesinger Library, Radcliffe College, Cambridge, Massachusetts.
David B. Mattern and Holly C. Shulman, eds., *The Selected Letters of Dolley Payne Madison.* Charlottesville, Virginia: University of Virginia Press, 2003.
Robert Rutland et al., eds., *The Papers of James Madison.* Presidential Series. 5 vols. Charlottesville: University Press of Virginia, 1984–.

William McKinley Papers, Library of Congress.

James Monroe Papers, James Monroe Museum and Law Library, Fredericksburg, Virginia.

Julie Nixon Eisenhower, *Pat Nixon: The Untold Story.* New York: Simon and Schuster, 1986.
Richard Nixon, *RN: The Memoirs of Richard Nixon.* New York: Simon and Schuster, 1978.

Franklin Pierce Papers, Library of Congress.

James Polk Papers, Library of Congress.
Herbert Weaver et al., eds., *Correspondence of James K. Polk.* 10 vols. Nashville: Vanderbilt University Press, 1969–.

Reagan Papers, Ronald Reagan Presidential Library, Simi Valley, California.
Nancy Reagan, *I Love You Ronnie: The Letters of Ronald Reagan to Nancy Reagan.* New York: Random House, 2000.
Kiron K. Skinner et al., eds. Reagan: *A Life in Letters.* New York: Free Press, Simon & Schuster, 2003.

Franklin D. Roosevelt Presidential Library, Hyde Park, New York.
Elliott Roosevelt, ed., F.D.R.: *His Personal Letters, 1928–1945.* 2 vols. New York: Duell, Sloan and Pearce, 1950.

Theodore Roosevelt Papers, Library of Congress.
Theodore Roosevelt Collection, Harvard College Library, Harvard University.
H. W. Brands, ed., *The Selected Letters of Theodore Roosevelt.* New York: Cooper Square Press, 2001.
Elting E. Morison et al., eds., *The Letters of Theodore Roosevelt.* 8 vols. Cambridge, Massachusetts: Harvard University Press, 1951–54.

William Howard Taft Papers, Library of Congress.

Harry S. Truman Papers, Truman Library, Independence, Missouri.
Monte M. Poen, ed., *Letters Home by Harry Truman.* New York: G. P. Putnam's Sons, 1984.

John Tyler Papers, Library of Congress.
Lyon G. Tyler, *The Letters and Times of the Tylers.* 3 vols. Richmond, Virginia: Whitten and Shipperson, 1884–85 and Williamsburg, Virginia: [William and Mary College], 1896.

George Washington Papers, Mount Vernon Ladies Aid Association.
Tudor Place, Carostead Foundation, Washington, D.C.

John C. Fitzpatrick, ed., *The Writings of George Washington.* 39 vols.
Washington: GPO, 1931–44.

Edith Galt Wilson Papers, Library of Congress.
Woodrow Wilson Papers, Library of Congress.
Woodrow Wilson Papers, Princeton University, Princeton, New Jersey.

Secondary Sources

Carl S. Anthony, *America's First Families.* New York:
Simon and Schuster, 2000.

Robert A. Caro, *The Years of Lyndon Johnson.* 2 vols. New York:
Alfred A. Knopf, 1990, 2002.

Betty Boyd Caroli, *The Roosevelt Women.* New York: Basic Books, 1998.

Thomas L. Connelly and Michael D. Senecal, *Almanac of American Presidents
from 1789 to the Present.* New York: Oxford, 1991.

Frank Cormier, *LBJ: The Way He Was.* New York: Doubleday & Co., 1977.

W. H. Crook, *Memories of the White House.* Boston, Massachusetts:
Little, Brown and Company, 1911.

Kathleen Dalton, *Theodore Roosevelt: A Strenuous Life.* New York:
Alfred A. Knopf, 2002.

William A. DeGregorio, *The Complete Book of U.S. Presidents.* New York:
Dembner Books, 1989.

Gerard Gawalt and Ann Gawalt, *First Daughters:
Letters between U.S. Presidents and Their Daughters.* New York:
Black Dog & Leventhal and the Library of Congress, 2004.

Joseph E. Fields, *"Worthy Partner": The Papers of Martha Washington.*
Westport, Connecticut: Greenwood Press, 1994.

Doris Kearns Goodwin, *Lyndon Johnson and the American Dream.* New York:
St. Martin's Press, 1991.

Doris Kearns Goodwin, *No Ordinary Time: Franklin and Eleanor Roosevelt, The Home Front in World War II*. New York: Simon and Schuster, 1994.

Joseph N. Kane, *Facts about the Presidents*. New York: Harper & Row, 1978.

Margaret Leech and Harry J. Brown, *The Garfield Orbit*. New York: Harper & Row, 1978.

William Manchester, *The Death of a President, November 20–November 25, 1963*. New York: Harper & Row, Publishers, 1967.

Eleanor Wilson McAdoo, *The Woodrow Wilsons*. New York: Macmillan Company, 1937.

_____, ed., *The Priceless Gift: The Love Letters of Woodrow Wilson and Ellen Axson Wilson*. New York: McGraw-Hill Book Company Inc., 1962.

David McCullough, *John Adams*. New York: Simon & Schuster, 2001.

_____, *Truman*. New York: Simon & Schuster, 1992.

Edmund Morris, *The Rise of Theodore Roosevelt*. New York: Coward, McCann & Geoghegan, 1979.

Sylvia Jukes Morris, *Edith Kermit Roosevelt: Portrait of a Lady*. New York: Coward, McCann & Geoghegan, Inc., 1980.

Paul C. Nagel, *The Adams Women: Abigail and Louisa Adams, Their Sisters and Daughters*. New York: Oxford, 1987.

_____, *John Quincy Adams: A Public Life, a Private Life*. New York: Alfred A. Knopf, 1997.

Allan Nevins, ed., *Letters of Grover Cleveland, 1850–1908*. Boston: Houghton Mifflin Company, 1933.

Geoffrey Perret, *Ulysses S. Grant: Solider and President*. New York: Random House, 1997.

Monte M. Poen, ed., *Letters Home by Harry Truman*. New York: G. P. Putnam's Sons, 1984.

Ishbel Ross, *An American Family: The Tafts—1678 to 1964*. New York: World Publishing Company, 1964.

Frances W. Saunders, *Ellen Axson Wilson*. Chapel Hill, North Carolina: University of North Carolina Press, 1985.

Dorothy Schneider and Carl J. Schneider, *First Ladies*. New York: Checkmark Books, 2001.

Robert Seager II, *And Tyler Too. A Biography of John Tyler & Julia Gardiner Tyler*. New York: McGraw-Hill Book Company, 1963.

William Seale, *The President's House: A History*. 2 vols. Washington, D.C.: White House Historical Association, 1986.

Harry J. Sievers, *Benjamin Harrison: Hoosier President, White House and After*. New York: Bobbs-Merrill Company, 1968.

John Y. Simon, ed., *The Personal Memoirs of Julia Dent Grant*. New York: G. P. Putnam's Sons, 1975.

Marie Smith and Louise Durbin, *White House Brides*. Washington, D.C.: Acropolis Books, 1966.

Nancy Kegan Smith and Mary C. Ryan, eds., *Modern First Ladies.: Their Documentary Legacy*. Washington, D.C.: National Archives and Records Administration, 1989.

Hans L. Trefousse, *Andrew Johnson: A Biography*. New York: W. W. Norton & Co., 1989.

Margaret Truman, *The President's House*. New York: Ballantine Books, 2003.

T. Harry Williams, ed., *Hayes: The Diary of a President, 1875–1881*. New York: David McKay Company, 1964.

ACKNOWLEDGMENTS

This book was compiled with the assistance of Jane Cavanaugh Gawalt.

A special thanks to those people who generously donated their time and effort to locate letters and photographs and provide valuable information—Wallace F. Dailey, Nan Card, Joanne Drake, Daniel Preston, and Mike Hill.

First, to those staff members in the libraries and offices of presidents, many thanks for their extra assistance: Nancy Lisenby and Linda Casey Poepsel, the Office of George H. W. Bush; Joanne Drake; Nan Card, Rutherford B. Hayes Presidential Center; Elizabeth L. Plummer, Ohio Historical Society; the anonymous staff members who processed for public use the collections utilized at the Library of Congress; the presidential libraries of George H. W. Bush, Lyndon Johnson, Ronald Reagan, Harry S. Truman, Dwight D. Eisenhower, Franklin Roosevelt, and Rutherford B. Hayes; Harvard University; Forbes Library, Northampton, Massachusetts; Ohio Historical Society; Massachusetts Historical Society; George Washington's Mount Vernon; and the Schlesinger Library on the History of Women in America.

We would also like to acknowledge those representatives and members of the Truman, Kennedy, Ford, Carter, and Clinton presidential families who were not able to locate, grant access, or give permission to publish letters, but were, nonetheless, willing to spend their time and efforts trying to meet our requests.

Heartfelt thanks to Iris Newsom of the Library of Congress Publishing Office who, in the spirit of true camaraderie, volunteered to complete this book in a professional and timely fashion after her retirement; Aimee Hess of the Library of Congress Publishing Office, for critical assistance in acquiring permissions and photographs and her general support work which we could not do without; W. Ralph Eubanks, Director of Publishing, for his critical support in bringing this project to fruition and completion; and Laura Ross, our New York editor at Black Dog & Leventhal, for her patience, good advice, professional work in all things editorial, and overall project coordination.

PERSONAL ACKNOWLEDGMENTS

Gerard W. Gawalt would like to personally thank George A. Billias for more than four decades of mentoring; Jane, his wife, friend, and co-compiler of this book for all her support and assistance; his daughter, Ann Geraldine, for her ideas and support for this series on letters between presidents and their families; his daughters, Susan Jane and Ellen Sarah, for their support and encouragement; his sons-in-law, John, Brian, and Patrick, for making history a family endeavor; his grandchildren, Caitlin, Sarah, Emma, Mary Elizabeth, Jonathan, and Abigail, for proudly introducing him to their friends and classmates as just "my Grandpa."

PERMISSIONS

Permission to publish material included in this volume was kindly and generously granted by the following institutions and individuals: Theodore Roosevelt Association, Oyster Bay, New York; Ohio Historical Society; The Seeley G. Mudd Manuscripts Library, Department of Rare Books and Special Collections, Princeton University Library;

Julie Nixon Eisenhower and The Firm Books; Houghton Library, Harvard University; Schlesinger Library on the History of Women in America, Harvard University; Dwight D. Eisenhower Presidential Library; Massachusetts Historical Society; Herbert Hoover Presidential Library; Franklin D. Roosevelt Presidential Library; Harry S. Truman Presidential Library; HarperCollins Publishers; Rutherford B. Hayes Presidential Library; Forbes Library, Northampton, Massachusetts; Lyndon B. Johnson Presidential Library; Nancy Reagan and the Ronald Reagan Presidential Library; Illinois Historical Society; American Philosophical Society; James Monroe Museum and Law Office; Hillary Rodham Clinton and Simon and Schuster, New York; George H. W. Bush and Scribners, New York; Houghton Mifflin Company; and Harper & Row, New York.

INDEX